Under the
City Streets

UNDER THE CITY STREETS

Pamela Jones

Holt, Rinehart and Winston
New York

Published simultaneously in Canada by Holt,
Rinehart and Winston of Canada, Limited.

Library of Congress Cataloging in Publication Data

Jones, Pamela.
Under the city streets.

Bibliography. p.
Includes index.
1. Public utilities—New York (City)—History.
2. New York (City)—History. I. Title.
HD2767.N75N47   363.6'09747'1   78–4691
ISBN: 0–03–021596–X

FIRST EDITION

Designer: Joy Chu

Printed in the United States of America
1 2 3 4 5 6 7 8 9 10

*To Mother
for her unending faith*

CONTENTS

ACKNOWLEDGMENTS

In my search both above and below ground for the hidden mechanisms that make New York City function, I met and read about countless men and women without whose experiences I would have had no book to write. Thousands among these are the immigrants whose labor created this marvel among cities. Sometimes—too often—they gave their lives for it.

Those experts whom I came to know personally, I should like to thank for their unstinting generosity and patience, for the wealth of information they gave me, and for the enthusiastic encouragement they offered throughout. To do justice to each of them, I have listed their names in alphabetical order: Leandra Abbott, Albert K. Baragwanath, John F. Barra, Carol S. Clifton, Alan Cox, James Daniels, Kevin T. Doherty, Linda Edgerly, Robert

P. Edney, Dorothy B. Ellison, William Fotopulos, Marie Gangemi, Martin T. Gearaghty, Edward M. Gillespie, Sheldon Hadden, William Haley, Donald W. Harold, Louis J. Hartmann, Martin T. Hauptman, Susan C. Holahan, Stu Jaffe, David Katz, Edward L. Lincoln, Jr., Phil R. Marciano, William Moore, Robert A. Olmsted, Peter Rickert, Lynn Roshen, Jack Sawinski, Louis P. Scaltro, Fred Schenk, John Tauranac, Robert J. Tracy, Tom Young, and Steve Zabel.

To Dorothy Pawlowski and Peter Jones I owe a particular debt of gratitude. Throughout the months while this book slowly emerged, they were never too busy to spend hours in New York's libraries and museums in pursuit of fact and accuracy, to ferret out little-known details, or to question, advise, and cheer me on.

Under the City Streets

INTRODUCTION

It rises majestically out of the world's largest natural harbor, its skyline piercing the sky, known the world over. It is a capital of finance and fashion. It is Broadway, Wall Street, Fifth Avenue. It is the United Nations. It is theater, music, and dance. It is great universities, museums, and libraries. It is a concept. It is New York.

First, there is Manhattan. The city's four other boroughs surround it, protect it, stand independent. Brooklyn, the Bronx, Staten Island, and Queens—they, too, are a part of New York, the city's pulse. Nearly eight million people in all. Yet the heart of New York is, has been, and always will be Manhattan.

Manhattan for centuries absorbed millions of the world's "tired and poor . . . huddled masses yearning to breathe free." They soon developed many "cities" within

the city—Yorkville, Chinatown, Little Italy, Harlem—
where Germans, Chinese, Italians, English, Irish, Swedes,
Poles, Blacks, and Puerto Ricans could congregate, where
even the native Indians retained a role.

It is a city of such racial and ethnic diversity as to
defy all belief, a city where history never stands still, because history is daily in the making. For more than three
hundred years, immigrants from every land across the
globe have found their way to Manhattan, which, as
Frances Trollope wrote in 1831, "rises, like Venice, from
the sea, and like that fairest of cities in the days of her
glory, receives into its lap tribute of all the riches of the
earth." Each wave of immigrants brings its own special
skills, customs, physical characteristics, and modes of
dress, which blend into a city of the world. And, like all
those immigrants who came before them, the new arrivals
are greeted with suspicion, scorn, and doubt, their heritage
put to the test.

Walk along any street, ride any subway, and sooner
or later you can hear any language in the world. Eat your
favorite memories of Russia, Denmark, Brazil, or Ceylon.
You will be at home. It *is* home—after seven years or
seven generations.

You are in New York, the Big Apple. It is bankrupt,
noisy, dirty, rude. It is brash, exciting, fashionable, hot,
cold, different. It is at all times *news*—everywhere. People
hate it, love it, want to leave it, come to it, return to it—
but never do they ignore it. It is unique.

Before the white man came, the island was loosely settled
by far-flung Indian villages. The Indians were peaceful
agricultural people who hunted deer and bobcats, lions
and otters in the island's rugged terrain, kept warm in
winter with the skins of beavers, caught oysters and clams
along the shores of the two great rivers east and west,
and grew tobacco, beans and corn, peas and pumpkins.

They prepared a richly mixed vegetable they called "sick-quatash," which we know today as succotash. The clam shells they ground into wampum, or money, and they clothed themselves "with the feathers of birds of various colours." They drank the sparkling water of countless springs and swam in the freshwater streams and lakes of the island. They caught perch and pickerel and trout, and roasted wild turkeys and heath hens. They ate the berries that grew in abundance in what was to be called Lispenard Meadows, and the nuts of the hickory and chestnut trees. They watched dolphins leap playfully, glistening in the river we call Hudson, and the waterspouts of whales rise jetlike toward the sky along the island's western shore. In their sleek canoes, they paddled silently, swiftly among the islands of the harbor, to the far shores of New Jersey and Long Island.

Then on September 6, 1609, an eighty-ton ship called *Half Moon* dropped anchor in the Lower Bay. Its captain, Henry Hudson, sent five of his crew in a rowboat to sound the Narrows. Suddenly, as they rounded a bend in the harbor, two large canoes manned by Indians came flying toward them. In a flash, the frightened natives sent a black whirr of arrows into the air. An instant later, one of the crew, an Englishman, fell back, a slow ooze of blood rising about the arrow which had pierced his throat.

John Coleman was buried the next day at Sandy Hook.

Later that same day, Hudson traded beads and knives for the tobacco and corn other Indians brought alongside his ship. He then continued his journey up the Great River of the Mountains, in search of a westward route to the Orient, for the Dutch East India Company. A month later, unsuccessful in his quest, a disappointed man, he pointed the bow of his ship homeward to Amsterdam, where he officially claimed for Holland the Mauritius River (Hudson) in honor of Prince Maurice of Orange.

The following year, a group of Amsterdam merchants dispatched a ship to the Hudson, "called Manhattes from the savage nation that dwells at its mouth." By 1614 several more ships had arrived at the shores of the New World. Soon after his own arrival on May 4, 1626, Peter Minuit began to establish the first settlement of the newly created Dutch *West* India Company. It was during the summer of that year that he negotiated the purchase of Manhattan with the Indians who inhabited the island.

By September, the trading post numbered "200 souls" who lived in "thirty ordinary houses on the east side of the river." Two years later, there were 270 people. That it would be a lucrative station there was little doubt. The very first shipment of produce consisted of "7,246 beaver skins, 675 otter skins, 48 mink, 36 wild cat, and various other sorts." A fort built at the southernmost point facing Noten or Nut Island (Governors) was named Nieuw Amsterdam, and the land beyond became New Netherland. A few wooden houses clustered near the fort, along the mouth of the East River. Yet despite the fort's presence, settlers who ventured farther afield found their properties razed again and again by fire in Indian attacks. Still the white man probed doggedly northward. In 1639 the fur trade, which had been reserved exclusively for the company, was "thrown free and open to everybody." And so, George Holmes and Thomas Hall, two of eight Englishmen who came to trade in the New World, were given a grant of land at Deutel (Turtle) Bay along the East River, roughly between Forty-seventh and Fifty-second streets, where they established a tobacco plantation. Slowly, the village around Fort Amsterdam grew into a small town, and by 1664 some eighteen languages were spoken there, though as late as 1759 half the population was still Dutch.

In describing the island in the late 1620s, Secretary de Rasières, the chief commercial agent of the company, wrote, "It is about seven leagues in circumference, full of trees, and in the middle rocky to the extent of about two leagues in circuit. The north side has good land in two places. . . . On the east side there rises a large level field, of from 70 to 80 morgens of land [140–60 acres] through which runs a very fine fresh stream; so that the land can be ploughed without much clearing."

The topography of the island, south to north, was divided roughly into three uneven portions. First were the shores of the southern end, which "were deeply indented with frequent marshy inlets and salt marshes." Next came a range of well-drained hills. Approximately above what is today Twenty-seventh Street, sandy soil gradually gave way to large formations of rock and granite, flanking stony valleys through which meandered several large streams. (Central Park today most closely resembles this part of the island's original contours.) Then, while the rocky formations continued on the west side to the far northern shore, they broke suddenly on the east at "the fertile plains and meadows of Harlem."

In 1647 the Dutch West India Company sent a new governor to rule New Amsterdam. As a young man, Peter Stuyvesant had fought the Spanish until a cannonball shot off his right leg. Known as "Old Peg Leg" behind his back, Stuyvesant was a stern and moral leader who insisted that everyone attend the Dutch Reformed Church and work as tirelessly as he did. Although he was far from popular, New Amsterdam became a thriving center of industry and commerce for the company during the nearly two decades of his rule.

In March 1664, King Charles II of England granted to his brother James, Duke of York, all the land west of the Connecticut River as far south as the Delaware Bay, ignoring prior Dutch claims, although the two nations were at peace. That spring, English troops began raiding Dutch towns on Long Island. The town elders of New Amsterdam, certain they could defend their "lives and fortunes" without much difficulty, considered the raiders little more than "a ragged troop." When Peter Stuyvesant suggested that it might be practical to build palisades along the riverbanks of the town in case of attack, the elders replied that the burghers were "exhausted and unable to be burdened more." Besides, the city coffers were depleted. However, the elders were prepared to lend their personal slaves to the effort should Stuyvesant wish them to.

The situation was resolved swiftly late in August, when the Right Honorable Colonel Richard Nicolls, Commander-in-Chief of His Majesty's forces, cast anchor below the Narrows and sent word to Stuyvesant demanding that he surrender all "such Forts, Townes, or places of strength" as were "now possessed by the Dutch." Stuyvesant soon realized that with scarce ammunition and food the colony was lost against the vastly superior strength of the English. As he and his elders struggled to reach an honorable decision, Governor John Winthrop of Connecticut consoled them with the advice that they should resign themselves "under the obedience of his sacred Majesty," that by doing so, they "may enjoy all the happiness tendered, and more then [sic] you can imagine, under the protection of so gracious a prince. . . ."

On September 8, 1664, Colonel Nicolls and his men occupied the town and immediately claimed the entire island for England, something the Dutch had not done for Holland. Although the city of New Amsterdam had become incorporated in 1653, its name was immediately changed to New York in honor of the Duke of York, who twenty-one years later became King James II of England.

More than three hundred years have passed since then. There is little now that remains of the low hills and rocky cliffs, the forests, streams, and plains, or even the marshes, except perhaps in Central Park. As we rush about our daily business, along the streets and avenues of the island, we decry at times its lack of natural beauty. We complain if the subway is slow or delayed, the water pressure low, or the telephone out of order. We curse the potholes, the thick clouds of steam that rise from under our feet and momentarily blind us. We grumble our discontent at the roped-off sections of thoroughfares marked MEN AT WORK and only idly glance into the gaping holes which afford a passing glimpse into the world beneath the city's streets.

Flick a switch; turn a faucet, a dial, a valve; answer the phone. Take a bath, hose the garden, douse a fire. Get warm, keep cool. Wash the dishes. Empty the garbage. We take these conveniences of our modern lives so much for granted—the city without them is unthinkable.

Much has been written about Manhattan since its beginning. Visitors, residents, historians, and diarists have recorded a wealth of impressions, facts, and statistics. From the surface of the city, each has sought to convey the marvel and confusion, the squalor and urgency of an obscure outpost reaching for greatness. In the chapters that follow, I also have tried to relate and shed light upon this drama—but from below.

After 1837 a series of engineering feats took place—most of them within a span of only seventy years—that transformed a disease-ridden provincial town into a major metropolis. In the wake of the deep underground rumble of exploding dynamite, to the tune of picks and shovels, thousands of laborers constructed a tangle of pipes and tunnels in the city's underside, a tangle so thick that today it is often impossible to insert even a spoon between its threads. These laborers had no sophisticated machinery then, no push-button technology. They created the underground wonders by the strength of their backs and their hands: aqueducts, sewers and subways, tunnels and ducts to carry the city's steam, gas, and electricity.

These laborers also had leaders, men of vision and

guile, who joined their own fortunes and ingenuity to New York's future.

In my search for the city's past, I have had opportunity to observe some of the subterranean operations this work and technology achieved. I have smelled the dank air inside a manhole, heard the throb of Grand Central seven levels below the street, walked down the length of a storm sewer in Queens, edged my way along the darkness of a subway tunnel (in care of an engineer, of course). Most of all, I have learned to hear and see and recognize what goes on under my feet. My town and I have, in a sense, met for the first time. And now, I hope to avail others of this same opportunity—to celebrate with me, from a mole's-eye view, the wonders of a unique city.

one

A TWO-HUNDRED-YEAR THIRST

New Yorkers take few things so much for granted as water. They are surrounded by it. Water gushes freely at the turn of a tap, on the first floor or the fortieth. Except during a prolonged drought, there has always been an abundance of pure, clear, wholesome municipal drinking water in Manhattan and the other four boroughs. At least, so it appears.

What most New Yorkers do not even suspect, however, is the large quantity of water under their feet. Buried deep beneath the surface are the streams, springs, ponds, and marshes that for more than two hundred years were the only means by which New Yorkers could quench their thirst. As time passed and the city grew, these waters became more and more contaminated and the cause of widespread disease and death. So bad was the city's water in 1798 that one daily newspaper asked its readers: "Can you bear to drink it on Sundays in the Summer time? It is so bad before Monday morning as to be very sickly and nauseating; and the larger the city grows, the worse this evil will be."

We owe it all to the Dutch. To Peter Minuit, to be precise. In 1626 this third director of the new colony achieved what is probably one of the most phenomenal real estate coups in the world—for trinkets worth about 60 guilders. Since 2.5 guilders equaled one daalder (the pronunciation of which has been corrupted to "dollar"— the first American dollar was not coined until 1794), and since one guilder equals $.4020 on a par, Manhattan Island—all 22.3 square miles of it—was bought for 24 daalders, or $24.12. At current exchange rates, that is surely history's greatest bargain.

The southern tip of the island was perhaps not the most sensible location to choose for settlement. The land was flat and porous, with only modest undulations. Much of it was waterlogged, and the contours of the shoreline were deeply wrinkled and pocked with salt inlets and swampland. Only a short distance away, there were hills of "considerable height," fresh ponds, sparkling brooks, and meadows. The Dutch, however, had come far from home, most of them never to return, and this part of the island was reminiscent of Holland. It commanded the harbor and its islands. It guarded the approaches to the Hudson and the East River from the harbor. So they built their small wooden houses with steep thatched roofs on the sandy reaches of Manhattan, amid a network of canals which they dug, and near enough to the fort to be protected by its guns. The Stadthuys on Pearl Street at Coentis Slip was their City Hall. (City Hall was later moved to Wall and Broad streets and eventually to its current location opposite the Brooklyn Bridge.)

The largest of the inlets, under present-day Broad Street, was named Heere Gracht. The canal was flanked by streets lined with elegant homes, and at its mouth was the city's first dock. By 1654 a "convenient and durable lock" had been constructed "to keep said Gracht at all times full of water, so that in time of need because of fire ... and at other occasions it may be used and that especially the great and unbearable stench may be suppressed, which arises daily when the water runs out." From the northern end of the canal and stretching all the way to Pearl Street was the Sheep Pasture, which amply fed the livestock. A little farther north "a continuous swamp extended from river to river, separating the lower part of the island from the higher land above, and spreading out on its western edge into an extensive morass, long famous for its malaria and mosquitoes."

Before long, the Dutch began to fill the marshes with earth and extend the shore. They learned to grow corn, tobacco, and watermelons. They traded for furs with the Indians, often cheating them, refusing to pay them at all, or wantonly attacking them. By the 1640s the Indians more and more frequently retaliated with attacks on outlying farms—burning crops and homes and stealing animals—or even the fort, nearly destroying the village of New Amsterdam. Things were so bad that in 1643 one young settler wrote, "On the Island of Manachatas, from the north even unto the Fresh Water, there are no spots inhabited at this date. All places are mostly in their [the Indians'] power." The Indian War continued for seven years.

Still, the Dutch persisted, sending thousands of beaver pelts to Holland each year, first tanning these by the canals until the stench of curing leather grew so foul that tanners were forced to conduct their trade farther and farther away. From Heere Gracht they moved to the Swamp, and from there they were edged up to the marshlands east of the Fresh Water. As time passed, they were joined by the breweries, distilleries, and slaughterhouses, which were also noted for their offensiveness to the human nose.

Not far away, at Bowery and Chatham Square, the Jews established their cemetery in 1656; a part of it remains even today as the oldest existing burial ground in Manhattan.

Fresh water had to be found ever farther away. Although the Dutch were remarkably adept at dredging canals, it seems never to have occurred to them to dig wells. The English, however, under the command of Colonel Richard Nicolls, wasted no time in correcting this oversight. One reason may well have been that they soon discovered that the taste of tea was not particularly improved when brewed with stagnant water. And so, in 1666 the first well in New Amsterdam, which was now called New York, was dug inside the fort, which had been renamed Fort James in 1664.

Within eleven years there were six more wells, and by 1700 there were ten. Although there is not a trace of them left today, these wells were important landmarks in their time, and a sign of progress for the city. There was Suert Olpkert's Well near Broadway and Exchange Place, not far from Rombout's Well; Tunis De Kay's Well at Broad above Beaver Street; William Cox's Well at Coentis Slip by the Stadthuys; Ten Eyck & Vincent's Well at Broad, between Stone and South William streets; De Riemer's Well near Whitehall, and Frederick Wessel's Well on Wall Street, west of William. The water in all of them was mostly brackish, but the volunteer firemen often found it to be a "valuable resource."

The English also had the decency and good sense to cover the Broad Street canal. For the most part, though, they continued a largely agricultural tradition. The first English-language description of New York in 1670 reported that tobacco grown within the colony was "as good as is usually made in Maryland: Also Horses, Beef, Pork, Oyl, Pearl, Wheat, and the like . . ."

Suddenly, in 1673, just as the colony had settled down to being English, the Dutch fleet attacked and re-captured "this entire Province of New Netherland, con-sisting of three cities and thirty villages." The fort was renamed Fort Willem Hendrick, and New York became New Orange. After all that bother, the land was restored to Great Britain by the Treaty of Westminster only one year later, and the names were changed back. It was all very troublesome. Less than a hundred years later, when George III ascended to the throne of England, Fort Am-sterdam/James/Willem Hendrick/James became Fort George. In time it was entirely demolished, and the United States Custom House was erected on the site.

From the beginning, however—whatever the city was called—it regularly succumbed to fires. As early as 1648, Governor Peter Stuyvesant had recognized the danger of fire. He forbade wooden chimneys within the town and ordered that roofs be made of tile. In spite of these pre-cautions, New York remained a constant victim of mas-sive conflagrations. Beginning in 1677, the English appointed "overseers of chimneys and fires," or Brandt Meisters, who were to check that chimneys and hearths were routinely cleaned. The first regular volunteer firemen made their appearance in 1680. Three years later, the city authorities passed the first fire prevention law. It provided not only for inspection tours but also for a penalty of twenty shillings for every defect. "No person," the law stated, "shall lay hay or straw or other combustible matter within their dwellinghouses." Houses with two chimneys (the most common arrangement) were required to keep one bucket of water on the premises, those with more than two chimneys were ordered to keep two buckets, while brewers and bakers were each to have six buckets "under penalty of six shillings for every bucket wanting." A few years later, the city fathers elaborated on this law by also fining the Brandt Meisters if they failed to carry out their weekly inspections. Constables were pressed into service at the turn of the eighteenth century to make certain the Brandt Meisters were on their toes. Nevertheless, Governor Stuyvesant's residence, White Hall, was razed by fire in 1715. It was not until 1731 that the first two fire engines arrived from London, and another eleven years passed before the arrival of two others.

Being a fireman had its compensations. These "strong, able, discreet, honest and sober men" who volunteered to be available whenever the cry of "Fire!" echoed through the streets were granted exemption from military and jury duty. But their volunteer work was far from easy. In winter, when fires smoldered more regularly in the hearths of every home and blazes erupted frequently, the water in the buckets and wells was often a solid mass of ice. The men were then required to take a pick, clamber down the wells, and chip through the ice until they reached free-flowing spring water. Then, as now, vandals roamed the streets looking for mischief, and cutting the ropes that suspended the buckets deep into the wells was one of their pastimes—until pump guards were appointed to keep watch.

Although they were much preoccupied with water and fires—too little of the one, too many of the other—for a short time in 1735 New Yorkers turned their attention to the trial for libel of the New York *Weekly Journal's* editor, John Peter Zenger. After Zenger was acquitted, most citizens agreed that freedom of speech and of the press had been rightly judged an inviolable right. But ever-recurring fires soon brought their thoughts back to the more important everyday matter of survival. As the population grew and the number of fires increased, buckets were often lost in the confusion of the citizen bucket brigades. So owners were obliged to paint their names on the buckets, which could then be retrieved from outside City Hall after a fire had been extinguished. As there was little prosperity among New Yorkers, the loss of a bucket could be a serious misfortune.

Although in 1737 the Legislature passed "An Act for the better Extinguishing fires," in which it offered praise to New Yorkers, saying "the Inhabitants . . . of all Degrees have very justly acquired the reputation of being Singularly and Remarkably famous for their Diligence and Serviceableness in Cases of Fire," the very next year, the "House at the old Bowling Green took Fire and in a few Minutes was reduced to Ashes." To escape the flames, the occupants "were Obliged to leapt [sic] out of the Windows one Story high." The scourge of fire continued unabated. The already scarce water in the wells, pumps, and cisterns was simply not equal to the task of filling the town's four fire "Ingens." This led one citizen in 1750 to make an elaborate though sensible proposal: "It is well known," he wrote, "that the Fires in this Town of late . . . happen'd to be situate within Reach of the Rivers; by which Means, the Engines could be supplied without great Difficulty." He went on to say that "a Drain, or Brick Channel, may be carried up at Low-Water Mark" in Broad Street, with three or four strategically placed pumps along the way, and that "the Drain end in a Large Well or Bason [sic]" would "convey the Water issuing out of this inexhaustible Fountain" to serve the entire neighborhood. He suggested that a similar system could be established in other parts of the city, so that no matter how "remote from the River Side" a fire might be, there would be water to put it out. Forty years later the Common Council seemed to nod its head in agreement when it came up with the brilliant collective idea of appointing a committee to direct the making of "a Copper Pump for drawing Water out of the River in Cases of fire and thereby preventing the disagreeable necessity of the Inhabitants going down into the Slips & handling the water up in Buckets." Being a thoughtful, ponderous sort of body, the Council three years later in 1793 also required "the Regulation of the Tea Water Men in order that they may be compelled to assist in supplying the Engines with Water in case of fire."

By 1827, according to an eyewitness report, the problem seems to have been resolved to some degree. The engines were placed along the street, some two hundred feet apart, in a line to the riverbank, where "the suction hose of the last engine in the line . . . being plunged into the river, the water was drawn up, and then forced along a leathern hose or pipe to the next engine, and so on, till . . . it came within range of the fire."

Long before that time, however, as the trades expanded to satisfy the needs of the growing town, women had been driven from the canals to the grassy slopes of Maiden Lane, where in sunny, dry weather they washed and bleached and dried their linen at a "little stream of sparkling spring water" which "rippled and danced over a pebbly bottom." It must have had other charms besides, because it was known as Maagde Paetje, or Virgin's Path. That is, until the spoilers came—a blacksmith and the tanners who set up shop at the corner of what is now Pearl Street and Maiden Lane—and drove the laundresses away. In due course, the area became known as Smit's Vly, or Smith's Valley. And when the first market sheds appeared on the reclaimed land at the mouth of the stream, the name changed to Fly Market, which it is quite likely we have corrupted still further to "flea" market. A little to the north was the Swamp, Beekman Swamp, or Kripplebush, which in spite of its apparent connotation meant tangled briars. This was located a little behind the present South Street Seaport Museum and almost under the Brooklyn Bridge.

As the population grew from 1,500 people in 1664 to

12,000 in 1746, and to between 26,000 and 30,000 at the start of the Revolution, people were forced to look ever farther afield for amusement. There was swimming in the rivers, promenades in the various public gardens, turtle feasts at Turtle Bay, or short boat rides to Ellis Island for oyster roasts and clambakes. Excitement was provided by bear- and panther-baiting on Bayard's Mount at Grand and Centre streets and by public executions on Gallows Hill, a little west of the Collect. While the Pond at the Battery outside the fort had long offered refreshing coolness in summer, and the tree-lined paths surrounding it a pleasant promenade, the Collect or Fresh Water Pond was by far the most popular resort. In time, of course, it became less fresh water and more collect (and today it lies buried beneath Foley Square, the Tombs prison, and the city's judicial buildings). But in the early days it was a place of unsurpassed beauty, ringed by woods and meadows, a rocky promontory called Kalk Hoek (Lime-Shell Point, so named for the heaps of oyster shells left by the Indians), which jutted into the Collect, a corruption of the Dutch *Kolk*, meaning small body of water, and not to be confused with *Kalk*, although it often was.

As early as 1730, parts of the marshlands around the Collect had already been filled. At the end of the eighteenth century, an engineer estimated the pond to be only twelve feet deep and about five acres in area. Earlier records had estimated it as between forty and seventy feet deep, seventy acres in all, the abode of "hideous and terrible seamonsters," and fed by a number of large springs.

For generations, the Collect was a favorite resort for fishing, boating, and picnics in summer, and for skating in winter. King William IV of England, the "Sailor King" and first royal visitor to America, learned to skate on it and amused himself by tossing coins on its glistening surface and watching the skaters chase them across the ice.

Fishing was so good in the pond that in 1734 a law was passed that, upon pain of a fine, severely restricted the sport. There were snipe and grouse in the eastern marshes, huge shade trees and wild flowers. The air was pure and fresh, the water clear. Here and there were still some signs of the earlier Indian encampments, flints and arrowheads, shells of clams and oysters which the Indians had dug as far away as Hellgate and along the Long Island and New Jersey shores. Toward the north were endless miles of meadows and compact woods crisscrossed by streams and rocky crags and dotted with sprawling farms.

It was a day of great excitement, during that summer of 1796, when John Fitch launched his newest invention, the steamboat, in the Collect. Curious New Yorkers vying for high-lying vantage points streamed to the water's edge to see the ship's yawl, eighteen feet long with a six-foot beam and a "square stern and round bows, experimentally fitted with a screw propeller. A ten- or twelve-gallon iron pot served for a boiler. The little craft made the circuit of the pond several times, at the rate of about six miles an hour"—to the loud cheers of the populace.

More than ten years before, Fitch had determined that he would build a steamboat. Two years later he had launched his first effort near Philadelphia. His second boat, launched in 1788, was capable of carrying thirty passengers, and although with financial backing he went on to build a third and a fourth, the public remained quite indifferent to his invention. When the fourth boat was wrecked before completion, he lost all financial support, even though he received both French and American patents. Ill and destitute, he made one final effort and built that first screw-propelled steamboat in New York. It was a futile attempt. The financial wizards of the time were simply not interested, and soon afterward Fitch died a broken man. His little four-passenger steamboat was eventually abandoned on the shore of the Collect and its parts carried off for firewood. A few years later Robert Fulton gained the world's applause for "his" invention, the steamboat.

By 1805 the Collect had become a repository for all the filth and garbage of the town. Its shade trees were cut to stumps and used for fires. A thick, putrid bilge which the Common Council described as "dangerous to the public health" swilled around the shoreline. Nearby hills were leveled to fill the marshes, and soon there was nothing left of the Fresh Water Pond which only a few short years before had been described as "too remote" from the town for development. However, even though the Collect rarely attracted large numbers of picnickers toward the end of the eighteenth century, it still played a major role in the city's search for fresh water.

Although a variety of pumps and wells had been sunk throughout the town, the water they yielded was limited invariably in quantity and certainly in quality. Even the "tea water pumps," so called for the fine tea which one could supposedly brew with their water, rarely provided a taste treat. Often as not their water contained mud and pebbles as well as dead vegetable and animal matter, so that boasts of the tea water pumps' healthy purity were in most cases something of an overstatement. In fact, the water caused an assortment of ailments, such as dysentery, diseased livers and kidneys, and, at the very least, upset stomachs.

There was, however, one pump, *the* Tea Water Pump, at Chatham Street and Roosevelt, which for decades was the source of the city's purest water. Or so it was said. Six feet in diameter, some twenty feet deep, with never less than three to four feet of water at its base, it was truly a bottomless pit. Of course, there were the inevitable skeptics who maintained that this was hardly surprising when one considered the proximity of the pump to the Collect, a suggestion immediately rejected by others who insisted the pump was supplied by its own spring.

Whatever the truth of the matter may have been, the pump was the source of one extremely profitable trade. The cartmen were a rough and boisterous crowd, well over a hundred of them before long, whose trade soon flourished into a very lucrative enterprise. Lined up every day, shouting and jostling each other's carts and horses, these men daily took their carts to the pump where they filled their 130-gallon hogsheads (barrels) at a cost of three-pence per hogshead and then drove through the city's streets, selling the water door to door at a charge of one penny per gallon! Although they drew an average of 110 hogsheads per day and, on hot summer days, as many as 216, the water level at the bottom of the pump never varied! Theirs was a highly competitive business as they whipped their horses through the streets, until an ordinance was passed forbidding them to drive faster than walking speed and ordering the men themselves to walk beside the horses, upon penalty of a six-shilling fine.

The city's wealthy merchants, meanwhile, sent slaves to fetch their water at the pump. It was not long before the Tea Water Pump became what the neighborhood bar is today, a popular gathering place. In fact, it was so popular that a 1741 law forbade Negroes to fetch water there. It appears that when a group of them was convicted of conspiracy to burn the town and fort that year, the general consensus held that the plot had been hatched over the pump.

By 1798 the pump had developed a reputation which, like its water, was not altogether wholesome, as is suggested by the following newspaper report: "the Collect behind the Tea-water Pump is a shocking hole, where all impure things center together and engender the worst of unwholesome productions; foul with excrement, frogspawn, and reptiles, that delicate pump is supplied." To which another New Yorker responded: "The inhabitants of New York have already as much good water as they can use . . . the spring will never fail us."

As early as 1784 one citizen had complained that during warm, dry weather, a large number of people gathered around the Collect from which the tea water was drawn and "washed their dirty linen therein." But New Yorkers went on drinking the water, although they liberally drowned its taste with "those beverages most noted for their purity." As for the poor people who could not afford the cartmen's prices, they were compelled to go on drawing their water from wells guaranteed to contain putrid and contaminated water, although it ultimately cost them a great deal more—their health and often their lives.

During the city's first two hundred years, probably no subject was discussed by more people more often than fresh water. There simply was not enough of it. As early as 1748 the Swedish botanist Pehr Kalm had observed that "there is no good water to be met within the town itself." He went on to say that those who were less delicate "make use of the water from the wells in town, though it is very bad. This want of good water lies heavy upon the horses . . . for they do not like to drink the water. . . ." A little more than ten years later, an English tourist, the Reverend Andrew Burnaby, wrote about the "want of fresh water; so that the inhabitants are obliged to have it brought from springs at some distance out of town." And yet, decade after decade, New Yorkers had no choice.

In spite of the extreme shortage of fresh water, people continued to settle the island. Elegant and stately mansions sprang up along the river fronts, far away in the country, and near the farm and orchards of Sir Peter Warren's "Greenwich" estate, which overlooked the Hudson at what is now West Fourth and Perry streets. Nearby was imposing Richmond Hill Mansion, north of Lispenard Meadows, with its view over the city, once the headquarters of General Washington, later the home of John Adams as well as Aaron Burr—a place of which Mrs. Adams wrote, "The venerable oaks and broken ground, covered with wild shrubs, which surround me, give a natural beauty to the spot which is truly enchanting. A lovely variety of birds serenade me morning and evening. . . ." There were grand estates still farther away, near the Bloomingdales, and at distant Nieuw Haarlem.

Generally, the city's cultural life was somewhat limited, even though it could boast a good amount of theater. As late as 1831, Frances Trollope noted that "often where a liberal spirit exists, and a wish to patronize the fine arts is expressed, it is joined to a profundity of ignorance on the subject almost inconceivable." Of New York women's clothing, she wrote, "the dress is entirely French . . . to say that an unfortunate looks like an English woman, is the cruellest satire which can be uttered."

In spite of its obvious disadvantages, New York continued to attract immigrants who found a wealth of opportunity in the city's healthy economic life. The majority of the city's inhabitants, however, were poor. They lived in crude hovels, often only a single room, with dirt floors. Theirs was a life not to be envied, and when the waves of epidemics struck—yellow fever, cholera, smallpox—they were the most severely afflicted.

From the beginning, the town had expanded more rapidly along the East River, overlooking the bluff of Brooklyn Heights, leaving much of the Hudson's shoreline to the mosquitoes whose sting carried a powerful venom which caused yellow fever. The fever began with the onset of high temperature and nausea. It destroyed the liver, which in turn yellowed the skin and eyes. Its course was rapid, survival unlikely. It tore through the city with ever more frequent ferocity (1791, 1795, 1796, 1798, 1803, and 1819), decimating the population with each assault, until finally the death toll was so high that in 1798 there could no longer be any doubt that contaminated water was largely to blame. Between August 20 and October 30 of that year alone, 1,310 people in a population of about 60,000 died of yellow fever. A Dr. E. H. Smith recorded that "within the last week the greater part of Pearl Street from Wall to Cherry Street and the eastern part of the town, has been evacuated . . . 600 people have been and are sick, and about one in ten have died." In a letter to Noah Webster, Dr. Samuel L. Mitchell, who later became a United States Senator, wrote on September 17, 1798, that "it seems to be admitted on all sides to be a homebred Pestilence. The Inhabitants have really poisoned their City by the accumulation of Excrement, putrid Provisions, and every unclean thing." In addition, he also firmly believed that the "long use of strong malt liquor, Wines and distilled Spirits" had contributed heavily to the spread of the fever by weakening the resistance of the imbibers. Certainly, an opinion expressed ten years earlier by a French visitor that "the healthfulness of the city rendered the medical profession unprofitable" was dramatically reversed.

Even the hospital west of Broadway, at Church and Duane streets, was unequal to its mission of mercy. Built as a private undertaking by a group of wealthy merchants, it had been totally destroyed by a flash fire just before its completion. Rebuilt immediately, it was completed just in time for the Revolution, when it first became a barracks for the Provisional Congress and, later, for the British. It was 1791 before the first patients were admitted.

Those who could afford to do so in 1798 began a mass exodus to the pure air, untainted water, green hills and valleys of faraway Greenwich, that quiet little country village some two or three miles to the north. Long before, it had been the Indian village of Sapokanickan, surrounded by woodlands where elk, deer, and wild turkeys roamed freely. Now it became a self-sufficient village with hastily thrown together ramshackle houses, shops, and businesses, as New York's refugees crowded into the wholesome climate—and promptly contaminated it.

Others less fortunate were forced to remain behind. Robbers looted and burned abandoned properties. The inmates of the Bridewell debtor's prison, their creditors long gone, pleaded for mercy and freedom. Confined in filthy, crowded conditions, with foul water and barely enough food to subsist, were "the great number of vagrants daily skulking about this city, from every part of the continent." Their view was of the gallows in what is now City Hall Park.

The city was more desperate than ever for fresh water. The Common Council appointed committees, and the committees appointed other committees which sought and encouraged ideas to supply New Yorkers with "pure and wholesome" water. One man suggested diverting water from the Bronx River which would, he claimed, produce 11,457,000 gallons every twelve hours, or nearly forty times the 300,000 gallons which New York needed every day. He felt this would be far better than supplying the city "out of that stinking mud-puddle the Collect." As an additional suggestion, he advised a "further alteration in the name, and call it Colic—it will then be descriptive of its effects." Bronx River water was, in fact, under serious consideration by the city, but it was finally rejected on the grounds that the water would "congeal" in cold weather.

While the search continued, people went on drinking from the Tea Water Pump. They refused to believe it could be other than pure. Wherever a well was dug, water was found in such quantity that a single well could supply whole neighborhoods, even though it was usually stagnant ground water or a drain of surrounding marshes.

The earliest recorded effort to build a municipal water system took place in 1774, when Christopher Colles, an Irish inventor and "promoter of internal improvements," proposed to the Common Council "to Erect a Reservoir, and to Convey Water thro' the Several Streets of this City." The Common Council, in its infinite wisdom, shelved the idea to "Some future Time."

Nevertheless, Colles dug a well east of Broadway between Franklin and White streets and waited for the appropriate official signal to proceed. He also began to prepare the wooden pipes through which he planned to funnel his water system. It is to be hoped that Colles found other gainful employment, because after the British landed at Kip's Bay and captured New York on September 15, 1776, even the subject of water took a back seat to politics. A week later, Nathan Hale was executed as "a spy from the enemy" outside Artillery Park at Sixty-sixth Street and Third Avenue. Besides, in one of the city's worst conflagrations, which in 1776 destroyed virtually all the buildings up to St. Paul's Chapel, the Colles infant waterworks was ravaged by fire and the site of his reservoir became a redoubt. Two years later sixty more houses and many stores succumbed to yet another fire. All the same, the question of a municipal waterworks was put aside for another twenty-four years.

At last the Common Council remembered. Late in 1798 it appointed a committee to "draw up a law for a municipal water company to alleviate the suffering of the inhabitants." But a group of citizens led by Aaron Burr warned the Council that the State Legislature at Albany would never consider incorporating a municipal water company because the company's powers were insufficiently well defined and the revenues potentially too low to warrant state aid. The group advanced the alternate suggestion that they form a stock company, a suggestion the city elders did not find distasteful.

It was a golden opportunity for Aaron Burr, an astute, vain, spendthrift lawyer, whose political affiliation with the Republicans had long restrained him from his political ambitions to attain the presidency of the nation. The Federalists controlled the city's and the state's banking and business, and therefore their politics. And the Federalists were controlled by Alexander Hamilton. While Federalist merchants were readily favored with loans and other courtesies, merchants of Republican persuasion were firmly, though politely, turned away. Since there were only two banks in the entire state at the time, both of them under Hamilton's domination, it is not difficult to recognize the incontestable stranglehold they had over the state's economy. For all intents and purposes, this single factor was destined to prevent Aaron Burr from ever becoming president. Except . . .

Except that Aaron Burr thought he saw in the water issue a way out. Not untainted by ruthlessness and guile, Burr, who was a master of persuasion, decided that he would break the Federalists' control of the banks by means of a public-spirited enterprise—a municipal waterworks.

Quietly he introduced a bill at the 1799 State Legislative Session entitled "An Act for Supplying the City of New-York with Pure and Wholesome water." In order to perform this miracle, the bill, to be capitalized at $2 million, empowered the Manhattan Company to dig wells and canals, buy or confiscate land, build reservoirs, and lay pipes, "*provided* That the said company shall, within ten years from the passing of this act, furnish and continue a supply of pure and wholesome water, sufficient for the use of all such citizens dwelling in the said city, as shall agree to take it on the terms to be demanded by the said company; in default whereof, the said corporation shall be dissolved." *But.* Attached to the bill was a rider, a seemingly innocent, innocuous proviso which permitted "That it shall and may be lawful for the said company to employ all such surplus capital as may belong or accrue to the said company in the purchase of public or other stock, or in any other monied transactions or operations not inconsistent with the constitution and laws of this state or of the United States, for the sole benefit of the said company." The most important part of that rider was the portion that began with "not inconsistent with the constitution . . ."

In these words was buried a most audacious and explosive plot. In these words Aaron Burr saw future power, economic power, the support of merchants and the people, the means by which he could at last challenge Hamilton and the Federalists. The rider was a brilliant inspiration.

On March 28, 1799, the bill passed the largely Federalist Assembly without so much as a recorded vote. The Federalist Senate bothered not even to dwell on it but referred it for consideration to a select committee of three. Burr's persuasive powers prevailed. Although the Chief Justice in the Council of Revision, who had to approve all bills, recognized the ruse and foresaw the uses to which the bill might be put, he was overruled in the Council. On April 2, the bill become law.

In no time, the Manhattan Company was oversubscribed, and with this additional money the *Bank* of the Manhattan Company was born. The Federalists promptly shouted treachery. To no avail. Burr had outmaneuvered them. Yet, indirectly, this proved to be his undoing. Hamilton used the incident to intensify his abusive public and private criticism of Burr and to support the consensus that Burr had used the disease-ridden city of New York to further his personal aims by creating a bank instead.

That bank lives on today, after amalgamation with the Chase National Bank, as the Chase Manhattan Bank.

His foes notwithstanding, Burr's Manhattan Company set about honoring its charter. The first step, as always, was to find likely sources of uncontaminated water, and again the discussion centered around the Collect. The Bronx River was again suggested to the public, but the Manhattan Company rejected it on the grounds that, among other disadvantages, it would prove too expensive. Elias Ring, an expert in such matters, wrote:

> The Collect has unjustly been stigmatized with the name of a filthy stagnated pond;—that it is not so is evident; for a stagnated pond neither proceeds from springs nor has it any stream issuing from it. . . . Nor is it ever discolored, putrid or thick, except sometimes near the banks, where it receives the wash of the streets, and is rendered in some measure filthy by throwing dead carcases into it.

Another report stated that there was "every reason to believe the Springs which supply water to the Tea-Water Pump and to the Collect are very copious, and many probably [are] adequate to the supply of Water for culinary purposes, *at least*."

William Weston, an engineer of note from Philadelphia, was invited to turn his attention to the matter of water for New York. It was his considered opinion that Bronx River water would probably be better for the citizens, although he felt it would be less costly and time-consuming to use water from the Collect. He also offered the Manhattan Company an estimate of costs. For constructing and laying wooden pipes and sheathing these in iron for greater durability; for digging trenches; and for building hydrants, cast-iron cylinders, a steam engine and engine house, the pump well and reservoir, including all materials and allowing for contingencies, the total estimated cost was $24,535.

It was decided to clean out and reopen Christopher Colles' well and to build the Manhattan Company's reservoir on Chambers Street behind the City Hall. The reservoir had walls twelve feet high and a capacity of 132,000 gallons of water. A pair of emaciated dray horses drove the pump initially, until the nags were put out to pasture in favor of a steam engine. It was calculated that if the pump were worked continuously, it could produce 691,000 gallons of water a day—a good deal more than the city then required.

The Manhattan Company had decided that iron pipes were too expensive and ordered wooden pipes to be manufactured, one end of each section to be a tapered "male" end and inserted into the next section's "female" end to lock into a watertight line. These pipes were buried several feet under the city's streets, constituting the first effort to drive Manhattan's utilities under the ground. In the process, of course, there was much disruption of the streets and halting and diverting of traffic, aided by the "sidewalk superintendents," ordinary mortals who advised the workers—until the company was ordered by the Common Council to make the necessary repairs and fill in the ditches it had dug.

Amid much rejoicing and public fanfare at the new-found wealth of fresh water, the Manhattan Company had laid six miles of pipe and was supplying four hundred houses by the end of the first year, although the company's boast had been that one well alone would be capable of yielding "to five thousand families a daily supply of at least fifty gallons each, of a quality excellent for drinking and good for every culinary purpose." Eventually, there were twenty-five miles of pipe supplying two thousand houses.

Since the island's lower end has a natural downhill

Above: The Manhattan Company's Chamber Street Reservoir as seen in an 1825 view. Opened in 1799, New York's first municipal system supplied the population with "pure and wholesome" water for more than forty years. From a lithograph for *Valentine's Manual*, 1865. *Museum of the City of New York*

Right: Wooden pipes buried several feet under Broadway, with lateral pipes to both river shorelines, became the city's first effort to drive its utilities underground. "Gates" inserted at intervals theoretically regulated the flow of water. *Juschkus Photo, Courtesy of Chase Manhattan Bank, Photo Studio*

grade, the water mains were laid along Broadway, while lateral pipes fitted with spigots carried the water as far as the rivers, with connections to the outside kitchens of individual homes. These lateral pipes had to be applied and paid for by homeowners. A charge of $5.00 per year was made for houses with up to four fireplaces, with a $1.25 surcharge for each additional fireplace. Bills were payable quarterly, and in cases of default the pipe was cut off. The water was expensive, but at least it was water.

Manhattan Company water used at fires was free of charge. At times, if a fire lacked the good sense to erupt near a spigot, a hole was drilled directly into the main. After the fire was doused, the hole was plugged with wood, which is probably the origin of the expression "fire plug," another name that describes a hydrant. Before long, those fortunate householders who could afford fresh water (and those who needed it most could afford it least) were providing entire neighborhoods with free water, a custom the company did not view with kindness.

It was also found that houses closest to the reservoir received merely a trickle of water, while the houses farther away, down toward the tip of the island, received an increasingly strong flow. The farther a house stood from the reservoir, the greater the rate of its water supply. Although the pipes were fitted with valves, or gates, which, in theory, regulated the flow, the water gained momentum as it streamed downhill, leaving some very unhappy customers near the reservoir. One such subscriber angrily denounced the company when he wrote: "Not long since I discharged my tea-water man and had a Manhattan cock introduced into my cellar, and for the first ten days I was highly pleased with it. . . . But, alas! for the last fourteen days, I have turned my cock repeatedly, but nothing comes from it. . . ."

In time, the Manhattan Company dug wells in several parts of the city, and its pipes sprouted some 150 hydrants.

One of the wells was in the broad pasture land north and west of City Hall, bounded by Duane, Broome, Church, Wooster, and Hudson streets. More than fifty years earlier, Anthony Rutgers had bought seventy acres of this pasture from the city, under the condition that he "clear and drain it within a year." Soon after Rutgers died in 1750, his daughter married Leonard Lispenard; and since they had inherited the Meadows, they gave their name to that land. It was a favorite resort and provided good skating in winter when the marshes froze over. It boasted snipe and woodcock, berries and cattails.

Before the first echoes of the Manhattan Company's "pure and wholesome Water" slogan had died away, the boast gagged on itself. On January 2, 1800, on a cold winter's day, a very beautiful and very dead young woman was found floating in the Lispenard Well. But New Yorkers were even then a good-natured crowd. Besides, they simply had not had time to acquire a gourmet's palate for the *je ne sais quoi* quality of pure water, and so they could not rightly say they had noticed anything unusual in the taste during the previous days. The body itself, however, stirred a good deal of interest and conjecture.

Miss Gulielma Elmore Sands, Elma to her friends (for she seems to have had no family), had disappeared eleven days earlier, on Sunday evening, December 22, at 8:00 P.M. She was a boarder in the home of Elias and Catherine Ring, Quakers, at Greenwich Street near Franklin, and seems to have been quite precocious for her time, having been "*very* intimate" with young Levi Weekes, another lodger. She had confided to a friend not long before her disappearance that she planned soon to be married privately. Her disappearance, it seems, did not create an exceptional stir. Even when her muff was found in Lispenard Well on December 24, nobody thought to see if Elma herself might be attached to it. Inevitably, the body rose to the top in the natural course of bloating and decomposition, and when it was found, her "hat was off; her dress was torn open about the waist; her shawl, handkerchief around her neck, and her shoes were gone."

Was it murder or suicide or an accident? There were those who argued that a person bent on suicide would hardly take off her shoes, tear her dress, and then jump in head first—the position in which she was found. Essentially, that also held true of an accident. But murder!

It was a sensational mystery. Levi Weekes was the most obvious culprit, and so he was duly apprehended and tried. He denied the charge, of course, and due to a lack of evidence, the court was forced to release him, although the judge did require Weekes to leave town immediately. The excitement died down, and New Yorkers went on with the business of drinking the city's water.

By now, the Volunteer Fire Department was equipped with the latest in fire engines. They were a proud group of citizens whom nothing, not even a wedding night (in one recorded instance), could stop from attending to a fire. On cold winter nights, when water froze in the pipes and fire-blackened buildings dripped with icicles, provision was made to furnish the men "with liquor, &c., at the times of fire." More often than not, however, they did not drink the brandy; rather, they poured it into their boots to keep their feet from freezing.

These early firemen were a special breed, with a strict code of behavior. Their evening entertainments consisted mostly of singing and storytelling. When they gathered in "the room in the City Hall," which was the forerunner of the modern engine house, they forswore to drink, eat, sleep, or misbehave there. It appears that in some instances even smoking and chewing tobacco were fined.

Many times, when fire hoses leaked or the city's water pipes carried too little pressure, the citizen bucket brigades had to come to the aid of the volunteers. In 1812, at one of the city's most devastating conflagrations, hundreds of houses on Chatham Street were burned to the ground. As blazing cinders threatened to set Dr. Spring's Brick Church afire, a sailor climbed high up on its steeple and extinguished them. Although a reward was offered to this brave and nimble man, he could never be found. In 1824 a shipyard between Houston and Stanton streets at the East River burned so fiercely that firemen were forced to leap into the river to save their lives. Fruitless attempts were made to launch the ships and save the equipment in the yard. It all happened too quickly. The vessels and all the shipyard property were totally destroyed. At another blaze, firemen in the process of dragging their water hose through one room of a burning house to fight the flames from the rear found two men sleeping peacefully in their beds. Their skin was so dark that they looked like blacks at first. Suddenly one of the firemen pointed at the two sleepers and let out a panicked scream: "The black small-pox!" At that, the men ran as if Satan himself were after them, hauling their hose as fast as they could out into the street. So justified was their terror of plagues that they were never reprimanded for this lapse.

The Bowery Theater burned down three times in all. The first time, in 1828, the fire was out of control for hours, in spite of the tireless efforts of 47 engines and 680 men. The water was pumped from the East River into the first engine in line, from this to the second, which in turn pumped it into the third, and so on, while the citizens stood in lines between the nearest pumps and the fire, frenziedly passing buckets of water one to the other. But still the theater was demolished.

By 1804 the friction between Aaron Burr and Alexander Hamilton had finally boiled to an open confrontation. On the morning of July 11, the two men stood on the heights of Weehawken, New Jersey, facing each other in the cool dawn, witnessed by seconds. Two shots were fired. A moment later Alexander Hamilton lay mortally wounded on the ground. He was rowed across the Hudson to a house in Greenwich Village, where he died. That pistol shot was to prove the end of Aaron Burr's presidential aspirations.

For another thirty-eight years Burr's Manhattan Company remained the city's only source of "pure and wholesome" water, although this claim became increasingly more questionable as the years went by. As the population grew far beyond the city's 1799 bounds, plagues and fires pursued the people without mercy and continued to take a grisly toll. New Yorkers were desperate for new sources of water.

More and more, pressure was applied on the Legislature to charter a municipal waterworks company which would once and for all time solve the endless question not only of quantity but of sufficient quality. "The drinking water in New York is very bad and salty," wrote Baron Axel Klinckowström, a visitor from Sweden, in 1818. "One finds in the streets dead cats and dogs, which make the air very bad." The Baron went on to say that "even the so-called Manhattan water . . . is not good. But in Brooklyn the water is splendid." Brooklyn was then a village beyond the bluff which rose sharply from the far shore of the East River.

A few years later, in 1824, Dr. David Hosack, in one of fifteen affidavits gathered from leading physicians, stated unequivocally that the city's water was "frequently productive of diseases of the stomach and bowels, especially with strangers upon their first use of it. Gravel, and other complaints of the kidneys, are of frequent occurrence among our citizens." To which the Manhattan Company replied in a public notice that "the quality of the water is as good as can be found; and the Company having lately replaced many of the old pipes with new ones, the water will be received clearly and in better order than heretofore." Fearful of losing its charter, the company was anxious to establish and maintain good public relations by undertaking prompt repairs and replacements of its equipment.

Nevertheless, the water issue remained a hot political football. Yet despite repeated and dire warnings of the consequences, the Legislature failed to act. It was generally considered that twenty-seven gallons of water per person was sufficient for their daily needs, and so among the various solutions attempted was the digging of artesian wells. One of these, at Bleecker and Mercer streets, plummeted 442 feet down, was 8 inches wide, and produced what was described as "a copious supply of good water."

Unfortunately, though, all such measures were merely illusive disregard of reality—at the people's expense. Houses sprawled farther and farther northward to above Grand Street, and that part of the city lay well out of reach of the Manhattan Company's pipes and their supply of drinking water. Equally dangerous in this section was the lack of access even to the rivers "for the purpose of extinguishing fires. . . . The breadth of the island at Grand Street, is about two miles; and does not materially differ as high up as Fourteenth street. . . . Now, to bring the water from either river, at the extreme distance by engines, would require 26."

In its crisis-planning attempt to confront this latest threat, the Common Council authorized the construction of the Bowery Reservoir on the corner of the Bowery and Thirteenth Street, which was to become both "the first public reservoir and the beginning of the public waterworks of the city of New York." The reservoir was duly built, and still it was not enough.

Slowly, though, a groundswell of ideas began to build: Twenty-eight-inch iron pipes might be laid to bring water from Rye Pond; water from the Croton River could be channeled to the city via an open canal; the Passaic River might be tapped above the falls at Paterson, New Jersey, and the water piped to Manhattan. . . .

two
THE THIRST IS QUENCHED

New Yorkers staggered under the repeated blows struck by fires and epidemics. Their lives were under constant siege. The air was foul with the stench of death. Burial grounds were filled to overflowing. Widespread hunger, poverty, and unemployment gnawed at the very bones of the city, as wave upon wave of poor immigrants landed at Castle Garden. The houses of these new settlers advanced steadily northward on Manhattan Island. Other immigrants established roots in Brooklyn, the Bronx, Staten Island, and Queens, or journeyed to other sections of the young nation. Yet for a period of adjustment in the New World, following often harrowing journeys across the Atlantic, countless people sought shelter, however temporarily, in the already overburdened city of New York. Between 1800 and 1840 alone, Manhattan's population increased by more than a quarter of a million souls, to a total of 312,710. And still there was no water, except what could be drawn from wells and streams or from the Manhattan Company's pipes at the lower tip of the island.

In 1832 an epidemic of Asiatic cholera struck the city and took the lives of 3,500 inhabitants—more than one percent of the entire population. Two years later cholera returned, killing hundreds more. Terror-stricken New Yorkers tried to flee the scourge of plagues, seeking the safety of the island's outlying areas on Murray Hill and beyond, in the villages of Harsenville, Bloomingdale, Yorkville, Harlem, and Manhattanville. As they did so, they compounded the water-supply problem through the city's expansion. Greenwich had ceased to be a country village almost ten years earlier; its streets were now linked to the city's mainstream.

Driven by extreme desperation, the citizens finally voted overwhelmingly in favor of "an Act to provide for supplying the City of New York with pure and wholesome water" through a municipal water-supply system. On May 2, 1834, like a giant hippopotamus at the riverbank, the Legislature finally bestirred itself into action. After decades of stopgap measures to cope with the disastrous shortage, the second of May proved to be a day which, in many respects, determined the future development not only of Manhattan Island but of the villages and townships that were to comprise the city's four other incorporated boroughs some sixty-four years later. However, eight more years were to pass before the promise became a reality—unfortunately, not in time to prevent the Great Fire.

On the night of December 16, 1835, flames erupted in a store on Merchant (now Hanover) Street. Fanned by gusts of wind, the fire spread within minutes to adjoining houses and raged uncontrolled through the heart of the city. Screaming New Yorkers poured into the streets, where the blaze heated the cold winter air and flushed their skin. All through the night, the sky burned in bright shades of orange and red. Thick dark clouds billowed over the harbor as the fire spread with a fury that devoured everything in its path, seventeen blocks in all between Wall and Broad streets and the East River. One New Yorker, who watched helplessly, wrote that it was "the greatest loss by fire that has ever been known, with the exception perhaps of the conflagration of Moscow. . . . I am fatigued in body, disturbed in mind, and my fancy filled with images of horror which my pen is inadequate to describe." Nearly seven hundred buildings were destroyed in that holocaust, two thousand merchants were ruined, up to eight thousand workers unemployed, and most insurance companies bankrupted. What had been spared of the old Dutch city in the fires of 1776 and 1778 now lay in ashes.

This latest catastrophe was proof beyond doubt that New York could not withstand many more assaults. Between 1834 and 1837 a grand and farsighted plan was conceived to divert the water of the Croton River to New York. The idea of an open canal had long been abandoned, since it would be structurally impractical and physically vulnerable to every kind of natural and man-made contamination. It was decided instead to conduct the Croton water to New York through an aqueduct and store it in two huge reservoirs to assure an abundance of pure and wholesome water, no matter how large the city grew. The newly formed Croton Aqueduct Committee undertook responsibility for surveying the region to be flooded and for compensating farmers who occupied the large land tracts which the city needed to purchase for the dam. Immediately, the city fathers faced the uproar of two hundred land owners who resisted such an incursion. Surveying parties were forbidden to cross property lines, "they were subjected to abusive language and, on one or two occasions, were actually assaulted." In the end, land that had been appraised at $65,400 cost the city $257,198.

At long last, on February 28, 1837, newspaper advertisements invited bids until April 26 "for furnishing the materials and completing the construction of *twenty-three sections of the Croton Aqueduct*, including the dam in the Croton, the aqueduct bridge over Sing Sing Kill, and the necessary excavations and tunnelling on the line of about 8½ miles from the Croton to Sing Sing village." A total of three years was allowed for the construction, and strict rules were to be enforced so that the three thousand laborers, most of whom were poor Irish immigrants, would have no access whatsoever to "ardent spirits," either on the job sites or in the hovels which constituted their living quarters while the work was in progress. Nevertheless, there were frequent riots, one of which was so savage that "bodies were maimed, heads were broken, and one man killed." Then, in the spring of 1838, the unskilled laborers went on strike, demanding a wage increase from $.81¼ to $1.00 per day. Their demands were met, although wages were again reduced two years later during the winter slack, bringing about another strike of such violence that the militia had to be called.

Work was begun in May 1837. Without the sophisticated equipment and tools available today, these men set about the monumental task of constructing the Croton Aqueduct through the sheer force and strength of manual labor. Under the supervision of Chief Engineer John B. Jervis, and a corps of engineers, tunnels were gouged out of rock faces, bridges were built, culverts laid. The massive foundation of the dam was buried deep in the ground below the valley which would soon be flooded to become Croton Lake, an earthen embankment was braced on the north shore of the river below the dam, and an elliptical aqueduct, seven and a half feet wide by eight feet high, was constructed through mountains, across valleys, and over newly built bridges. Soon the depth of the Croton Lake stood at forty feet, and the thirty-three-mile stone, brick, and cement aqueduct neared completion. Across the Harlem River and on Manhattan Island itself, an arched viaduct, 1,900 feet long, began to take shape across the Manhattanville flatlands and down the West Side near Tenth Avenue. The viaduct, which could compare proudly with any built by the ancient Romans, carried iron pipes down to grade to conduct Croton water in a wide sweeping arc east to the Yorkville Receiving Reservoir under what is today the Great Lawn in Central Park. From there, iron pipes traveled the final two and a quarter miles to the terminal reservoir at Murray Hill. Throughout its long journey, the aqueduct maintained a steady downward grade of thirteen inches to the mile. Supported by lofty arched bridges which allowed the water far below to run unimpeded, it crossed twenty-five streams and countless brooks whose waters were channeled through culverts. It traversed fields and plunged through forests.

Then, in the early dawn of January 8, 1841, disaster struck. It had been a particularly harsh winter. Snow lay eighteen inches deep on the ground. But the weather patterns had shifted dramatically, and warm moist air hung heavily over the whole area of Croton Lake. Thick black clouds pressed down on the valley, and when they burst, they let loose a rainstorm of such intensity that all the snow melted. For two days, the rain came in such torrents that the water level in Croton Lake above the almost completed dam rose at the terrifying rate of *fourteen inches per hour*, threatening the dam itself. Sheets of water gushed over the dam's overflow and pounded the earthen embankment at the river's edge below. The embankment began to give way. In anticipation of the impending calamity, one brave man, the son of one of the contractors, hurried off in the predawn darkness in a desperate attempt to warn several families who lived in the path of what would shortly be the lake's floodwaters. But the force of the water was so enormous that he could barely make any headway. Even as he ran, the water swept away several bridges below the dam. Miraculously, only three lives and several houses were lost in the storm.

After the winds and rains had died away, the water commissioners and engineers set about assessing the damage. Severe as it was, they soon realized that the storm had proved to be a blessing in disguise. An inspection of the dam demonstrated that although it had withstood the extraordinary onslaught, there was a severe flaw in its design. To correct this, the dam was promptly rebuilt upon a radically different plan and carried 50 feet high and 270 feet across the entire river. The earthen embankment was eliminated altogether, and the overflow extended to three times its original width, to a total of 260 feet. It was with some satisfaction that the water commissioners reported: "We are happy to say, that all the aqueduct work, on the line, has stood remarkably well, and the culverts have been found ample to discharge the water from the valleys and streams, and the embankments have been but little washed or damaged by this unprecedented storm."

The considerable additional expense notwithstanding, work went on with redoubled energy. Water had been promised to the parched city of New York by the summer of 1842, and nothing could stop it from flowing on time.

In June of that year, the water commissioners made their final inspection of the entire aqueduct, beginning six miles above the junction of the Croton and Hudson rivers. The lake behind the dam now spanned five miles in length and covered a total of four hundred acres. The commissioners traveled the entire length of the masonry conduit on foot, checking every inch. Their thirty-three-mile journey to the Harlem River took three days, and when

The Croton Aqueduct's terminal reservoir along Fifth Avenue between Fortieth and Forty-second streets. Built on the site of a potter's field, the Murray Hill Reservoir's upper rim was for decades one of the city's most fashionable promenades. *The J. Clarence Davies Collection, Museum of the City of New York*

they arrived, they were justly proud of having been responsible for the erection of a monument that could withstand the transition into the industrial age.

In the meantime, work was completed on the Croton Aqueduct's terminus, the Murray Hill Reservoir along Fifth Avenue, between Fortieth and Forty-second streets, where the Public Library stands today. Before work could be begun on the reservoir, the potter's field that had occupied the site was moved eastward, the bodies disinterred and then laid once more to rest between Fourth and Lexington avenues, from Forty-ninth to Fiftieth streets, in the block now occupied by the Waldorf-Astoria Hotel. In 1842 the reservoir was still well beyond the densely populated sections of the city, which were then concentrated below Fourteenth Street. The rocky mass of Inclenberg (Murray Hill) rose steeply above Thirty-fourth Street (and still does), with a commanding view far to the south.

At long, long last, on June 22, 1842, at 5:00 A.M., the first Croton water entered the aqueduct. As it made its way swiftly down the long masonry channel, it carried on its back a tiny boat, the *Croton Maid,* with four passengers navigating downstream toward the city. It was an arduous journey, interrupted twice by long portages—at the Harlem River and the Manhattanville Valley—where the water ran through iron pipes.

It was twenty-two hours before the eager crowds that had gathered at the Harlem River end of the line were rewarded with their first glimpse of Croton water. Four days later the new water was admitted through the remaining miles of pipe to the Yorkville Receiving Reservoir. To the shouts and cries of a jubilant multitude, to a thirty-eight-gun salute, to speeches by Governor William Henry Seward (who, as Secretary of State under President Lincoln, purchased the Alaska Territory in 1867) and by Mayor George P. Morris, to the stares of disbelieving dignitaries, merchants, tradesmen, bankers, and ordinary citizens, the sparkling water slowly, luxuriantly crept up the sides of the two huge basins with their total capacity of 150 million gallons. And when the *Croton Maid,* carrying the four commissioners, emerged from the aqueduct's tunnel and came alongside in the reservoir, there was no longer any doubt that a "*navigable* river was flowing into the City for the use of its inhabitants."

It was a day which few who lived through it could ever forget, and the festivities resumed on July 4, when the Croton water was finally introduced into the Murray Hill Reservoir. It was an Independence Day celebration unlike any other the city had experienced. In spite of the early hour of the wondrous event, "an immense concourse assembled to witness the introduction of the Croton water into the reservoir," noted the *Evening Post* the following day. The water "was successfully admitted at sunrise and continued to flow during the day, amid the roars of artillery and the cheers of the multitude." All that day, the citizens of New York crowded around the reservoir, peering with a greed and joy and satisfaction that surely even the wealth of King Solomon's legendary mines could not have elicited. From that day until it was demolished around 1900, the circumference of the Murray Hill Reservoir was one of the most fashionable promenades in the city.

That summer, water spouted freely, lavishly, in all the streets, from hydrants and faucets, from newly designed fountains, down avenues and alleys, from hoses and pipes. Women's skirts dragged heavily through the mud, horses trampled the soft dirt, and carriage wheels sank deep in the wet earth as water flowed clear and fresh and pure and wholesome, with a vigor and abundance never known before.

As Philip Hone, later the mayor of New York, wrote in his famous diary:

> Nothing is talked of or thought of in New York but Croton water; fountains, aqueducts, hydrants, and hose attract our attention and impede our progress through the streets. Political spouting has given place to water spouts, and the free current of water has diverted the attention of the people from the vexed questions of the confused state of the national currency.

So inured to the impurities of all city water were some people that George Templeton Strong was moved to write petulantly that the new water flowed through an aqueduct

In this view of "The Great Water Celebration" of October 14, 1842, the specially honored Volunteer Fire Department contingent in the five-mile-long parade rounds City Hall Park, where fountain jets awesomely display the day's theme. *The J. Clarence Davies Collection, Museum of the City of New York*

"which I hear was used as a necessary by all the Hibernian vagabonds who worked upon it." A year later, in 1843, his trust had quite clearly been won by Croton water when he wrote, "I've led rather an amphibious life for the last week—paddling in the bathing tub every night and constantly making new discoveries in the art and mystery of ablution. Taking a shower bath upside down is the latest novelty."

The date for the official celebration—"The Great Water Celebration"—was set for October 14, 1842. Hundreds of invitations were sent out—to President Tyler and all living ex-presidents, to chief diplomatic representatives, and to state and city officials in every state. The parade route was carefully determined, plaques and medals were struck, banners sewn, special costumes designed, and entertainment, food, and speeches prepared. It was to be a celebration such as New York or any other American city had never before witnessed.

The day began with the roar of a hundred cannons and the ringing of church bells at dawn. The bells of all the city's churches continued to ring every hour until dusk to proclaim New York's rescue. The festivities began at 9:00 A.M. with a special ceremony honoring the Volunteer Fire Department, which had served the city for so long against such imponderable odds. Not a soul slept late. People rushed into the streets in their clean, bright clothing to watch the parade which stretched five miles, winding through the city streets from the Battery up Broadway, around Union Square eastward to the Bowery, over to East Broadway, and from there to Chatham Street and westward to City Hall Park.

"The whole line of the procession," wrote Hone of that memorable day, ". . . embraced, besides the different regiments of troops, firemen, of whom there were fifty-two companies, including several from Philadelphia, Brooklyn, Newark, and Poughkeepsie." The contingent of firemen alone snaked a mile and a half through the city, accompanied by its highly polished engines and bright banners fluttering in the crisp autumn air. There were butchers on horseback, representatives of scientific institutions, temperance societies, printers and mechanic associations. Most notable of all, however, said Hone, was the "perfect order and propriety" of the masses along the route. "Not a drunken person was to be seen."

The fountain in Union Square "throws up a noble column of water to a height as great almost as the houses which surround the square," marveled the *Evening Post*. But by far the most spectacular sight was the fountain in City Hall Park, where from an as yet uncompleted one-hundred-foot basin, one main center jet and its twenty-four subordinates were capable of spouting watery sculptures fifty feet into the air. To the proud New Yorkers this display could surely not have been rivaled by the fountains of Versailles, Rome, or St. Petersburg. Riding in the carriage with Governor Seward was John B. Jervis, chief engineer of the Croton Aqueduct, the man under whose keen and vigilant eye it had all become a reality. As the carriage neared City Hall Park, two hundred members of the New York Sacred Music Society sang an ode written especially for the occasion by Mayor Morris. The fountain's jets played their awe-inspiring themes high into the blue sky—"The Maid of the Mist," "The Croton Plume," and "The Fan." And, as the sun sank over the Hudson, to the sound of the church bells, amid singing and cheering, a "cold collation" was served to dignitaries and hundreds of citizens at the end of that wonderful day.

Once the celebration was over, work resumed on High Bridge, 1,450 feet long and built to carry two iron pipes, 36 inches in diameter, over the Harlem River. When the bridge was finished in 1848, it marked the completion of the Croton Aqueduct system. High Bridge still stands today (amid a network of highways and apartment complexes), its elegant arches rising a hundred feet above the river.

To twentieth-century New Yorkers who have never experienced the desperation of prolonged thirst or of monstrous diseases, the following statement made by a witness to the Croton miracle may seem extreme. But to those who were saved by that miracle, these words were undoubtedly true.

The solidity of the general structure forbids the idea, for centuries, of other than slight occasional repairs. . . . The abundance of the source relieves from all solicitude as to adequate supplies for multitudinous population hereafter. It is for the future even more than for the present, and will attest to other lands and to other times, that, magnificent as may be the works of conquerors and kings, they have not equaled in forecast of design, and beneficence of result, the noble aqueduct, constructed at their own cost, by the freemen of the single city of New York.

All the same, less than ten years later, the Common Council, cognizant "that the means of storing a large supply of water upon the island, cannot with safety be much longer deferred," instructed the Croton Water Department "to purchase, without any unnecessary delay,

High Bridge across the Harlem River marked the completion of the Croton Aqueduct system. The columns to some of the bridge's lofty arches were eventually removed to make room for shipping. *The J. Clarence Davies Collection, Museum of the City of New York*

enough of suitable ground upon which to construct a new reservoir, of capacity sufficient with those already built, to contain a supply for at least sixty days consumption. . . ." Two years later, in 1853, the Legislature authorized the city to acquire lands between Eighty-sixth and Ninety-sixth streets, Fifth and Seventh avenues for the construction of this new Croton reservoir. Built of brick and granite, to an average depth of 40 feet, and covering 107 acres, Manhattan Lake is capable of holding more than a billion gallons of water.

As the city spread northward at an alarming rate, there were ever more vigorous efforts to reserve some acreage for park land. Among the proposed sites was Jones Wood, bounded by the East River and Third Avenue, from Sixty-sixth to Seventy-fifth streets. Two major arguments against this location were its obviously rich real estate value along the waterfront and its ludicrously small size. Landscape gardener Andrew Jackson Downing scoffed that such a 154-acre park was "only a child's playground!" With a population rapidly approaching the one-million mark, he felt that "five hundred acres is the smallest area that should be reserved for the future wants of such a city, *now*, while it may be obtained." It was on this assumption that he proposed a central reservation around the Croton Aqueduct's reservoirs.

In 1853 the Legislature passed two bills, one authorizing Jones Wood, the other Central Park. In due course it fell to Frederick Law Olmsted and Calvert Vaux to transform the disorderly topography north of Fifty-ninth Street into a recreation ground which would provide for New York's citizens not only a cultured garden in the manner of European parks but also a sense of spaciousness and variety which would give the illusion of open countryside. Hampered both by the park's central, rectangular location and by the existing Yorkville reservoirs, the park's design evolved slowly. It was a difficult task. There were several brooks running through the area, and the topographic undulations were of relatively unimpressive scope. Olmsted and Vaux therefore decided that "mere rivulets are uninteresting, and we have preferred to collect the ornamental water in large sheets, and carry off through underground drains the water that at present runs through the park in shallow brooks." Before the Yorkville Reservoir was eventually filled to become the present-day Great Lawn, Olmsted and Vaux coped with its awkward rectangular border by banking it with trees and leading paths away from it. Today, Manhattan Lake, the irregularly shaped reservoir to the north, encompassing 107 acres between Eighty-sixth and Ninety-sixth streets, could hardly look more natural in its surroundings.

As the work on Central Park progressed slowly and steadfastly, the topography was rearranged to fashion the beauty, variety, and charm that exist today. In all, ten million cartloads of stone, soil, and glacial outwash were removed or repositioned to give the park its present natural look. The lakes, which seem as if they had always been there, were created through massive excavations and the installation of a ninety-five-mile drainage system that carried off excess surface water and, at the same time, allowed for regular infusions of water from the reservoir.

Before the park could be finished, work was interrupted by a far greater tragedy than the city itself had suffered until then: the War between the States. A few days after the Confederate attack on Fort Sumter, New York's crack Seventh Regiment marched eagerly toward Washington, past cheering thousands, to defend the Yankee North. Four years later a shot was fired which plunged millions of Americans into deepest mourning. Charged with their saddest duty of the war, the Seventh returned home, as escort of the cortege which brought the body of President Lincoln to City Hall. Some 120,000 people who had only four years before cheered the regiment to war, now thronged past the coffin in stunned silence.

When peace once again joined the Republic, work resumed on Central Park.

The park has undergone many changes since its completion in 1876. It has become host to many more buildings than had been the vision of Olmsted and Vaux, though for New Yorkers it is indeed the oasis which was first imagined for them well over a hundred years ago.

As a generation of New Yorkers grew up to the commonplace of ever-present, ever-abundant water, others became only too painfully aware that the Croton supply would soon be insufficient. "More Water Wanted," stated *The New York Times* on October 15, 1882. It was found that "the amount of water supplied was inadequate to meet the requirements of households between 6:00 A.M. and 9:00 P.M., as during that time it did not run above the basement floors." The article went on to say that "the health of families . . . was jeopardized because sufficient water could not be secured to keep clear the sewer and other pipes and prevent the generation of gasses." One of the proposals was to stop using the two thousand wells that existed in the city and which, it was estimated, supplied some two million gallons of water a day with "all sorts of bad things" in it. Because of the expense of water meters, "a great many wells were being bored in cellars."

Although Bronx River water had been used by Bronx residents without ill effects for some time, the suggestion of its diversion for use by Manhattanites was once again rejected on the grounds that it was "a dirty stream." In a petition to the Commissioner of Public Works, a group of West Forty-third Street residents "prayed for relief" and agreed that probably the "best place to obtain a water supply was the Hudson, opposite Esopus Creek."

The time had come for a new aqueduct.

In 1883 the Legislature authorized the city to build a new Croton Aqueduct of tunnel construction, and to include not only the Central Park reservoirs but also a new reservoir at Jerome Park in the Bronx. Completed in 1891, the new aqueduct's capacity was 300 million gallons daily. Yet it, too, soon proved inadequate.

As the flow of immigration from the face of Europe assumed tidal proportions by the turn of the century, the city's development lurched uptown at an unprecedented pace. The island was covered shore to shore with buildings, from Grand to Fourteenth streets, from there to Twenty-third Street, approaching Forty-second in little more than fifty years. In 1890 Manhattan alone had a population of just under 1.5 million. Between 1860 and 1912 more than 25 million immigrants were admitted at Manhattan's port of entry, located at Castle Garden until 1892 and at Ellis Island thereafter. It was a flood tide of human dispersal such as the world had never seen before, nor has seen since.

On May 4, 1897—271 years after Peter Minuit's arrival in Manhattan—The Greater New York Charter became law. On January 1, 1898, it went into effect, uniting Brooklyn, Queens, and Staten Island with Manhattan and the Bronx. What had been a city of 22.3 square miles was suddenly transformed into a metropolis of 539 square miles, with a total population of 3.1 million. A population still desperate for water.

After a private company had sought an exclusive forty-year contract to supply the city with up to 200 million gallons of additional water from the streams of the Catskill Mountains, a careful survey indicated a need for at least 500 million gallons per day. And so, in 1905, Governor Frank W. Higgins signed into law two measures that simultaneously created New York City's Board of Water Supply and the State Water Supply Commission, the latter designed to safeguard the water resources of all the state's communities.

Almost exactly two years later to the day, on June 20, 1907, the first shovelful of earth of what has since become one of the finest municipal water systems in the world was turned. Built in two stages, the Catskill Water Supply System was to provide a total dependable water supply of 525 million gallons a day, 250 million gallons of which would be available by 1917, the end of the first stage of construction. It included the building of three reservoirs at elevations as high as 1,130 feet above sea level (measured at Sandy Hook, where Henry Hudson first landed) with a total storage capacity of 190 billion gallons and with drainage areas at elevations of up to 4,000 feet through heavily forested mountainous land which ranks among the most spectacular in the world. More than 25,000 acres of land and a water surface of 18.4 square miles were acquired for this project. Nine former villages were submerged, and a total population of 2,850 moved elsewhere. To make way for New York's water, more than 4,000 bodies in 39 cemeteries had to be reinterred, 11 miles of railroads relocated, 16 bridges built, and 67.5 miles of highways constructed.

A total of about 23 million cubic yards of rock and earth was excavated in tunnels and open cuts, and millions of cubic yards of stone masonry and concrete were applied by a work force of 5,300 men. From the Schoharie Reservoir to the Silver Lake Reservoir on Staten Island, tunnels and aqueducts carried water to the city over a distance of 159 miles.

Schoharie Creek, a tributary of the Mohawk River, together with some 314 square miles of land provides the watershed tributary to the Schoharie Reservoir in the New York State counties of Schoharie, Delaware, and Greene. Because the Catskill mountain streams are subject to floods, the tunnel leading from the Schoharie Reservoir was built large enough to carry more than twice the supply that is normally obtained from the watershed. The overflow portion of Gilboa Dam stretching across the lower portion of the reservoir was built on solid rock and constructed of large stone blocks embedded in concrete. The downstream face consists of large terraces which break the force of water spilling over the crest. From there, Shandaken Tunnel is capable of conveying more than 650 million gallons of water per day to Esopus Creek, which was deepened and enlarged to cope with the vastly increased flow. Itself a tributary of the Hudson River, the Esopus drains south and central portions of the Catskill Mountains and carries the waters to the Ashokan Reservoir west of the city of Kingston. With a maximum depth of 190 feet and a water surface of 12.8 square miles, this reservoir is as large as Manhattan Island below 110th Street, with a capacity of 130 *billion* gallons, a quantity that is sufficient to drown all Manhattan Island under thirty feet of water!

On leaving Ashokan Reservoir, the city's water is successively aerated (1,599 nozzles liberate any odor-producing gases and charge the water with oxygen), screened, and chlorinated. Below the reservoir, Olive Bridge Dam stretches 4,650 feet across Esopus Creek and funnels the water into the Catskill Aqueduct, a huge conduit that carries its precious cargo through Ulster and Orange Counties to Storm King Mountain, where it crosses the Hudson River. It travels from there down the east side of the Hudson to the Kensico Reservoir above White Plains, and from there to Hill View Reservoir in Yonkers, a total of ninety-two miles. From Hill View, the aqueduct continues as City Tunnel No. 1 and crosses the city line, deep under the streets of the West Bronx and Manhattan, traveling virtually in a straight line north and south down the center of the island, with large pipe conduits and siphons serving as the means of distribution as far as the borough of Richmond on Staten Island.

Portions of the aqueduct are as large as seventeen and a half feet high by eighteen feet wide (larger than a subway tunnel) and are driven through hills and mountains or buried by "cut-and-cover" construction. To cross broad valleys, it was decided to construct pressure tunnels deep in solid rock, so that the overburden of rock and earth could withstand the pressure of water in the tunnels. These, in turn, were met at each end of the valley by vertical circular shafts, all concrete-lined, with occasional steel reinforcement. All the voids around the tunnels and shafts were filled by forcing a thin grout of Portland cement into the spaces under pressure. The Hudson River, by far the largest of the valleys which had to be transversed, required particularly careful attention. Here a fourteen-foot tunnel was driven between the vertical shafts on both sides of the river through solid granite to a depth of 1,114 feet below sea level (only 136 feet less than the height of the Empire State Building), for a distance of 3,022 feet.

Kensico Reservoir north of White Plains was designed primarily to contain a sixty-day emergency supply of Catskill water, in case the aqueduct above it needed to be inspected, cleaned, or repaired. (Its dam spans the Bronx River, which allows that river at last to become a small part of the city's water supply.) With nearly a million cubic yards of masonry, the Kensico Dam, considered one of the great structures of the world at the time it was built, nevertheless contains only one-third the masonry of the Great Pyramid in Egypt. Fifteen miles south of Kensico, just north of New York City, the water reaches Hill View Reservoir, 295 feet above sea level. Here, through the reservoir's two outlets, City Tunnel No. 1 and City Tunnel No. 2, New York City's water supply is regulated to its hourly needs. Hill View's elevation allows the water to be delivered by gravity, with minimal need for pumping. City Tunnel No. 2 courses through the East Bronx, across the East River at Riker's Island just west of the river mouth into Long Island Sound, through Queens, and south to Brooklyn. Two delivery conduits extend to Silver Lake Reservoir on Staten Island and are carried across the Narrows by thirty-six-inch and forty-two-inch flexible-jointed cast-iron submarine pipelines known as Narrows siphons. They lie buried in deep trenches in the harbor bottom to protect them from ships' anchors and other hazards. (Since completion in 1971 of a rock tunnel ten feet in diameter and nine hundred feet below the Narrows, and a conduit eight feet in diameter under the streets of Staten Island, leading to storage tanks with a capacity of 100 million gallons, the two pipelines from the City Tunnel No. 2 system and the Silver Lake Reservoir have been used only intermittently.)

The city tunnels themselves, 38 miles in all and as much as 780 feet below the surface, were constructed deep through the rock underlying the Bronx, Manhattan, Queens, and Brooklyn. Vertical shafts dotted throughout the city contain "risers," which bring water to the surface to supply the local distributing mains and delivery conduits. The risers terminate at the tops of the shafts in underground valve chambers that control and measure the delivery of water to the street mains.

In case of a major break in the valve chamber or in the connected pipelines, a bronze riser valve can be closed automatically or by the mere pressure of a fingertip. To provide maximum security, these valves are located more than a hundred feet under the *top* of solid rock. To assure a constant equality of pressure throughout the city, large steel conduits connect the city tunnels in Brooklyn. Other connections admit Croton water from the original system into City Tunnel No. 1.

The Catskill system was an achievement such as few of the world's great cities have known. With immigration unrestricted, labor was abundant. Largely uneducated, accustomed through poverty to the crudest unsanitary living conditions imaginable, these immigrants provided plenty of cheap labor—although they brought with them all manner of disease. One of the first measures undertaken by the Board of Water Supply was to set advanced standards of campsite and watershed sanitation and hygiene. Strictly supervised model camps were constructed with recreational facilities and maintained in scrupulous cleanliness, with the help of health and sanitary experts, police, and fire protection. Extraordinary precautions were taken to prevent pollution of the watersheds, streams, and reservoirs. Runoffs from the campsites were regularly chlorinated and filtered to minimize the risk of contamination during the water system's construction.

The Board of Water Supply was also required "to provide proper police protection to the inhabitants of the localities in which any work may be constructed ... against the acts and omissions of persons employed on such works or found in the neighborhood thereof." This provision was well reasoned, since many laborers in those years were accustomed not only to carrying arms but to using them at the slightest provocation. A largely mounted police force of as many as 377 men maintained twenty-four-hour patrols, not only of the camps and working places but for a mile in either direction, covering some 240 square miles. Their duties included maintaining general order and sanitary regulations as well as suppressing riots, removing liquor and weapons from the camps, preventing crimes, and catching felons. Their task was far from easy, and they averaged 1,500 arrests per year. By 1918 they had obtained 4,998 convictions, including a case with the remarkable ratio of seven executions for two murders!

The first Catskill water reached Manhattan in 1916 and Brooklyn and Queens the following year, with city-wide celebrations marking the occasion in 1917—exactly seventy-five years after the Great Water Celebration of 1842—although construction of the City Tunnels Nos. 1 and 2 was not completed until 1936, by which time preparations were already underway for the new and larger Delaware System.

As soon as the first Catskill water had been introduced, the city's water consumption rose by a staggering 30 million gallons per day, and it was immediately recognized that, at this rate of increase, the city would shortly be in peril again. By 1938 the population of greater New York had reached 7.5 million and was still growing. It was estimated that, with the addition of the Delaware System, the city's water supply could be increased by 700 million gallons per day. The project was to be completed in 1939.

However, unlike the Catskill System, all of whose water sources lay within New York State, the Delaware System was to draw on sources which flowed through New Jersey and Pennsylvania as well as through New York. Action brought by the state of New Jersey in the United States Supreme Court caused serious delays until 1931, when the Court decreed that New York City could divert only a limited amount of water from the Delaware River and its tributaries. The decree also required the city to release water into the river during dry seasons. Actual construction did not begin until 1937, and not long afterward the requirements of the armed services during World War II delayed the project still further.

By the time the first limited supplies of the Delaware System were introduced at the end of the war, the city was again on the brink of disaster. The postwar population explosion proved so enormous that the combined capacities of the other aqueducts were incapable of meeting the city's demand for water.

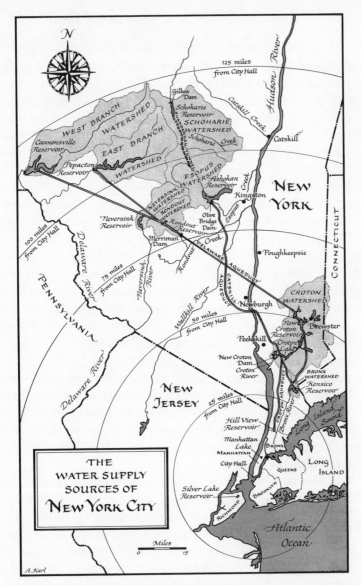

To obtain the 1.5 billion gallons of fresh water New Yorkers use every day, watershed areas are tapped as far away as 125 miles. The supply flows as deep as 1,114 feet below sea level and as high as 295 feet above to reach the city's 794,000 service connections. *The Board of Water Supply, New York City*

Traveling a total of 162 miles, Delaware water was obtained from near the river's head, necessitating the purchase of 65 square miles of land by the city. Once again, villages were flooded, cemeteries removed and bodies reinterred, highways built—all in preparation for increasing New York City's available water supply to 1.5 billion gallons per day. Four reservoirs, of which the Neversink at 1,440 feet is the highest, followed by the Pepacton, Rondout, and Cannonsville, have a total storage capacity of 330.4 billion gallons. However, because the Delaware System must be shared, the available storage for city use is often less.

With the advances in modern technology and equipment, tunnel excavations were accelerated to the incredible distance of 135–270 feet per week, as compared with 25–40 feet per week during construction of the original Croton Aqueduct and 55–70 feet per week during the Catskill System's construction. From two of the countless exploratory borings along the route gushed 2,300 gallons of water per minute, so that the contractor was forced to install a series of pumps to keep the tunnel from being flooded. On another occasion, under pressure of large quantities of water, some one thousand cubic yards of decayed rock in the form of mud, sand, and small stones burst into the tunnel.

Unlike its predecessors but just like City Tunnel No. 2, the 105-mile Delaware Aqueduct is a circular pressure tunnel buried deep in bedrock, making it by far the longest tunnel built anywhere for any purpose. As deep as one thousand feet below the ground surface, the tunnel traverses terrain containing deep earth-filled preglacial gorges in the bedrock or geological faults where the rock is crushed and deeply decayed. At these points the tunnel is deep enough to allow the cover of solid rock and overburden to resist the tremendous pressure which, under the Hudson River, for example, is more than five hundred pounds per square inch.

At the reservoirs, in addition to aeration and chlorination processes, Delaware water is subjected to the rigors of a coagulating plant which removes any traces of turbidity. By the time Delaware water reaches the city, it can be counted, together with Croton and Catskill water, among the purest, safest, and most wholesome of fresh waters in any municipality in the world.

The combined watershed areas that quench New York's lusty thirst cover more than two thousand square miles, or an acreage slightly smaller than the entire state of Delaware. Yet, even before the East and West branches of the Delaware System were completed, the Board of Water Supply was forced to anticipate future needs. To this end, City Tunnel No. 3 was begun to provide broader distribution facilities throughout the city. Already called "one of the engineering wonders of the world—the greatest nondefense construction project in the history of Western Civilization, greater than the Panama Canal or the St. Lawrence Seaway," City Tunnel No. 3's massive twenty-four-foot pipe will be large enough to accommodate two freight trains side by side (not that it will be asked to). It will be constructed in four stages and will course down through the Bronx, across the Harlem River just north of the approach to the George Washington Bridge, south through Manhattan's West Side, and then east across Welfare Island to Queens and Brooklyn, where it will connect with the Richmond Tunnel to increase water distribution to Staten Island. Because of the city's financial problems, Stage One of City Tunnel No. 3 has progressed in largely spasmodic bursts, at a cost already of $200 million and nineteen lives. Each passing year of continued delays brings the threat of a water shortage dangerously closer, while the empty rock tunnel itself, exposed to the air, is in constant danger of collapse.

City Tunnels Nos. 1 and 2 were engineered to outlast the city itself, drawing on the 600-billion-gallon capacity of their watersheds in New York State's mountainous regions (although, once completed, City Tunnel No. 3 is destined first to supplement and later replace the two existing tunnels). About ninety-five percent of the water New York residents drink every day, and take so much for granted, is sent under the force of gravity through a six-thousand-mile network of pipes ranging from four to seventy-two inches in diameter. This pressure is sufficient to reach the top floor of a five- or six-story building; the remaining five percent must be pumped to higher elevations. Branching out from the street mains throughout the city are some 794,000 service connections to individual buildings, and from here, still smaller pipes serve each apartment.

To secure service, and to keep a constant pressure at street level, the mains are interspersed with small underground reservoirs hidden all over the city. These eighty-four-inch prestressed concrete-sheathed mains are lowered into the rock in sixteen-foot lengths which weigh twenty tons each. Yet for all their size, only four bolts and a rubber grommet keep them from leaking.

It is within the system of street water mains, many of them more than a hundred years old, that trouble frequently stirs. Even though they are constructed of cast iron, many regularly succumb to old age. In fact, the city's water mains burst on the average of one per day. This usually happens at night when little water is used, when faucets have been shut off and pressure builds up in the pipes. It is not at all uncommon for about four hundred mains to burst in this fashion in any given year. But the all-time record was set in November 1957, when six mains erupted within a five-hour period—all of them in the vicinity of the Metropolitan Opera House, at Broadway and Thirty-ninth Street, with the opera house suffering considerable damage. Since the pipes were quite old, the collective pressure that had built up inside them forced the water to explode through several points.

Water mains break frequently during a sudden thaw following prolonged freezing temperatures, when the pipes begin to expand with the warmth—even though they are usually buried well below the frost line. At other times they break for no obvious reason, with water blasting upward in the predawn hours, gouging through the street surface, gushing forth in vast quantities and flooding streets, manholes, and rapid transit subways. The water threatens buried utility lines—often ripping them apart under its force—and pours into neighboring cellars. When this happens, a variety of emergency work crews from the city and utility companies rush to the scene within minutes. The water supply to the immediate area must be turned off to stop the flow through the ruptured main. Electric power must be shut off before conduits can be inspected. Manholes and subways have to be pumped, gas and steam leaks checked. It requires a swift and concerted effort by all the utilities involved to make the necessary repairs and to resume service.

One of the more ironic breaks took place in March 1977, near Foley Square. The water from a hundred-year-old, twenty-inch cast-iron main which exploded through the street there not long past midnight must surely have felt quite at home in the proximity of what used to be Collect Pond. It flooded the Federal Court House cellars to several feet, streamed into the office building of the United States Attorney, and ruined a twenty-five-day food supply at the jail. The gaping chasm on Pearl Street from Kent Place to Park Row laid bare a tangle of broken and cracked electrical conduits, a rusted gas main, the naked shaft of a telephone manhole, and a large jagged hole in the water main some ten feet below the street. It also revealed an old gas main, cracked and abandoned. Although electric power was restored within hours, judges and lawyers and office workers seized the unexpected opportunity to take time off on a beautiful sunny day and watch the show.

Thus New York's precious water supply is lost through water main breaks, just as it is through the wanton opening of fire hydrants in summer. As early as 1948 a New Sources Division devoted exclusively to New York City's future water supplies was established by the Board of Water Supply. It has been long recognized that building more aqueducts to far-distant sources is no longer practical, nor is there time. Sources must be developed within the context of existing aqueducts, tunnels, and reservoirs. To this end, as early as 1949, the Hudson River above Chelsea and Rhinecliff and above the salt water line from the ocean was chosen as a source from which up to a hundred million gallons of water could be pumped daily in times of extreme emergency. After thorough screening and superchlorination and the addition of copper sulphate to control algae and other organisms, this water can be introduced into the Delaware Aqueduct through the Hudson River pumping plant. With the addition of alum to the water to help remove turbidity, and allowing for a period of "quarantine" in the West Branch and Kensico reservoirs, as well as other purification processes that require several months, additional water can be provided for the city. Radioactive monitoring and laboratory analysis for alpha beta and tritium activities continue each week under the watchful eyes of the New York State Department of Health and the United States Environmental Protection Agency.

And so, deep into the city's fourth century, the search goes on for alternatives that will "once and for all time" alleviate New York's water shortage.

three
SPIRITS
WILD
AND
MAGIC

Gas: a word derived from *chaos*. It is a void and formless infinite, colorless, and, in its natural state, without odor. It has the capacity of generating heat and light and energy for myriad modern needs. It is used in the manufacture of chemicals as well as steel, glass, cement, china and pottery, automobiles, bread, and clothing.

It was in 1609, the same year that brought Henry Hudson to the shores of New York, that the Belgian alchemist and mystic Jan Baptista van Helmont began experimenting with fuels and discovered that they yield "a wild spirit." The same man who believed that buckets filled with wheat flour and dirty linen would spontaneously spawn mice now found that this "spirit" could be produced through combustion, fermentation, and the action of acids on limestone. "Seventy-two pounds of oak charcoal gave one pound of cinders and the seventy-one pounds remaining served to form the spirit Sylvester," he wrote. "This spirit, up to the present time unknown, not susceptible of being confined to vessels, nor capable of being produced in a visible body, I call by a new name—gas."

Seventy years later, in the early 1680s, John Clayton, an English parson from Yorkshire who experimented with steam engines fifty years before James Watt, developer of the steam engine, was even born, made a series of discoveries about the properties of gas which hold true even today. He wrote:

Having seen a ditch within two miles of Wigan in Lancashire wherein the water would seemingly burn like Brandy, the flame of which was so fierce that several strangers have boiled Eggs over it, I observed that there had formerly been coal pits in the same close of Ground & I then got some coal from one of the pits nearest thereto which I distilled in a Retort in an open fire.

Finding that this process at first produced only steam, followed by "a black oyle," Clayton was at last rewarded by a spirit which arose.

I observed that the spirit which issued out caught fire at the flame of the candle & continued burning with violence as it issued out, in a stream. . . . I then had a mind to try if I could save any of this Spirit, in order to which I took a turbinated Receiver & putting a candle to the pipe of the Receiver whilst the Spirit arose I observed that it catched flame & continued burning at the end of the pipe though you could not discern what fed the flame. I then blew it out and light [sic] it again several times, after which

I fixed a bladder squeezed & void of air to the pipe of the Receiver. The oyle & fleghm [steam] descended into the Receiver but the Spirit still ascending blew up the bladder.

With one single stroke, Clayton had discovered that coal could produce gas, that gas remained combustible even after passing through water, and that it could be stored. Although it appears that a number of ministers were drawn to the mysteries of natural gas (it is not quite clear what particularly attracted men of the cloth to the gas business), a century was to pass before its many uses began to be harnessed. While the civilized world advanced from lighting supplied by sperm oil to the age of the wax and tallow candle, in 1792 another Englishman, William Murdock, succeeded in lighting his Cornwall home with gas produced from coal. By 1798 he had joined James Watt as a construction and erection engineer in London's Soho and had succeeded in lighting an entire factory with gas.

Legend has it that inspiration for Murdock's development of the cockspur burner, or gas tip, came from his wife's thimble. Wishing to extinguish the gas flame at the end of an open tube, he capped it with the thimble. Since it was an old and well-worn thimble, it did not entirely stop the flow of gas. When Murdock held a light to it, he obtained from the tiny perforations a flame that was far more intense than the flame from the open tube. But even though Murdock had thus demonstrated the practicality of gas lighting, he failed to pursue this achievement on a broader scale.

At the same time that Murdock was experimenting in England, Philippe Lebon was active in France. By 1799 he had obtained a patent for producing gas by distilling coal or wood, and by 1801 he was lighting his Paris home and garden with gas. However, it was left to the Moravian promoter and mountebank, Albert Winsor (or Winzer, Winzler, Wintzler), an unscrupulous plagiarist of technical writings, whose own knowledge of chemistry was nonexistent, to take up the cause of gas. And this he did with flare and fervor, with courage, and above all with great vision. In 1803 he traveled to London to propose the organization of a company for "enlightening the inhabitants of London." He gave lectures and organized exhibitions, and in 1804 he obtained the first English patent for gas-making purposes. But Winsor's vision, which anticipated by more than a century the many uses to which gas is put today, was separated from realization by a chasm of ignorance and prejudice.

"Since the beginning of the world," he stated in an early appeal, "mankind has lost above eighty per cent in all combustibles by the mere evaporation of smoke. This very smoke, which often proves troublesome and dangerous to health and houses, is now discovered to contain the most valuable substances, and, if properly extracted, gathered, washed, purified and resolved, we gain no less than five costly products, viz: oil, pitch, acid, coke and gas. . . ."

His plea went unheeded. "There is a madman proposing to light London with—what do you think? Why, with smoke." So wrote Sir Walter Scott to a friend. The great Napoleon merely dismissed the idea as *une grande folie.* Actors and writers ridiculed Winsor from the stage and in verse.

Three years later, the tenacious Winsor gained the support of wealthy shareholders in the London and Westminster Gas Light & Coke Company; he won the applause of all Londoners for the first public street lighting in London's Pall Mall on January 28, 1807. Less than five years later, Parliament granted him a charter, and the world's first gas company came into existence.

During the same years, tremors of anticipation began to flicker in the United States when M. Ambroise & Company, Italian fireworkers and artists located in Philadelphia, mounted a gas-lighting exhibition. Then in 1812, David Melville, a pewter and hardware merchant living in Newport, Rhode Island, lighted his home and the street in front of it with gas he manufactured from coal. By 1817 he had induced the government to let him install gas lighting in the Beaver Tail Lighthouse. Even though his light could be seen as far as forty miles away, at Montauk Point on Long Island, Melville never gained popular recognition, and he died in obscurity.

It was Baltimore which broke through popular opposition and became the first American city to install public street lighting. Other cities eventually followed but not before a New England newspaper had published a bill of objections:

1. A theological objection. Artificial illumination is an attempt to interfere with the divine plan of the world which had preordained that it should be dark during the night time.
2. A medical objection. Emanations of illuminating gas are injurious. Lighted streets will incline people to remain late out of doors, thus leading to increase of ailments by colds.
3. A moral objection. The fear of darkness will vanish, and drunkenness and depravity increase.
4. Police objection. Horses will be frightened and thieves emboldened.
5. Objections from the people. If streets are illuminated every night, such constant illumination will rob festive occasions of their charm.

Nevertheless, the use of gas lighting soon spread to public buildings, although only wealthy citizens could afford to light their homes with gas. Because rates were high and progress slow, it was not until 1865 that home lighting with gas made any real headway. Today, gas is an industry which represents an annual utility investment of more than $50 billion.

It was Rubens Peale of Baltimore who introduced the charms and infinite possibilities of gas lighting to New York, and it was New York, with its customary drive and ingenuity, which made the manufacture of gas an industry of major proportions. In 1816 the Common Council appointed a committee to study the feasibility of building a municipal gasworks. After seven months and $6,000 of the taxpayers' money had been spent, a crude gas-making apparatus was erected near City Hall, with temporary tin pipes running down Chatham Street and on Broadway to Fulton Street. Shopkeepers along this short route were wildly enthusiastic about their newfound illumination, so much so that they were prepared to pay as much as $10 a year for gas lights. But still the committee soberly reported that gas lighting, though no doubt profitable for private individuals, would be far too expensive for the city to undertake. While the issue languished at City Hall, three influential men of vision—Samuel Leggett, Thomas Morris, and Josiah Ogden Hoffman—took matters into their own hands. They traveled the two-and-a-half-day journey by stagecoach to Albany, and when they disembarked at sundown on February 21, 1823, they were prepared to confront the State Legislature to seek a charter for a company to be known as the New York Gas Light Company and to be vested with "full power and authority to manufacture, make, and sell gas, to be made of coal, oil, tar, peat, pitch, or turpentine, or other materials, and to be used for the purpose of lighting said city [New York], or the streets thereof, and any buildings, manufactories, or houses therein contained or situate."

The charter was granted, but with the stipulation that the company obtain permission from the city. Six weeks of negotiations followed, at the end of which, on May 12,

1823, an agreement was reached between the company and city officials. The company agreed to build, service, and maintain all necessary equipment, lay pipes on Broadway between the Battery and Grand Street, and supply light to streets and public places, using gas of a quality equal to that used in the city of London and at an expense no greater than the cost of oil lighting. The city's part of the bargain was to bear the cost of lampposts and the gas they used. At the same time, the company could not prevent others who might wish to do so from setting up a gas apparatus on their own premises.

With Samuel Leggett as its first president the New York Gas Light Company was capitalized at $1 million, and on May 23, four thousand $50 par value shares were offered to the public. As had been the experience of the Manhattan Company some twenty years earlier, the new gas company was immediately oversubscribed.

That June, Timothy Dewey, who had been selected as superintendent of the new gasworks, sailed for Liverpool to study English gas practices and to purchase necessary equipment. The company's directors permitted him an absence of three and a half months—two months' travel time, and four to six weeks for his study. During this brief time he was charged with seeing, reading, and learning about all aspects of gas manufacture from oil and coal. He was to visit existing plants in several English cities to learn everything possible about gas mains and service pipes, burners and lamps, gas meters and fixtures—their construction, assembly, and operation. He was also to hire skilled workers and purchase all necessary apparatus for the construction of a plant in New York. It was a tall order, and therefore it was not surprising that more than seven months went by before Dewey returned with his report and an accounting for $18,500 in expenditures for machinery.

Armed with plans and drawings, he set about constructing an oil gasworks plant in which gas was to be manufactured from whale or various fish oils which were more economical than coal (although by 1828 these had also become too expensive and difficult to obtain, and beginning the following year gas was made from rosin). By December 1824, six miles of mains had been laid a few feet under the surface not far from the Manhattan Company's water pipes, and more than three hundred building owners had subscribed to the new service. At the end of January 1825, the Manhattan Company announced it was ready to supply two thousand hogsheads of water to the cistern surrounding the gasometer—a measure which not only allowed the gasometer to float but also prevented the gas from leaking.

Although we do not know exactly when the fire at the gasworks on the corner of Hester and Rhynder (Centre) streets was first lit, it can be safely said that gas service began in New York on February 14, 1825. By September, more than 1,700 burners had been installed, with demand rapidly outreaching all expectations. Only the Common Council viewed these developments with a certain skepticism and maintained a suitable indifference to all the excitement. However, when the gas company offered to install gas lamps in the council chamber and to provide gas free of charge for one full year, the city fathers accepted graciously. Yet two years went by before they bestirred themselves to any official action to permit gas lighting. Instead, they appointed yet another committee to engage in a study comparing the costs of lighting the city streets with oil or with gas. The result was a grand $2,000 appropriation to install gas lamps on Broadway for a distance of less than two miles between the Battery and Grand Street.

Presto! The "Great White Way" was born. The public, which had until then remained generally apprehensive, suddenly began flooding City Hall with requests for similar lighting on *their* streets. This caused a good deal of consternation for the city fathers, who were now bound by their own agreement with the New York Gas Light Company to assume the expenses of $24 lampposts as well as $8 annually per lamp for gas. Needless to say, each application and petition was given careful thought. But demand was so insistent that it was not long before other streets were lined with lampposts, and proportionate lengths of mains were laid underground.

In 1826 the Hester Street gas plant was already so strenuously overworked that its directors were forced to advertise a plea for caution and conservation so that there would be enough gas to go around. The public responded reluctantly. Free at last of the daily chore of cleaning and trimming lamp wicks, relieved of the expense of candles, New Yorkers basked in the magical new illumination. So the company resorted to hiring gas inspectors whose duty it was to patrol the streets in the evening, loudly rapping their canes on the sidewalk and crying, "Gas lights out." As the gas lights dimmed inside the houses, the light of candles and oil lamps appeared. If an inspector's command was not obeyed, he promptly turned the offender's gas supply off altogether.

Between 1830 and 1863 three other companies entered the field—the Manhattan Gas Light Company, the Harlem Gas Light Company, and the Metropolitan Gas Light Company—and with them came new manufacturing plants. Fierce competition sprang up between them all, and New Yorkers were caught in a crossfire of claims and counterclaims, rising and falling prices, and interrupted or multiple service, while the streets were torn apart and the noise of discordant shouts echoed through the city. Bitter propaganda and angry charges flew through the air, luring customers with cut-rate prices and the promise of better service, while stockholders were promised high dividends. The New York Gas Light Company's early agreement with the city soon proved economically ruinous because of the much better terms the rival companies had obtained, the rising costs of maintaining the lamps, and the required wages of the company's many lamplighters who carried their ladders through the streets every sunup and sundown to turn the lights off and on.

In the 1840s it was decided to meet the ever-increasing demand of the city's half-million population for gas by switching to the simple process of the high-temperature distillation of bituminous coal—English coal. Although it had to be shipped from Liverpool and New-castle, this coal proved less expensive than either rosin or American coal, which was not available in large quantities until the late 1850s. (The distillation process can be readily duplicated in a simple experiment: Fill the bowl of an ordinary clay pipe with small fragments of bitumi-nous coal, seal the top with clay, and place the bowl in a bright fire. Immediately, smoke begins to issue from the pipe stem. When the smoke stops and a match is held to the end of the stem, a bright flame appears. At the same time, a thin black liquid oozes out of the stem, and when the flame dies, a residue of char, or coke, remains in the bowl. It was on this same principle that New York's gas was manufactured on a large scale.)

Then in 1859 Colonel Edwin Drake struck oil in Penn-sylvania, and it was not long before his gushers were pro-ducing two thousand barrels a week. By 1861 there were more than two million barrels, and oil was selling at twenty-five cents per gallon. That same summer, more and more gushers were struck, and suddenly oil was flowing more cheaply than New York City water. At home and abroad, the markets were glutted to overflowing. Thousands of barrels ran to waste in Oil Creek, and prices dropped to ten cents for forty-two gallons! With the discovery of abundant oil came a revival of experiments with "kero-sene gas," which promised to revolutionize the lighting industry in New York and other cities, until just as suddenly, oil prices skyrocketed with the help of some astute manipulation. The gas industry heaved a collective sigh of relief.

By now competition was also centered around the size of gas mains. A far cry from the days of the earliest temporary half-inch tin pipes, miles and miles of cast-iron gas mains measuring as much as twenty inches in diameter were lodged under the streets by 1853. Day and night, gas flowed through at the same pressure. "Consequently," according to William Chauncy Langdon, "unless a consumer used a patent regulator or took the trouble to adjust the cocks with which his fixtures were provided, he found the brilliance of his illumination varying at different times of day in inverse ratio to the number of people using gas." When he least needed it, at noon, he was rewarded with astounding brightness, and when he needed it most, in the evening, he could barely get a flicker. As people went to bed, so the flames grew higher again. It was not an entirely satisfactory system.

In addition, gas customers frequently became startled and angry pawns in the gas wars, and the new box contraptions in their cellars were alternately ripped out, others installed, or a "spare" left by its side to measure the amount of gas for which customers were billed each month. The gas meter, developed by Samuel Hill of Baltimore in 1832, became a source of endless aggravation for customers who, as often as not, were billed by several companies for their gas and were likely not to know themselves whose gas they actually received. To add to their troubles, these meters had to be filled with water, and in winter New Yorkers were forced to add alcohol or whiskey to prevent the water from freezing. The New York Gas Light Company eased this burden by selling whiskey to their customers at $1 per gallon. Another company's ledger reads, "1,200 gallons of whiskey at 25¢ per

Left: Once the gas meter was developed in 1832, New Yorkers often became startled pawns of the warring gas companies, which sent out meter men alternately to rip out and to install the new box contraptions. *American Gas Associates*

Below: Because gas meters had to be filled with water which often froze in winter, meter men sold whiskey "for use in gas meters to prevent freezing." Being a meter man had its compensations. *Con Edison*

gallon for use in gas meters to prevent freezing." It is safe
to assume that, even if the gas meters were not entirely
frost-free, the customers and meter men were. However,
as is always the case with a good solution, a better one
was found in 1844 when two inventors named Croll and
Richards patented a dry gas meter which eliminated the
need for both water and whiskey. Eight years later another meter designed to regulate the flow of gas into
the home was patented, and all the fun was gone.

A far more offensive problem arose before long as the
foul smell of lime in the manufacture of gas pervaded
the city's air. Upon orders from the Board of Health, all
but one of the companies worked toward perfecting a
system that ventilated the lime so that its stinking gases
did not escape into the atmosphere. Only Metropolitan
staunchly denied responsibility for the stench that hung
in the vicinity of its West Forty-second Street plant. When
the company was finally confronted with the evidence
gathered by olfactory detectives, however, Metropolitan
blandly claimed the smell's great medicinal value for the
cure of whooping cough and other diseases, a claim they
advertised loudly, with the result that the gas plant soon
took on the semblance of a health resort. Gullible New
Yorkers sent their diseased children off to the gas plant in
the hope of a miracle cure, and "even gentlemen brought
children in carriages."

Then in 1870 a fifth gas company, the New York Mutual Gas Light Company, headed by Cornelius K. Garrison, came on the scene. Armed with a charter, though
without a franchise to open shop in the city, Garrison had
the good fortune to own a considerable interest in the
Gas Light Company of America, which had just acquired
the rights to a new process by which gas was made from
petroleum distillates, notably naphtha. Not only did this
gas provide a far greater candle power, but it could also
be produced much less expensively. Immediately, the

Mutual mounted an assault on New York's existing gas companies with a ruthlessness none of the original four had ever indulged in. It was wholesale slaughter, as twenty-four-inch mains went down into the ground and customers' meters were ripped out overnight and replaced by Mutual's. By 1876 Mutual boasted ten thousand customers and ranked as the second largest gas company in New York.

While the city's gas lighting pioneers began to slip fast under the murderous onslaught, desperately cutting their prices in a vain attempt to halt the stampede of customers over to Mutual, yet two more companies entered the fray with the even more recently patented hydrogen and oxygen gases and the so-called water gas. In this "carbureted water gas process," steam and an enriching material such as naphtha (later crude oil, and today gas oil) were used with coke or anthracite to produce a gas light which achieved 21¼ candle power, as compared with 16–18. It was a major step forward in the manufacture of what was then the leading source of illumination. By now, the gas wars, waged for nearly a half century, had reached proportions that threatened financial ruin for all participants.

It was a brilliant young man from Port Huron, Michigan, who was destined to ring the death knell for the gas lighting industry. As a boy, he and some friends had already constructed a primitive telegraph system between their homes by stretching "stove pipe wire with bottles, set on nails driven into the trees for insulators." In his teens he had devised an ingenious contraption for the electrocution of cockroaches. Haunted all his life by the "mystery of electrical transmission," he was to receive more than a thousand patents in his lifetime for, among other things, electric motors and generators, continuous nickel and copper plating, the motion picture camera and projector, and cylinder and disc phonographs. He was a handsome man, tall and slender, a shy retreating individual possessed of a fine whimsical turn of mind who, in one entry in his diary, referred to the practice of chewing gum as "the mastication . . . of illimitable plasticity—a dentiferous treadmill so to speak . . ." and who proposed to his second wife, the great beauty Mina Miller, by tapping Morse Code on her hand (she nodded her "yes"). He was a tireless inventor of undisputed brilliance, the man who perfected a machine called the typewriter, the man whose development of a carbon transmitter made the telephone a universally usable instrument. But it is for his refinement of the incandescent lamp that he gained his greatest renown and the world's acclaim and gratitude. His name was Thomas Alva Edison.

Although he was not the first to make an incandescent lamp, it was Edison's refinements that made it practical on a large scale. He began work on it in 1877, realizing that one of the most important elements for prolonged light-giving had to be the filament. He tested hundreds of materials in his laboratory in Menlo Park, New Jersey, and was finally rewarded when he came upon the common sewing thread which, once it was carbonized, provided filament, although it worked for only two days before it burned out. Edison knew that before his work could be commercially successful he needed to find a material that would provide longer light.

During the same years, several electric light companies came into being in America to provide electric arc lighting in the streets, and gas lighting retreated more and more into the home. It was an infant industry which attracted a large variety of inventors. They developed a number of arc generators which powered the arc lamps, a mechanism in which two carbon rods a small distance apart were continuously regulated as the current consumed them. But the arcs hissed and fluctuated and frequently threw hot embers on unsuspecting passersby. Carbon rods had to be replaced and the lamps cleaned daily. Voltage was so high that it posed a wanton threat to life and limb. In fact, so serious was this menace that a new word appeared in the English language—*electrocution*.

There were other problems with the arc lights as well. Often the lamps "stuck," and the posts had to be shaken to get the mechanism moving again so the carbons could strike an arc. It is said that one serviceman's horse, Jericho, was so used to this procedure that he would help his driver in his daily rounds by stopping at a recalcitrant lamppost and giving it one sharp rap with his hoof. If the lamp still refused to light, Jericho kept kicking until it did.

Downtown New York had by now come to resemble a forest of poles, with crossarms supporting rows of glass insulators for branches. A heavy tapestry of wires ran from pole to pole and from insulator to insulator. In the cold of winter these thousands of wires were covered with icicles and snow, posing a constant danger. "There were telegraph wires, gold and stock ticker wires and private lines; and later high tension arc light circuits were being added," Edison's chief electrical engineer, Francis Jehl, wrote sixty years later. Taut or corroded wires snapped under the weight of ice and snow, and these high-tension menaces whipped through the air, swooping down on the citizenry, into windows and against wooden walls, lashing out their violent deathblows. Some hideous accidents occurred during these years, until the dense thicket of wires which blocked the natural light from above was more feared for its lethal potential than loved for the convenience it provided.

It was left to Edison to save New Yorkers from these horrors. Day and night he worked, testing and experimenting, searching for a new and stronger filament that would make his incandescent lamp a commercial reality. Jehl reported that, after long hours, when fatigue finally overcame Edison, "he would then crawl into an ordinary roll top desk and curl up" to take a nap. On October 22, 1879, he discovered that carbonized paper could provide several hundred hours of light. (By 1880, Edison lamps were made with bamboo filaments, and in later years still other substances were used.) Edison knew he had succeeded where no other inventor had, and he became determined to greet the new year, the year 1880, with a burst of light such as the world had never seen. He was keenly aware that, in order to make his new electric light system practical, he would first have to invent a large number of other parts. He would need a way to distribute the power; a suitable lamp and meters to read customers' current usage; a means of maintaining even "pressure" throughout his system; generators or dynamos and a way to regulate them; and lamp holders, fixtures, switches, and wires.

Nevertheless, New Year's Eve 1879 was set as the day to bring light to the world from Edison's laboratory at Menlo Park. The story broke in the New York *Herald* on December 21, 1879.

EDISON'S LIGHT

The Great Inventor's Triumph in
Electric Illumination

A SCRAP OF PAPER

It Makes a Light, without Gas or Flame,
Cheaper than Oil

SUCCESS IN A COTTON THREAD

There is a story that when Thomas B. Connery, the *Herald*'s managing editor, read the "scoop," he rushed to his city editor in a raging fury. "How did that stuff get into the paper? Lights strung on wires! You've made a laughingstock of the *Herald*. Don't you know it has been absolutely demonstrated that such a light is against the laws of nature? Who wrote that article?"

But Marshall Fox, the *Herald's* star reporter, was not fired. In fact, years later Edison remarked that it was the most accurate story of the time concerning his invention.

Although it was a stormy night, hundreds of people made their way across the river from New York and many other areas that New Year's Eve. Extra trains were run by the Pennsylvania Railroad, and when visitors reached the depot at Menlo Park, they were greeted by a line of twenty lights along the street leading to Edison's laboratory, which was itself brilliantly lighted with twenty-five electric lamps. Edison was there to welcome them all, to explain his entire system in great detail and subject it to tests. "Among others," said the *Herald*, "the inventor placed one of the electric lamps in a large glass jar filled with water and turned on the current, the little horseshoe filament when thus submerged burned with the same bright steady illumination as it did in the air, the water not having the slightest effect upon it." In another test, one of the lamps was turned on and off with great rapidity, without the brilliance or durability of the lamp being affected. Edison further demonstrated how the supply of electricity could be regulated at the central station and explained the workings of the electric motor, which could as easily light a lamp as work a sewing machine or a water pump. He also showed how current is produced and how electrical consumption is measured. By far one of the most popular items on view was the horseshoe filament, which could be simply prepared. While one assistant punched tiny horseshoes out of cardboard, another placed them in an iron mold which he then put into a furnace. After about an hour, the cardboard horseshoes had become carbonized filaments, which were subjected to the action of electric current to strengthen them.

Edison, dressed in a rough working suit, led his audience through every stage of his invention, explaining every aspect in detail and answering every question. Many visitors had expected to find a dignified scientist and were astounded by his youth—he was thirty-two—and his simplicity of language and manner as he guided them through his laboratory. Confronted by a few skeptics who argued that gas could successfully compete with electricity in price, Edison gave convincing evidence that even if gas and electricity cost the same to produce, the electric motor would be capable of providing power day and night without variance, while gas provided light for only a few short hours at night and lay idle all day. He also assured them that under no circumstances could gas without an electric motor be produced as cheaply as electricity.

By January 1 and 2, the crowds were so large that it became necessary to put up signs warning observers not to touch the apparatus, and Edison's assistants were constantly rescuing valuable and delicate instruments. In the crush, it was discovered that eight electric lamps had been stolen. The *Herald* reported that "hundreds of those who came were well-bred people ... but it is to be regretted there were others ... who regarded the laboratory as they would a circus."

As a result of Edison's open house, there suddenly appeared swarms of patent pirates, technical experts, and capitalists, who spared no expense or effort, including the use of detective agencies, to ferret out Edison's "secrets."

Edison's first commercial contract was the installation of an electric plant on the S.S. *Columbia*. Throughout 1880, visitors from all over the world continued to make their way to his laboratory. Even the "divine" Sarah Bernhardt traveled through "rain mingled with soft snow" to meet *"le Grand Edison,"* a man who totally captivated her both by his person and his invention. Under the guidance of Grosvenor P. Lowery, Edison's guardian angel, preparations were made to bring the new system into the field of commerce, and so a group of New York City aldermen was invited to inspect it.

It was already dark when the aldermen arrived. Edison led his guests through every part of his laboratory, explaining the system in broad terms and demonstrating its safety elements, including the use of fuse wires. Inevitably, the conversation turned to the arc lights and the great danger of their high-tension wires suspended over the streets. At this point Edison explained that his system used only a hundred volts and that, in any case, he planned to run his conductors underground. This produced a murmur of considerable interest. Edison then led the aldermen to his upstairs laboratory. Just as their eyes were beginning to grow accustomed to the darkness there, Edison clapped his hands, and suddenly the place was brilliantly lighted. At one end of the room were long tables laden with the finest foods and wines catered by the famous Delmonico, with waiters dressed in swallow-tail coats and white gloves, ready to serve.

A spontaneous cheer went up from the startled city fathers as they sat down and did justice to the meal. There were speeches and three cheers for Edison, and all the aldermen agreed that his system was a decided success. It was said that the inventor was entitled "to the thanks of the world for bringing this light to such perfection that it now can take the place of gas."

Edison knew that New Yorkers were ready for electricity. A survey he had conducted himself had revealed that large numbers were prepared to pledge themselves to use his light and power as soon as a central station could be readied. They had grown weary of being constantly victimized by the warring gas companies and were impatient to do away with kerosene lamps and the horses and mules they needed to operate their elevators from their basements. For some years these poor beasts had been corralled to do duty in apartment buildings.

But it was more than a year before Edison gained the franchise that allowed him to create New York's first central station for supplying electrical light, heat, and power. He immediately set about making good his promise to bury his "Edison tubes," copper bars insulated with hot asphalt inside iron pipes. He personally supervised 1,500 hard-working men, most of them immigrants, as they tore up the streets for nearly a year. Once more, as had been their fate off and on for close to a century, New Yorkers learned to tolerate traffic jams and bottlenecks and deeply gouged trenches outside their homes. But Edison's work promised at last to bring peace as well as light into their daily lives. Carefully, meticulously, he plotted the entire underground distribution system, frequently working feverishly himself to wire office buildings and connect them to the copper tube mains in the streets.

At last, on September 4, 1882, the nation's first commercial, ninety percent efficient generating station to produce electricity for incandescent lighting, the Pearl Street station in New York, was ready for service. Two of Edison's initial fifty-nine customers were *The New York Times* and the New York *Herald*. If the lights failed to go on, the press was bound to notice, and electricity would be buried before it was born. Late that afternoon, Edison and Francis Jehl took a deep breath. "Two steam engines were turned on and immediately thirty little balloon shaped globes, ranged at intervals on either side of the long room containing the machinery, glowed with incandescent horseshoes," Jehl recorded later. "Mr. Edison, wearing a white high-crowned derby hat and a shirt without any collar stood about looking greatly pleased. 'I have accomplished all that I promised,' he said."

The gas war came to an abrupt end. Incontestably

The Pearl Street station began to deliver electricity for incandescent lighting to Thomas Edison's first fifty-nine customers on September 4, 1882. *Con Edison*

defeated by electricity, six of the companies joined forces in 1884 and organized the Consolidated Gas Company of New York. Quietly, they also acquired the stocks of several electric companies in the city and, while they switched to the promotion of gas for cooking and heating, they soon led a united effort to encourage the growth of their affiliated electric companies.

Often in the cold dawn, two tense young men could be seen pausing a moment to discuss their respective projects. Both were there to oversee work being done: trenches being dug in the streets, pipes being laid with minimal disruption of city life and disturbance of the residents. As they tried to keep warm, their breath evaporating in the semidarkness, they compared their difficulties working in New York streets, conferred on problems, and provided encouragement to each other in ventures which would many decades later be taken as much for granted as the air they breathed. One of the men was Charles Edward Emery. At the time, his men were laying pipe mains packed in mineral wool to supply the financial district of New York with steam heat. The other man, Thomas Edison, commented later, "I thought he had a harder proposition than I had, and he thought that mine was harder than his." These were nervous months for both men, as their years of research and labor were finally being put to the ultimate test.

As early as 1769, the Scottish instrument maker and inventor, James Watt, had developed a condensing steam engine that was able to convert heat into mechanical energy. A pioneer in the use of steam for heating, he created what was probably the first steam radiator in 1784 by piping steam from a boiler on the ground floor of his house to an iron box in his upstairs study. Some years earlier, Sir Hugh Plat, an Englishman, had devised an ingenious steam heating system for his greenhouse. By extending a long pipe to the greenhouse from an iron container in which water was simmering over an open fire, he was able to keep his flowering plants warm and properly moist during the winter months.

It was not until the early 1840s that isolated steam heating systems supplied by boilers in the basement were incorporated into the design of individual buildings. And it was another thirty years before the idea of piping steam to a variety of buildings from a central station took root.

Experimenting in his home in the upstate village of Lockport, New York, the American inventor Birdsill Holley looped a pipe a short distance underground from a boiler in his basement back to his own radiator—and catapulted the concept of steam heating into the realm of commercial reality. He immediately secured a franchise and laid steam pipes throughout Lockport.

It was not long before the tall, elegant millionaire Wallace C. Andrews, a former partner of John D. Rockefeller and a director on the board of Standard Oil Corporation, heard of Holley's invention. At once he recognized its potential and set out on the two-and-a-half-day stage coach journey to Albany. From there he took a six-day boat trip along the Erie Canal to Buffalo, then went northeast some forty miles again by stage to Lockport. He was so impressed with what he found that he hurried back to New York and sent a technical expert to investigate the proposition from every angle. The expert he selected was "the eminent engineer Charles Edward Emery, who as early as 1869 had begun the study of steam distribution and had done much valuable work for the United States Navy during and after the Civil War." Emery's report totally substantiated Andrews's own opinions and observations.

While it was clear from the start that constructing a central steam heating system on Manhattan Island would be infinitely more difficult than it had been in Lockport, Andrews wasted no time in using his financial prominence and considerable reputation to obtain from the State Legislature in Albany the necessary franchise and exclusive right to use the Holley system in New York City. By July 24, 1879, he had organized the Steam Heating and Power Company of New York and appointed Emery as chief engineer. The following year, when another group was granted a franchise with considerably more comprehensive terms, Andrews was quick to nip such competition and duplication of services in the bud by acquiring control of the newly organized New York Steam Company and combining the two organizations under the latter's name. Among the first stockholders of the new entity was Mrs. Ulysses S. Grant, whose husband that year had lost his bid for a third term as president.

Andrews devised a plan to divide Manhattan into

ten districts with a central steam station in each district. While Emery worked day and night, planning, testing, and purchasing materials, as well as checking the work in progress in the streets, yet another company, American Steam, plunged ahead in what soon became a race to provide steam heating to New Yorkers. American's mains were designed quite differently from Emery's, though neither had ever been used on such a large scale. The public and the press appeared to support American's design and were quick to jeer "Andrews's Folly." It was during this anxious time that the forty-one-year-old Emery, who frequently met the competitor's engineer during their nocturnal inspection tours, was considerably reassured by the strong support he got from Thomas Edison. Edison found it commendable that "Emery used mineral wool to surround his pipes, which was of a fibrous nature and was stuffed in boxes to prevent the steam in the main from condensing, whereas his competitor was laying his pipes in square boxes filled with lampblack."

Then one night it happened. As Edison later described it:

> Emery had finished all his pipes and [while he] was working in the street one night, he heard a terrible rush of steam. It seems that his competitor had put on steam pressure to test out his pipes. There was a leak in the pipe; the steam got into the lampblack and blew up, throwing about three tons of lampblack all over the place, and covering the front of several stores in Maiden Lane. When the people came down the next morning, everything was covered with lampblack—and the company busted!

While steam mains were being laid under the streets, amid the complaints of querulous citizens, the central steam station was rising in what was then the heart of the

The American Steam Company was working against time to complete the first steam line before Emery did when one of its mains blew up in Maiden Lane, spewing lampblack over the street and storefronts. *Con Edison*

city, a full block bounded by Cortlandt, Dey, Greenwich, and Washington streets. Its chimney was the second highest structure in all of New York, second only to the Trinity Church spire.

On March 3, 1882, six months before electricity began coursing through Edison's underground tubes, steam was sent through the first half-mile of steam mains to service the company's first customer, the ten-story United Bank Building at 88 Broadway. By July of that year, steam mains totaled one mile in length, and by November another two miles had been added. By 1886 there were five miles of mains and three hundred customers—among them the Liberty Street annex of Edison's Pearl Street generating station. Customers were delighted. They were relieved of the burdens of maintaining a boiler plant, buying and storing coal in their cellars, and removing ashes. They had already adjusted with ease to the luxuries of constant fresh water and electricity, and now steam heating provided additional comfort.

One of the first problems the New York Steam Company had to solve was what to charge its customers. Rates were based on the cubic feet of space in a customer's building, not on the amount of steam used. Residents rarely took the trouble to adjust their steam valves when their homes became too hot, but instead opened their windows. As a result, the company was frequently heating large tracts of the outdoors. But the ever-resourceful Emery soon designed a recording steam-flow meter to correct this problem.

Despite the popularity of steam, the company was beset by financial troubles from the very beginning, in part because customers often did not pay their bills on time (making it not unusual for shareholder customers to be asked to pay their bills a month in advance so that the steam company's payroll could be met). For almost three years, Wallace Andrews sold his Standard Oil stock at the rate of $1,000 per day to keep his steam company puffing. Even so, he decided to expand by building another boiler plant at Madison Avenue and Fifty-eighth Street to supply the new uptown district, which had rapidly blossomed into a showplace of great wealth, dotted with the fine mansions of many of the nation's foremost families. Because a number of the company's early mains had begun to leak at the joints, causing considerable loss of steam which further aggravated financial problems, it was decided that the uptown mains should be made of heavier iron pipe, with screwed cast-iron flanges at the joints.

Then came the year 1888. On March 11, the New York *Herald* published Walt Whitman's "The First Violet of Spring" and predicted that the weather would be "cloudy, followed by light rain and clearing." Nobody suspected that the worst part of that winter—the Blizzard of '88—was yet to come.

The rains came as promised, but they soon changed to sleet and then to snow. By Monday morning, March 12, the snow was piling up to unprecedented levels, and winds howled at eighty-four miles per hour. A number of people, exposed to temperatures below zero, died during the storm, and countless others required medical attention as the city was buried under several feet of snow. Traffic was paralyzed. Thousands of New Yorkers were stranded at home or in their offices until tunnels could be dug through the snowdrifts to free them. The fires in stoves and ovens all over the city died and the ashes grew cold as supplies of coal and oil dwindled to nothing. Water froze in the pipes. People were forced to wrap themselves in coats and blankets to keep from freezing. Food supplies ran short or spoiled on the shelves of shops whose owners and customers were unable to get through the snow.

Only steam customers could count their blessings. Throughout these days of hardship, steam services continued uninterrupted. The coal company that supplied the steam stations hired snow shovelers to clear paths for the horse-drawn wagons that delivered fuel to the steam plants. No effort was spared, not a man allowed to rest, to keep the steam flowing freely. For several days even the coal company president climbed aboard a wagon and whipped his horse through the streets to keep the coal deliveries on time. The blizzard was like nothing anyone who lived through it had ever witnessed, or would ever witness again.

At about that time, Wallace Andrews's brother-in-law, Gamaliel St. John, devised a method of strengthening the steam mains by welding steel flanges at the ends of each length of steel pipe, and then bolting the flanges together with a gasket in between. Experts claimed that it could not be done. Yet six months later, after repeated trials and tests, a welded-flange pipe was produced, the design of which has changed very little in the years since. Now, when leaks did occur, they could be easily stopped by repairing the flanges, replacing the gaskets, and then bolting the pipes together again.

Following this successful venture, St. John next applied himself to the redesign and simplification of the steam-flow meter for which Emery had obtained a patent in 1897. (Although the St. John meter has undergone a number of changes and was replaced altogether in 1928 by the English Shuntflo meter, many of the original St. John models are still being used—reliably—throughout New York City.)

In April 1899, just when the New York Steam Company appeared to be headed toward resolving some of its financial problems and the Andrews and St. John families had decided to take a well-earned vacation together, tragedy struck. On the eve of their departure, both families were staying at the Andrews's home on East Sixty-seventh Street. Gamaliel St. John planned to join them on the following morning upon his return from a business trip. That night, while everyone was asleep, a devastating fire broke out in the mansion, raging through the house with incredible speed and intensity. When St. John arrived the next morning, he learned that thirteen people were dead, including his wife and three children, his sister, and his dearest friend and brother-in-law, Wallace Andrews. This tragedy, which might have broken a lesser man, instead created in St. John a driving force to keep the company afloat. Slowly and painstakingly, as funds could be spared, he built short extensions to the steam distribution system in the downtown and uptown districts. Though the demand for steam increased steadily through the years, the company struggled along for financial survival, until St. John retired in 1915. Even with the completion of the Burling Slip station at Pearl and John streets, with its advanced 2,000-horsepower boilers (earlier equipment had used 250-horsepower), the company's financial troubles prevented it from expanding its mains into new territory. After World War I, the Public Service Commission approved a surcharge or credit on each customer's monthly bill, based on the rise and fall of coal prices, but it was not until the company was reorganized in 1921 as the New York Steam Corporation, with new financing through city banks, that it appeared to be on the road to financial stability.

In 1926, Kip's Bay, the world's largest district steam station, with a capacity of two million pounds of steam per hour, began operation along the East River between Thirty-fifth and Thirty-sixth streets. Thanks to new technology, its pulverizing mill was able to grind coal to powder at the rate of fifty tons an hour. The increased temperatures and pressures gave a single boiler at Kip's Bay a capacity greater than the combined capacity of all forty-eight boilers in the company's first plant.

To obviate the need for at least ten steam company plants in Manhattan alone, the practice of leased plants came into being. Beginning in 1928, individual buildings could produce their own steam in privately owned boiler plants in times of excessive demand, and also send steam into the central system in case of need. In that same year, Con Edison pioneered the dual use of electric generating station boilers to produce both electricity *and* steam. In 1931 the steam system gained further flexibility when a transfer main running north and south on Seventh Avenue made possible an interchange of steam between the downtown and uptown districts. New technology also made it possible to transport high-pressure steam as far as three miles without great loss of temperature or pressure.

By February 9, 1934, when temperatures dropped to fourteen degrees below zero—the coldest day recorded since the American Revolution—steam plants were capable of producing seven million pounds of steam in one hour—two million pounds above the normal demand. By 1948 it was possible to send steam either way between Manhattan and Astoria, Queens, through a main installed in an old gas tunnel under the East River.

The following year, turbines at the Waterside electric station had increased steam capabilities to 1.8 million pounds per hour. By this time, the technology of air-conditioning was beginning to make strides, and the burdens placed on the electric system became intolerable—until the steam system came to the rescue. The load of 27,500 tons of cooling capacity placed on the steam plants in 1950 grew to 680,000 tons by 1971.

With the city's population now hovering at approximately 7.5 million, it has long been recognized that, without central station steam service, in Manhattan alone some 400 million gallons of oil would have to be burned annually in individual boiler plants. It would have to be delivered in 100,000 truckloads. And if coal were used instead of oil, it would produce 3 million tons of ashes every year, as well as an intolerable level of air pollution.

The simple system of steam heat designed by Birdsill

Holley a century ago has grown into a system more versatile than either he or Wallace Andrews could have imagined. In today's world, steam heats and cools buildings, cooks food in restaurants, heats towels in barber shops, serves Turkish baths, cleans subway tunnels and the exterior of buildings, blocks hats and presses clothes, sterilizes medical equipment, dishes, and utensils, is used in the manufacture of phonograph records, preheats commuter trains at Pennsylvania and Grand Central stations, keeps the outdoor overhead ramp at the Port Authority bus terminal free of snow, and protects bank vaults ("steam jackets" around the vaults are prepared to give any would-be burglar a somewhat warmer reception than he might expect). It was steam that the dragon in "Siegfried" belched during the Metropolitan Opera's *Ring* cycle —when the Met was still at Broadway and Thirty-ninth Street—and it was steam that the famous Camel smoker puffed from the Times Square billboard for many years.

Somewhat less beneficent was an unprecedented event that occurred in the early morning hours of March 21, 1973, when steam billowed hundreds of feet into the air above Avenue C and Fifteenth Street, creating a spectacular display. The blast from a ruptured expansion joint in the north-south steam main under the intersection sent stones and pieces of concrete flying, dented several automobiles, and broke windows in the nearby Stuyvesant Town apartment complex, where debris and mud damaged some apartment furnishings. Incredibly, nobody was hurt. Within less than two hours, Con Edison work crews had valved off the rupture and moved in to begin repair work. By late afternoon that same day, they had completely restored normal service. Although there are some four thousand such expansion joints within the steam system, this was by far the most dramatic incident of its kind in the company's near-century of operations.

By the mid 1970s the total capacity of the city's steam system had reached more than fifteen million pounds per hour. And still the steam system continued its century-old "tradition" of financial uncertainty and struggle to meet increasing demands.

four
TWO
GIANTS

"Mr. Watson, come here, I want you!"

It was not the most inspired line to usher in the age of communication over the airwaves. But as Alexander Graham Bell later wrote in his laboratory notes, "To my delight he came and declared that he had heard and understood what I said." It was March 10, 1876, a momentous day for Bell and his assistant, Thomas A. Watson.

Bell was only twenty-nine when he invented what was to become known as the telephone. He had already spent much of his life working on various ways to help the deaf to speak, an interest founded on the elocution work done by his grandfather and father, and/or the loss of his mother's hearing when Bell was only twelve.

At sixteen, he had built a speaking machine with his

brother. After constructing an artificial skull of gutta-percha (the gummy, milky fluid from certain Malayan and Brazilian trees, once also used for making chewing gum), the boys added vocal parts made of tin, India rubber, and a lamb's larynx. When they blew through this contrivance, they were able to make it cry "Ma-ma!"

Young Bell was not yet twenty when he began to teach music and elocution in exchange for his own lessons. Two of his first pupils were George Sanders and Mabel Hubbard, both deaf children from prominent and wealthy Massachusetts families. It was during this time that Graham, as he preferred to be called, began experimenting with the resonance of vowel sounds in relation to the position of mouth and tongue. These experiments led to his first contact with acoustics and electricity.

In 1874 he constructed a device which could translate sounds into visible markings. One part of this "phono-autograph" was the actual ear of a dead man! It was this same human ear which led Bell to a major breakthrough. He noticed that whenever words were spoken, the ear's membrane vibrated, causing a lever to scratch a wave pattern on a piece of smoked glass. Although his knowledge of electricity was minimal at this stage, a delighted Bell realized at once that with such a membrane an electric current could be made to conform to the precise variance in the airwaves produced by the sound. And so the principle of telephony was born in July 1874.

With financial backing from two grateful fathers, Thomas Sanders and Gardiner G. Hubbard, Bell moved his experimental work from his parents' home to a garret above an electrical shop in Boston. It was here that he met Thomas A. Watson, the young machinist whose exceptionally sensitive hearing endeared him to Bell from the start. The two men took an immediate liking to one another and began a close collaboration which, little more than a year later, would amply justify Bell's often expressed "Watson, we are on the verge of a great discovery."

At precisely the same time, Elisha Gray, the cofounder of Western Electric Company in Chicago, was on the verge of the same discovery.

In mid-1875, Bell excitedly wrote Hubbard, "I have read somewhere that the resistance of a wire . . . is affected by *the tension of the wire.* If this is so, *continuous current of electricity* passed through a vibrating wire should meet with a varying resistance. . . . The *timbre* of a sound could be transmitted."

On June 2, 1875, there was a lucky mistake. Bell's transmitter was equipped with strips of flexible, magnetized steel reeds, clamped at one end. The free end of the reeds vibrated at a specific pitch whenever a current flowed through the electromagnet under them. Each reed was able to transmit a current that was received by a second reed tuned to exactly the same pitch. That day, one of the transmitting reeds had been too tightly screwed down and did not vibrate at all. When Watson plucked at it to free it, the reed emitted a loud "twang."

The too tightly adjusted contact screw had changed the intermittent current into a steady current. Because the reed was magnetized, its vibrations over the pole of the electromagnet had induced an electric current which ran through the wire to Bell's receiver some sixty feet away. The intensity of the current varied exactly as the density of the air, and therefore the sound.

Seized now with the excitement of an imminent discovery, Bell instructed Watson to make what has come to be known in telephone history as the "gallows" telephone. It was a diaphragm (like a little drumhead) for the transmitter, with the free end of the reed resting on its center. When someone spoke down into the diaphragm, the sound caused the tautly stretched membrane to vibrate, which in turn made the reed vibrate, thus inducing a current that varied according to the sound.

On the morning of February 14, 1876, Bell decided to file his patent application for the gallows telephone. That same day, just a few hours later, at the same patent office in Washington, Elisha Gray filed a caveat warning other inventors against claiming the telephone invention. Less than a month later Bell was granted U.S. Patent No. 174,465, often considered the most valuable patent ever issued and the center of a bizarre drama in litigation for many years. Entitled "Improvements in Telegraphy," it neither mentioned electrical transmission of speech nor the word "telephone." Crucial in Bell's battle against Gray's claim to the invention, however, was his almost casual inclusion of the variable resistance principle in the margin of his application.

Although neither contestant had as yet actually transmitted human speech, the world had long been ready for such a development. Since the beginning of time, man had sought to communicate with his far-off brothers. Through the use of drums, gongs, smoke signals, runners, and riders, there had always been the desire to bridge the distances. "Whispering rods," long, thin, trumpet-shaped instruments, were used during Colonial times in American homes too small to provide much privacy. Young people particularly enjoyed this ingenious method of communicating their precious secrets without fear of being overheard. The word "telephon," derived from the Greek meaning "far speaking," appears to have been first used in Germany in 1796 to describe a system of directive megaphones. In writing of his "enchanted lyre," an instrument which transmitted music acoustically through the use of rods of wood, glass, or metal, Sir Charles Wheatstone used the word "telephonic" in 1821 and called an electric telegraph device he invented in 1839 a "rhythmical telephone." Six years later another Englishman invented what he bluntly termed "the telephone"—a non-electrical device "for conveying signals during foggy weather by sounds produced by means of compressed air forced through trumpets." Soon after the first telegraph cables were laid across the English Channel, some French and English newspapers speculated that the cables could transmit speech using the following recipe: "A plate of silver and one of zinc are taken into the mouth, the one above, the other below the tongue. They are then placed in contact with the wire, and words issuing from the mouth so prepared are conveyed by the wire." But they failed to explain *how* words were to issue from a mouth stuffed with silver and zinc! Generally, however, public reaction to the very thought of telephony clung stubbornly to the fear of the supernatural. Human speech was a gift from God not to be tampered with. And besides, it was self-evident that electricity was incapable of carrying the human voice over a wire.

Bell's patent was issued March 3, 1876. A week later, he spoke the first words ever carried over a wire, and the telephone as we know it today was born. Years later Bell remarked: "I should never have invented the telephone if I had been an electrician. What electrician would have hit upon so mad an idea?"

In June 1876 he was prepared to demonstrate his mad idea at the Centennial Exposition in Philadelphia. The weather was hot and humid, the panel of judges tired by the time it was Bell's turn to exhibit his invention. In the audience that day was none other than Dom Pedro II, the English-speaking emperor of Brazil. His response to Bell's telephone was so enthusiastic—"My God, it talks!" he exclaimed—that the weary judges finally bestirred themselves to examine it. To their amazement, they could hear Bell reciting Shakespeare over the contraption.

Within months, news of this thing called a telephone had spread around the world. People crowded to pay admission to see and hear the marvel with their own eyes and ears. Bell would appear before one audience, while Watson positioned himself on another stage elsewhere. The two men then spoke and sang to each other over the telephone, proving without a doubt "its practical work of conveying INSTANTANEOUS COMMUNICATION BY DIRECT SOUND," as contemporary advertisements announced.

"Most extraordinary," commented Queen Victoria, a lady not easily given to superlatives, in 1877.

"By physical impulse the voice travels through the air, as in ordinary talking, singing, or yodeling, at a speed of about 1,100 feet a second. . . . By electricity the voice goes at the rate of 185,000 [*sic*] miles a second. This was the basic element in Bell's invention . . ." wrote William Chauncy Langdon in 1933.

The Bell Telephone Company was formed in July 1877 by the Hubbard and Sanders families, Bell, and Watson. That same year Bell married his former pupil Mabel Hubbard. In August the Telephone Company of New York was organized. One of its first customers was J. Lloyd Haigh, a manufacturer of wire for the suspension cables of the Brooklyn Bridge, which was then under construction. Three years later there were already four telephone cables across the bridge, which itself was not completed until 1883. New York and New Jersey could communicate via a cable drawn under the Hudson River. By 1881 the company's annual report stated that it registered 132,692 telephone customers. By 1934 more than one-sixth of all the telephones in the nationwide Bell System were concentrated in the New York metropolitan area, which composes only about 1/1200th of the land area of the continental United States. But as early as 1880, Bell himself, having succeeded in launching the world into a new era, lost interest in his invention and returned once more to his real mission in life—teaching the deaf to speak.

Before long a new proliferation of overhead wires

appeared in New York, creating problems of a quite un-expected nature. Since single-wire circuits relied on the earth as a conductor to complete the circuits, they in-ducted a variety of other electrical impulses. Speaking over the telephone therefore proved a deafening expe-rience. Thunderstorms could be detected over the tele-phone long before the first cumulus cloud drifted over the horizon. Sputtering electric arc street lamps and trolley car switches produced a painful cacophony. Other disturbances, according to Herbert N. Casson, included:

> spluttering and bubbling, jerking and rasping, whis-tling and screaming. There were the rustling of leaves, the croaking of frogs, the hissing of steam, the flapping of birds' wings. There were clicks from tele-graph wires, scraps of talk from other telephones and curious little squeals that were unlike any known sound. The lines running east and west were noisier than the lines running north and south. The night was noisier than the day, and at the ghostly hour of midnight, for what strange reason no one knows, the babel was at its height.

Americans took the telephone to their collective bosom, making it an extension of themselves, using it to replace letter writing and long-distance travel, to pay debts, to make business deals—and even love. The tele-phone also created the "call girl." Some early telephone booths were veritable works of art, made of ornately carved golden oak, with glass doors and silk draperies. On occasion, these were also mistaken by the uninitiated for *pissoirs*!

The telephone was *the* fashionable thing to own. The New York *World* felt compelled to instruct an ignorant public in the manners of telephone speech. "It is not necessary to roar into the instrument so that you can be heard eight blocks away," the writer explained. "The telephone don't [*sic*] work on that principle. . . . Stand back *two or three feet* [italics mine] from the mouthpiece of the transmitter and speak slowly and distinctly in your ordinary voice. The telephone is not deaf."

By far the most enthusiastic response in Europe came from the Swedes who, by the turn of the century, owned one telephone for every 115 people.

Although the telephone could hardly be described as a smash hit in England—where it was generally considered a "scientific toy" or passing fancy—Bell was granted a British patent for the receiver (Thomas Edison already held a British patent for his carbon transmitter). This unwieldy situation was resolved in 1880 when the United Telephone Company was formed to join the Bell and Edison interests—using the former's receiver and the latter's transmitter. In France, bureaucracy found innumerable ways to make the telephone something less than desirable. Among other requirements, the government, which controlled the new enterprise, insisted that telephone operators not be allowed to "marry policemen, cashiers, foreigners, or mayors of towns, lest they betray the secrets of the switchboard."

By the mid-1880s downtown New York resembled nothing so much as a forest of poles. West Street, home of one of the telephone company's offices to this day, had the thickest concentration of all—ninety-foot poles carrying thirty crossarms each, which in turn were laden with three hundred wires! Although the one-wire circuits had already been replaced by two-wire circuits which eliminated the "earthly" sounds, the proliferation of wires—telephone, high and low tension, and telegraph—permanently darkened the city's sky. The wires were not only unsightly but extremely dangerous. Telephone service was regularly interrupted for days and even weeks during winter, when as much as three pounds of ice weighted

By the mid-1880s, overhead wires permanently darkened the city's sky. The Blizzard of '88, as seen here on New Street looking toward Wall Street, changed all that. High winds and the weight of snow snapped dozens of poles and whipped thousands of live wires through the streets. *Museum of the City of New York*

each foot of overhead wire. In 1884 mounting public outrage at last moved the New York State Legislature to pass a law requiring all wires to be placed underground. But because insulation techniques were as yet only in the research stage, the law was largely ignored.

Then came the Blizzard of '88. As the snowdrifts piled higher and the winds roared with hurricane ferocity, miles of poles came down all over New York. Although the "forest" stood firm at West Street, the wind shrieked through the wires at an ear-splitting pitch. Along Twelfth Street, it was a different scene altogether—one pole was snapped at the top, and with a searing scream its thirty crossarms and three hundred wires sliced through the roof of a nearby house. Farther along the block and elsewhere, dozens of poles and thousands of wires were draped over buildings and streets, or whipped through the air. The blizzard was the proverbial straw that broke the camel's back. Those wires *had* to go underground. Living through a New York City winter had become a grand game of Russian roulette.

It is said that Mayor Hugh P. Grant took matters into his own hands and chopped down the first poles himself after the snow from the blizzard had settled. That year the search for the "perfect" insulation technique was begun.

The relatively new Board of Commissioners of Electrical Subways was flooded with some six hundred schemes and designs for executing the mammoth task of laying cables beneath the ground. Each of these was given careful thought, although most proved eminently impractical.

A major consideration in all underground insulation techniques was the need to adapt to weather conditions. The insulation had to be strong enough to withstand assaults of rain, wind, sleet, heat, cold, ice, and lightning. Ice in the ducts would destroy the cables, so the conduits were built on a slope to allow water to flow easily from the ducts into the manholes.

A trench was dug in Brooklyn some thirty inches below street level and an iron trough placed at its base. Cables were then laid over insulite bridges which spanned the trough at eighteen-inch intervals. Each cable contained fifty wires, each about a quarter-inch in diameter. Once the cables were placed, vulcanized bitumen, or

Bitite, was poured into the trough, cementing everything in it into a solid mass.

At the Thirty-ninth Street exchange in Manhattan, cables containing between 50 and 100 wires insulated with cotton and soaked in paraffin were placed in wooden boxes filled with sand. At the Twenty-first Street exchange, 100 to 270 wires covered with cotton and treated with an insulating compound were bunched together and inserted into thirty-foot lengths of iron pipe which were then filled with asphalt.

Another method of insulating was the Dorsett Conduit constructed of a mixture of asphalt and sand molded into three-foot cylindrical sections under high pressure, each section containing seven two-inch holes. Five miles of this "duct" system were installed in Brooklyn. Initially hailed as gas-tight, within a year it was discovered that this rough material scratched cables so badly during the "hauling in" process that not only was it not gas-tight, it was not even water- or mud-tight. Although gutta-percha had been successfully used to insulate telegraph cables, it soon proved too expensive for telephone cables. Then came the Brooks system, in which each wire was covered first with cotton, then wrapped with a light copper wire which was also insulated with cotton. Bunched together, the wires were drawn into an iron pipe filled with oil. To keep the oil under constant pressure and to prevent water from entering the pipes in case of a leak, a standpipe and reservoir containing several gallons of oil were connected to the system.

The Johnstone system used a conduit made of cast-iron plates which could be assembled to provide any even number of ducts between four and sixteen. The top plate sections contained removable caps which allowed for substitution of a section either for service connections or repair. Access manholes made of cast-iron rings set upon a pan also served the function of supporting a length of plate castings.

One of the more eccentric insulation techniques was to draw each of twenty wires into tiny glass tubes. A group of these tubes, together with a mixture of grease and rosin, was then drawn into a lead pipe. Even if a glass tube broke, it was thought that the compound would hold it in place.

The problem with all these early methods was that telephone conversations were successful only over short distances. The greater the distance, the more indistinct became the voice transmission.

Today's duct systems are constructed of plastic in a concrete "envelope," capable of containing as many as 3,600 *pairs* of wires (although the average is 1,500–2,400 pairs) sheathed in plastic for durability and strength. A telephone "subway," or conduit, can contain as few as 3 ducts or as many as 318—the average is 6.

As the New York Telephone Company developed and its service spread throughout the five boroughs, it subcontracted the actual subway construction to outside firms (and still does). To do this work in Manhattan and the Bronx, a unique company came into being in 1891, when New York City still consisted of only these two boroughs. Although at first it was thought that a single underground system of electrical conductors could accommodate all the city's wires, it soon became clear that it would be highly impractical to have high-tension wires lying side by side with low-tension wires. And so while the Consolidated Telegraph and Electrical Subway Company was charged with burying high-tension conduits, a new company, the Empire City Subway Company, Ltd., was formed to provide, build, equip, maintain, and operate the conduits for telegraph and telephone cables, as well as for low-tension electric light and power conductors in Manhattan and the

Bronx. Even though all five boroughs became incorporated into Greater New York City in 1898, Empire City has retained its unique position within the Bell System for nearly a century. A wholly owned subsidiary of New York Telephone Company, Empire City leases the ducts it has been building over the decades, at an annual rental, to a variety of customers. Of these, the telephone company occupies some ninety-seven percent of the duct space. The remaining three percent is used by such varied agencies as the Holmes Electric Protective Company, Western Union, television and cable television companies, the New York City Transit Authority, and the city's police, fire, and traffic departments—the latter three rent-free.

Under normal conditions, Empire City prefers to lay its cable ducts within four feet of the street surface. But nothing in New York's subsurface is normal, and the company's engineers have had to go as far down as fifty feet— under the rapid transit subway—before they could find some unoccupied space. There is no other city in the world whose subsurface is as impenetrably crowded with cables, mains, pipes, and tunnels. Construction of a new conduit with as direct a route as possible requires uncommon ingenuity and is a problem faced by all the utility companies.

Perhaps Empire City's most incredible achievement was the construction of the Harlem River crossing in 1931. Cables buried in a muddy river bottom are not only virtually impossible to maintain, but they often become so entangled by shifting currents that isolating a single defective cable can mean days of fruitless search. It was decided that the main toll circuits between New York and New England would need a special conduit. To accomplish this, first a large trench was dredged across the river bottom, so deep that the topmost part of the finished structure would be 27 feet below the mean water level. A

614-foot pipe tunnel, 7 feet in diameter and made of 1¾-inch cast iron, each 12-foot length weighing ten tons, was constructed next. Timber piles were driven along the trench at 12-foot intervals, while the pipe lengths were assembled and jointed on barges near the shore. When a riveted steel truss, or "strongback," was tied to the 72-foot jointed pipe lengths, a floating derrick could pick up the entire unit and lower it into place on top of curved cast-iron saddles which had been emplaced on the support timbers.

Once the pipe was in place, precast concrete saddles contoured to fit the pipe were placed on top of it at intervals to add to its weight against prevailing currents. Side forms were then constructed against these saddles, and concrete was forced through a tube between the side forms. The final protective thickness around the pipe tunnel was twenty-four inches top and bottom and eighteen inches on the sides—and almost all of the work had been done under water! When the tunnel was completed, the pipe was pumped dry and construction crews built a narrow-gauge track for transporting materiel inside it. Only then could the actual cable conduit installation begin. In all, 206 ducts were installed, completely filling the deep tunnel. In the decades since its completion, the tunnel in the Harlem River has proved totally safe from the hazards of dragging anchors and dredging operations.

All told, Empire City Subway Company, Ltd., with a staff of only 265, has built and equipped a total of twelve thousand duct miles and some ten thousand manholes in its two-borough territory—all of which it regularly maintains and repairs.

Today, when New York Telephone determines where a cable "plant" is needed in Manhattan or the Bronx, it calls on Empire to draw up the requisite plans for the new conduit, for which Empire must then obtain approval from the city. One of the most confounding aspects of building any new facility in New York is the lack of any one map showing the placement of *all* the utilities.

Each of the hundreds of thousands of manholes installed throughout the city has involved the same careful process of surveying and plotting. As soon as the most direct route of a conduit is determined, a utility company consults all subsurface utilities and city departments whose facilities are indicated as being present along the proposed route. This may include any—or all—of the following systems: electric, gas, steam, and sewer lines; low- and high-pressure water mains; and transit subways. Each company or agency then updates its own records based on the information it obtains through this system of close cooperation. Within such a planning process it is not at all uncommon to utilize existing subsurface structures, and so it is quite possible to find telephone conduits in abandoned steam and water mains, in transit subway vent chambers, in and through depressed bays of existing vehicular tunnels, on bridges, and even under subway tunnels.

Empire City's engineers determine which method of rock fragmentation should be employed, depending on geological variations found throughout the city. There is the standard drill-and-blast method, often impractical because of noise, vibration, and flying debris. (Another technique that can be used is electrical rock fragmentation in which a high-voltage electric current passed through the rock generates electrothermal stresses which then produce fragmenting stresses.) The most prevalent method uses drills, breakers, air rams, and splitters. Noisy though this type of work is, even to the already desensitized ears of most New Yorkers, it is the one safe method that eliminates potentially dangerous ground vibrations in the congested spaces both above and below the surface.

After Empire City has "spoon dug" its way through

Caution, dexterity, and highly developed skills are required of the men who regularly check New York's underground lifelines. Working in the congested spaces of the city's manholes, they must steel themselves against heat, cold, noise, and dirt. *Con Edison*

the tangle and completed a "plant," the telephone company's linemen take charge of pulling the cable through the conduit. Once the cables are in place, their care is taken over by splicers.

It was a hard day's labor years ago when splicers were called upon to sit for hours in the confined solitude of a manhole and make the wire connections by spinning, or twisting, them together. A later development which allowed them to solder the joints provided considerable relief for these men, although the work was unenviable during summer months when the heat of their soldering irons added to nature's discomfort. Today their task is a matter of connecting wires with a mechanical device that simultaneously applies pressure and heat, producing the equivalent of a soldered connection—a job that now takes seconds instead of hours.

The older lead-sheathed cables regularly fall victim to electrolysis, in which stray electric currents from other utilities flit around in the earth in search of low-resistance conductors. They are most interested in finding a water pipe, but failing that, they are quite happy with a bit of lead. And so lead sheaths are being forever eaten away by electrolysis, necessitating a constant watch over the cables they contain. Luckily, the modern plastic sheaths are not

Daily water-main breaks throughout the city can wreak havoc among the tangle of utility lines. Sometimes, however, they expose a length of the Manhattan Company's wooden pipes, a flintlock, or, best of all, a disused pipe that can be used to carry new conduits. *Pamela Jones*

prone to the problem. There are occasions, however, when high-tension (Con Edison) electric cables burn out. At such times, even though the current released into the earth again prefers to dive toward a water pipe, it is not at all opposed to a juicy low-tension telephone cable—which it promptly fries in a somewhat startling manner. First the current burns the sheathing, and then—bypassing the cable's outer wires—it welds the core into a solid mass. Fortunately, this does not happen too often.

Water is one of the most constant problems telephone company teams have to contend with. Let a water main break anywhere in the city, and the telephone crews are on the spot, since there is every likelihood that wherever there is a water main, telephone "plants" are not far away. A centrally located Electronic Switching System can scan the affected lines to determine whether or not any cables are in trouble. Since all cables are color-coded and classified by pair numbers, the computerized scanner can isolate and identify a break within seconds, and repairmen can immediately begin work on the line without disrupting service on any others in the vicinity.

Once the affected wires have been repaired, any remaining dampness in the cable must be "boiled out." For many years this was done by driving hot paraffin along the sheath toward the break. But for the past twenty-five years, a drying agent called Desiccant, a finely powdered, chemically superheated, saltless type of sand, has been applied to the affected area.

Cable sheaths can also be damaged or broken by vibrations of rapid transit subway traffic, the steady rumble of cars above the ground, blasting from a nearby construction site—or the teeth of a hungry rat!

Sometimes escaping steam from a nearby main or, worse still, a break in a steam main causes cables to become brittle and damaged. "Blowing the cable down" with chemicals such as bottled nitrogen (occasionally visible on city streets in large 3,640-cubic-foot tanks), cools the fever.

Even as the New York Telephone Company installs, maintains, and repairs its approximately twenty-five thousand miles of cable containing the billions of pairs of wire which course under the city's streets, new developments will make it possible in the years to come for a single cable the width of a thumb to carry fifty thousand simultaneous conversations. By using light transmitted over hair-thin solid glass fibers, this new cable will refine the basic principle Alexander Graham Bell tinkered with more than a century ago in his Photophone, an instrument that could transmit sound for a short distance over a beam of light. By the year 2000, fiber optics, as the field is called, will revolutionize the industry and dramatically change much of the work done by Empire City and New York Telephone.

Modern-day Consolidated Edison, generally known as Con Edison, can boast a long line of forefathers since the days of the Edison Electric Illuminating Company of New York. It is a giant corporation which directly or indirectly supplies all the electricity and steam needs of New York City and much of its gas (Brooklyn Union Gas serves Brooklyn, Staten Island, and several other areas). Producing energy is its business. Producing electric energy is its major business.

The same year that Thomas Edison introduced his incandescent light bulb, Nikola Tesla, a brilliant Serbian-born inventor, discovered the principle of the rotating magnetic field, which led to his development of the induction motor and the polyphase, alternating-current (AC) system—its generating, transmission, and distribution. Although Tesla worked briefly for Edison, he met with resistance whenever he tried to interest Edison in his new theory. Still flushed with the success of his own invention, Edison stubbornly refused to consider Tesla's alternative. Unlike Edison's direct current (DC), which flows in only one direction, Tesla introduced the theory in which current reverses its direction of flow periodically. Thus, with a sixty-cycle alternating current, for example, the current goes from zero voltage to its maximum in one direction, back to zero, then to its maximum in the other direction and back to zero again, sixty times per second.

Not until 1889, when George Westinghouse decided to introduce alternating current in New York City, did the controversy between direct and alternating currents become a central issue between the two leaders of the infant industry. While Edison continued to oppose alternating current, Westinghouse defended it just as emphatically.

Although Edison's system was most reliable, it required a large number of generating stations which could supply only a limited area, whereas an AC network system was capable of supplying large areas from only a few generating stations. The battle lasted well into the 1920s. In the end, Tesla's alternating current predominated, although even now large services—notably Grand Central trains and the Transit Authority's subway network—are powered by direct current. To serve DC-using customers, it is first necessary to feed electricity produced at AC-generating stations through rotary converters or rectifiers. Once these have converted AC to DC, the current can be fed into the DC network.

In the meantime, cable insulation among the various utilities kept apace—until Con Edison's chief electrical engineer heard of the advances made in the field by the Italian firm of Pirelli in 1925. The Pirelli cables, paper-insulated and sheathed in lead and laid in groups of three in parallel ducts, were capable of carrying 132,000 volts. The multiple layers of paper insulation were completely and continuously saturated with oil specially treated to remove all traces of oxygen and other contaminating gases. The oil also prevented the cable from being damaged through heating and cooling as a result of the system's alternating peaks and lows.

By 1963 the 132,000-volt cables were outranked by the newer, extra-high-voltage transmission systems of 345,000 volts, or 345 kv. Insulation techniques changed too when it was found that polyethylene was not only cheaper than paper but also offered greater resistance to moisture—a constant danger to all electrical cables. By 1952, in response to the ever-growing shortage of copper resources, Con Edison began testing and installing a significant amount of aluminum cable. Today eighty-five percent of all its new secondary cable installations consist of aluminum. A large portion of this is concentrated in the relatively small New York metropolitan area, which receives some eighty percent of the company's entire load within its six-hundred-square-mile territory.

Since high-voltage transmission systems are only as reliable as the cables carrying the current, every foot of cable that leaves the factory is meticulously inspected. Even brand-new cable can contain "soft" or "hard" spots. Specialists are relied on to ferret out any possible weakness before the cable is placed in service. "What may start as a perfectly manufactured cable is coiled onto a large take-up reel; then it is coiled onto a smaller impregnating reel; then onto another reel, after protective covering has been applied; and finally onto a shipping reel," writes Con Edison's historian, Dorothy B. Ellison. "Each time the cable is re-coiled, it is in a reverse direction from the previous coiling," and in the process "the perfectly applied paper insulating tapes" may shift and thus produce soft spots.

A network of thirty-seven "bulk" substations capable of interchanging electricity through a vast complex of high-voltage lines, or even to neighboring systems if the need arises, keeps a reliable supply of power flowing through the 80,000-mile underground cable system and the 34,000 miles of overhead transmission wires.

Transformers reduce the power voltage at these bulk substations before sending it along to more than two hundred distribution substations. There, the voltage is reduced once more, and the power is sent into the underground network. Almost all the substations are controlled by an automated system equipped with alarms and flashing lights which alert the District Operator at the company's Energy Control Center in Manhattan to anything from a fire to a switchman entering or leaving. The District Operator's control board also provides continuous load readings on all transformers and feeder lines.

Throughout its citywide system, Con Edison has some five hundred thousand manholes, including street transformer vaults, which are small "rooms" in which cable joints and transformers are installed, tested, and repaired. Often, before the men can even start on their electrical work, they have to do a spot of housecleaning. In fact, every year Con Edison crews remove about ten thousand tons of dirt, sludge, and garbage from New York City manholes!

Before manholes were prefabricated in the 1930s, they had to be dug and then lined with bricks. Later, concrete mixed at the job site was poured into wooden forms lining the hole. Once the concrete was dry, the forms were removed. Precast manholes of reinforced concrete changed all this. What had earlier been a task that could take several days, is now a matter of no more than eight hours. There was one instance, however, where all did not go quite according to plan. A manhole in front of the New York Telephone Company's West Street office had no sooner been installed than the Hudson River's high tide, which had washed in through the landfill of that part of town, lifted it right out again. Since the tide was clearly destined to repeat this prank every twelve and a half hours, the manhole had to be weighted down to keep it in place.

There is also the story of the man who lived in one of Con Edison's cable vaults somewhere in the Bowery area during the bitterly cold winter of 1966. A work crew, having found the lock of a manhole cover broken, entered the vault and discovered the man fast asleep. His clothes were neatly hung up, and he had hooked up an electric hot plate to a secondary cable. There was a light in the ceiling, and the six-by-eight-foot "room" under the ground was altogether cozy. In fact, the man was quite indignant when he was evicted.

Since gas leaks are fairly common in many manholes, work teams must take a gas reading before it is considered safe for them to enter a manhole. For these readings, they carry a gas meter to which a long thin hose is attached. Once the manhole cover is removed, they attach the meter to the guard stand around the hole and dip the hose into the darkness below. Depending on the size of the manhole and the amount of gas, it can take as long as an hour for the exhaust pump or fan to clear sufficiently the underground atmosphere so the men can begin working. "No wonder the bills are so high," passersby occasionally grumble when they see telephone or Con Edison workmen lounging in their trucks for what seems a longer-than-necessary "coffee break."

The men who work in Con Edison's manholes and transformer vaults learn to tolerate biting cold and sweltering July heat, are able to make some sixty different kinds of splices, and at times must also be equal to events that have little or nothing to do with electricity. "They have revived heart attack victims, discovered late night or early morning fires, and guided potential victims to safety, given first aid to seriously injured people . . . chased and caught muggers and robbers, and stopped runaway trucks," writes Ellison. An off-duty Con Edison man once thought he saw a building tremble on Manhattan's Second Avenue. As he ran across the street to make certain his eyes were not deceiving him, the foundation walls began to crumble, bricks slipped loose, and a fine shower of mortar rained down on him. Without further thought, he rushed into the building to warn its occupants, and led them to safety. Then he called Con Edison's emergency service to shut off the building's gas and electricity, and also notified the police. Moments later the building collapsed! Thanks to James Day, nobody was hurt.

Once a Con Edison crew had to contend with a police horse stuck in a manhole. Fortunately, the policeman himself had dismounted moments before the pavement buckled and the manhole cover gave way. While poor Joyce was wedged into the three-by-four-foot opening, Con Edison workers spent a couple of hours carefully enlarging it with jackhammers until they could retrieve the frightened gelding. Another time, an unsuspecting Saint Bernard skidded into an open manhole, much to the surprise of the men working below. Con Edison work crews are quite accustomed to snakes and bees and rats— even unexpected "showers" from open hydrants—but not dogs. Once they were even asked to recover one of Elizabeth Taylor's diamonds. More disconcerting finds have included a gun believed to have been used in the murder of an eighty-nine-year-old woman—and a man's skeleton, which turned up in another manhole.

The common plight of all utilities is the lack of underground space. In addition to electric, telephone, and traffic cables, gas, sewer, steam, and water mains, and rapid transit structures, the precious space is shared with police and fire alarm systems. Con Edison's electric cables alone snake a total of eighty thousand miles under the city. Not only does it seem impossible at times to get more than a teaspoon between utility lines, but it is frequently necessary to move and relocate them if the city requests it. This is a task akin to removing one particular strand of spaghetti with a fork from among a bowlful. Utility companies generally have a franchise to use the area above or below the street to conduct their business. However, a franchise does not guarantee them any right to a particular section of the street. And so they must constantly be prepared to make way for new civic structures, such as sewers, water mains, bridges, tunnels, and housing developments. They must do so with minimal interruption of service and at their own expense.

One such instance occurred under Flatbush Avenue in Brooklyn, where the city asked Con Edison to lower one of its duct lines. In order to avoid interrupting service or damaging the line by merely pushing it into a deeper trench, Con Edison solved the problem by digging under the ductline, then bracing the excavation with support timbers. Once this was done, they slipped huge cakes of ice under the line and removed the timbers. As the ice melted, the ductline sank gently and gradually into its lower trench.

Soon after World War II, the utility companies as well as the city itself were faced with a seemingly insurmountable challenge. With the site of the United Nations headquarters selected along First Avenue, it was decided that the only way to eliminate the constant roar of the avenue's traffic was to construct a seven-block vehicular tunnel between Forty-first and Forty-eighth streets. So all the electric, telephone, and telegraph cables, gas and steam mains, fire department alarm cables, water pipes, and sewers that already occupied that space had to be moved out of the way. Representatives of each affected group began a series of meetings. Engineers and planners from the companies and city departments involved began to shuffle cables and pipes on paper in innumerable drafts and revisions, until at last a firm relocation plan emerged. Even so, to relocate all the facilities merely a matter of feet and yards cost millions of dollars. Con Edison alone relocated some thirteen miles of high-voltage cables and almost twenty-two miles of low-voltage ones.

What could be an intensely trying and costly problem under similar circumstances is generally made more bearable by the close cooperation between the utilities and various government agencies. Since hundreds of contracts are negotiated in any given year, with the city having priority over all others in its installations, and since the private companies must underwrite all expenses involved in relocation, such cooperation is essential—the difference between utter chaos and frequently no more than a minor design change that costs the city nothing and saves the companies thousands of dollars.

The first tunnel ever built under the East River was completed by the East River Gas Company, a predecessor of Con Edison, in 1894—nine years before the first subway tunnel. By October of that year, gas was being sent from the Ravenswood plant in Long Island City to Manhattan via a 3-foot main in the 2,516-foot tunnel, which is 137 feet below sea level at the Ravenswood end. Today that tunnel also carries electric, steam, and fuel oil lines. The company's Astoria tunnel between the Bronx and Queens became a landmark of construction history. Except for the aqueducts, it is the city's deepest tunnel, 261 feet below grade and 4,662 feet long. Other Con Edison tunnels carry steam, electric, and fuel lines across the East River from Brooklyn to lower Manhattan, span the distance between Hunts Point and mainland Bronx, Flushing and Corona, and Long Island City and Greenpoint. Hundreds of heavy-duty cables lie under the waters of the Harlem, East, Bronx, and Flushing rivers, Gowanus and Motthaven canals, Pelham and Wallabout bays, the Little Hell Gate tidal strait, Bronx Kill, and Newtown and

Coney Island creeks. It is a system of almost unimaginable electric power, which New Yorkers notice only when it fails as it did during the blackouts of 1965 and 1977.

By the early years of the twentieth century, manufactured gas production had shifted into high gear. Two huge plants located in what was then still the periphery of the metropolitan area and controlled by the Consolidated Gas Company (which became Con Edison in 1936) supplied the city's gas needs in conjunction with Brooklyn Union Gas. The Ravenswood plant sent its "water gas" through the East River tunnel to Manhattan, while the Astoria plant carried gas to the Bronx through six-foot mains. It was not until 1926 that the Hunts Point plant in the Bronx was put into service. Long before then, coal imports from England had become unnecessary when the coal fields of West Virginia and Kentucky were opened, producing high-quality bituminous coal.

In the intervening years, a series of coal by-products began to make their appearance. Among these was toluol, an essential ingredient in the production of TNT. During World War I, Con Gas produced enough toluol to manufacture more than twenty million pounds of the explosive. Since it was always one of the most basic principles in the gas business to waste nothing, it became possible to make more than two hundred thousand different by-products from gas manufacturing wastes. The most important of these was coke. Other products included ammonium sulfate, light oils, and coal-tar stuffs to make drugs, dyes, antiseptics, perfumes, fertilizers, and roofing materials. Some twenty million gallons of road tar, another by-product of gas manufacture, were sold annually.

The last remaining gasworks on Manhattan Island was shut down in 1945, marking the end of the "gashouse district" in New York. On that site today stands the vast and complex sprawl of Stuyvesant Town and Peter Cooper

Village. During the postwar population explosion in the city, Con Edison began to feel the growing strain of meeting concomitant increases in the demand for gas. A particularly harsh winter in 1947–48 caused a large number of gas pipes to break, because the gas had been saturated with vapor when it left the plant and service pipes had collected frost which often impeded or stopped the flow of gas. Vibrations caused by heavy trucks passing several feet above the cast-iron pipes could also cause them to break, sending their toxic carbon monoxide into the air. The experience of such a winter, with its attendant emergencies and miseries, hastened the company's plans toward augmenting gas manufacture with natural gas in 1951.

Natural gas was used as early as two thousand years ago when the Chinese captured it at the surface of the earth and conveyed it through bamboo tubes to illuminate distant cities or to boil the brine in salt mines. For centuries, natural gas was the focus of legends and superstition in many parts of the world: fire worshipers built temples to appease this "god," a temple near Baku on the Caspian Sea housed an eternal flame from the early seventh century to modern times, and the Oracle of Delphi imparted its wisdom with "the breath of Apollo."

Natural gas is thought to have been formed over thousands of years through the decay of billions of tiny plants and animals whose remains were washed millennia ago into lakes and oceans and covered by mud and sand. As these materials gradually turned to rock, the heat, pressure, and perhaps the effects of bacteria and radioactivity caused the organic matter to decay, forming compounds of what we know today as hydrocarbons. Held between particles of sand and porous rock, they became gas and petroleum. Where these particles were covered by layers of impermeable rock through which the gas could not pass, fields of gas were stored and can be drawn upon for our use today. In other areas, where the gas was not trapped, it escaped to the surface. Today one can see a similar process at work in the formation of marsh or swamp gas, where small quantities of gas bubble up through stagnant water.

One of the earliest discoveries of natural gas in modern times occurred in seventeenth-century England. In Thomas Shirley's report to the Royal Philosophical Society of London in 1667, he referred to a phenomenon he had observed about eight years earlier at a spring "where the water did burn like oyle and did boyle and heave like water in a pot." He found this to "arise from a strong breath, as it were, a wind which ignited on the approach of a lighted candle," and "did burn bright and vigorous."

In 1783 a balloon filled with gas carried three unlikely travelers aloft, to the cheers and applause of French royalty and commoners alike. As they drifted over Versailles, nudged by a gentle breeze, a sheep, a duck, and a cock made aviation history. Upon their landing, only one injury was recorded—the cock had been kicked by the sheep!

A "spring" of natural gas was discovered in the small town of Fredonia, New York, at the shore of Lake Erie as early as 1821. The gas was conducted through the town in wooden pipes—the first attempt in the United States to harness natural gas.

But more than a hundred years went by before modern technology was ready for natural gas. Following World War II, a group of Texans formed the Transcontinental Gas Pipe Line Company (TRANSCO), offered to build a giant gas line to New York, and began looking for customers. They did not have to look long. The costs of manufacturing gas had skyrocketed, so New York's gas companies were only too eager to commit themselves. Con Edison alone contracted to buy 100 million cubic feet a day. And so, TRANSCO set about building a 1,840-mile pipeline—one of the longest continuous pipelines in the world. Traveling through varied geography and a wide range of climates and built with a series of compressor stations to maintain even pressure and volume throughout the route, the largely thirty-inch diameter line was to carry gas from vast fields in Louisiana and Texas to the New York metropolitan area.

At the same time, Con Edison began installing 350-pound-per-square-inch mains underground, overhead, over bridges, through tunnels, and under rivers throughout the company's territory. For greater efficiency, a pool known as the New York Facilities System, consisting of Con Edison, Brooklyn Union Gas, and Long Island Lighting, was formed to cooperate on construction, operations, maintenance, and joint delivery points, thus promoting considerable economy and flexibility.

Con Edison's design and planning engineers set to work to develop a master plan for the distribution system. Before straight natural gas could be introduced into any part of the system, existing mains and pipes had to be "purged" and customer appliances "converted" to burn gas with twice the Btu content of manufactured gas, with minimal interruption of service to its millions of customers.

Among the preparations necessary for the arrival of natural gas, which burned with a much higher flame than manufactured gas, was the testing of every conceivable type and vintage of domestic and industrial appliance that Con Edison's men were likely to encounter during the conversion work. A training school went into operation to teach the conversion crews every procedure they would need to know. In all, some 1,100 men were involved in the pipe-to-pipe, house-to-house, room-by-room conversion work throughout the city.

Customers were alerted well in advance with a booklet explaining what the conversion mechanic would do, and describing how natural gas would work. And then C-day, as it came to be known, arrived. While the city slept, conversion crews went to work at midnight. First, all valves in a particular section were turned off. Work crews then set up their eight-foot "purge burners" and introduced natural gas into the mains, lighting the burners until the manufactured gas in that section was burned off and replaced by straight natural gas. In the early morning hours other crews then went about converting individual appliances so that service was rarely interrupted for more than four hours.

By 1954 the Con Edison men knew the work they had done so far in Riverdale and a section of Queens (in Westchester, the first area to be converted, the work was done by outside contractors) had been merely a rehearsal for the big job—Manhattan and the Bronx—where 1.5 million gas-burning appliances would have to be adjusted for more than a million customers. One Bronx housing development alone contained over twelve thousand apartments. An early estimate, when conversion of Bronx-Manhattan was still in the "maybe" stage, was that it would require four years.

Work on Manhattan, which was divided into fifty-one sections, began in September 1955. More than a thousand men were involved. They took a collective deep breath and set to work. It was a herculean task—over five hundred industrial customers; thick webs of mains and pipelines under heavily traveled major thoroughfares with rapid transit structures beneath them; universities and medical centers with thousands of Bunsen burners; printing plants; dental laboratories; precious-metals craftsmen with thousands of torches and crucibles; the garment center; hotels, restaurants, night clubs. In private homes, rooming houses, tenements, apartments, hotels, and schools throughout the city, work crews replaced outdated rubber hose connections on hot plates with permanent piping at no charge. Where they found illegally installed appliances or safety hazards, they disconnected them. They also replaced refrigerator burners, laboratory burners, torches, heaters, and more than nineteen thousand hot plates, where replacement proved cheaper than conversion or repair.

Whatever fears conversion crews or the public might have had, they remained unjustified. The only incident that did occur and that threatened to ruin the crews' near-perfect record proved instead just how incredibly efficient they were. A large commercial bakery had been hostile to the whole conversion program from the beginning, even though its management had been advised that the bakery would *have* to be converted if it wished to continue receiving gas. It was then that the bakery's manager notified Con Edison that each hour of oven production was worth $8,000, and demanded that he be compensated in full for time lost on his eight enormous ovens. The prospect of shutting the bakery down for even one hour was a bleak $64,000, and the thought of shutting it down longer, as had been necessary in a number of other bakeries, was positively ruinous. Faced with this grim proposition, Con Edison engineers worked out a plan whereby the entire eight-oven conversion could be made by interrupting service on only one of them for merely ten minutes. Even though company attorneys found the manager's claim questionable, Con Edison decided not to contest, and paid the $1,100 the bakery demanded.

By July 1956, all Con Edison customers were receiving straight natural gas. The conversion had cost $36.5 million. Work in the Bronx and "impossible" Manhattan, which had been estimated to take four years, was completed in less than two. An added bonus of conversion was the elimination of 260 miles of duplicate underground mains.

When the last of the city's gas plants was shut down in 1968, it marked the first time in 131 years that gas was not being manufactured in New York every minute of every hour of every day. Now the city was relying entirely on a product transported under pressure from thousands of miles away.

But with the advent of natural gas, a new problem arose. For example, an average of five hundred New Yorkers had died annually from the carbon monoxide poisoning of manufactured gas during the four years before natural gas was introduced. For years, gas employees in the distribution department had been required to undergo regular "smell tests" to differentiate between such odors as ammonia, kerosene, lemon oil, and drip oil. With the advent of odorless natural gas, there was suddenly no way to detect a gas leak. And so began a major effort to develop an odor with which natural gas could be artificially treated—an irony since the earlier companies had struggled for years to minimize the foul odor produced by manufactured gas. Today, a mercaptan base compound, nicknamed skunk oil, is added to natural gas before it is sent into the distribution system. Of course, inevitably one day a customer complained of a gas leak, and a careful search by both police and Con Edison employees finally revealed no fewer than six skunks in the man's cellar.

Because natural gas is "dry," as opposed to manufactured gas whose oil vapors keep it moist, a slightly higher percentage of natural gas does leak into the atmosphere. For this reason, the Leakmobile was developed. It is a vehicle specially equipped with a tube hanging from its front which regularly cruises through the streets "sniffing" the air at ground level. In certain sections, when an underground gas buildup not easily accessible from a manhole is suspected, small round holes, two inches or less in diameter, are drilled into the ground.

Although these holes occasionally produce inconveniences, they are far more tolerable than a gas buildup of explosive proportions.

There are some seven thousand miles of gas mains under the city's streets. When any of them become defective, replacement with minimal traffic interruption becomes a true challenge to engineers. One of the methods used whenever possible is the pipe-in-pipe technique utilizing special machines which can pull a sixteen-inch main, for example, through an already existing twenty-four-inch main. Vertical digging is necessary only where the pipe dips or turns.

There are three categories of gas—firm, winter, and storage. Firm gas is the amount contracted for by Con Edison, winter gas is supplied during the colder days of the season, and storage gas is "borrowed" from the pipeline companies' underground storage areas in case of a particular winter emergency and must be returned to storage during the summer months. To store gas, it must be liquefied by lowering its temperature to 260 degrees below zero (600 cubic feet of natural gas will occupy only one cubic foot of space after liquefication). For this purpose, Con Edison has built a storage facility of its own at its Astoria electric generating station by constructing a huge double-walled steel storage tank with a capacity of one billion cubic feet.

Because of the growing threat of a serious natural gas shortage by the late 1970s, plans have been put in motion to develop ways to supplement natural gas with limited quantities of synthetic gas derived from coal, oil, oil shale, and tar sands. With gas needs reaching about 140 billion cubic feet per year, it seems likely that "synthetic natural gas," although it is extremely expensive to produce, will be called upon more and more in the future.

five
TUNNELS, TRACKS, AND TRIPPERS

Every weekday of the year, New York City's subways carry about 3.5 million people over 230 route miles, across ten bridges, through thirteen tunnels, to far-distant places within four of the five boroughs (Staten Island excepted). It is a feat akin to twice daily evacuating the entire metropolitan populations of such cities as Havana or Hamburg, of Milan, Saigon, or Kiev. In fact, there are only seventeen cities in the *world* whose populations exceed the daily number of New York's straphangers.

The development of an efficient transportation system in the city was bogged for decades in the mire of political expedience and indecisiveness. Beginning in 1827 with a twelve-seat horse-drawn vehicle named Accommodation, citizens could ride all or part of the length of Broadway from the Battery to Bleecker Street for a flat fare of one shilling. This first "omnibus" was so successful that by 1831 there were two others. By 1832, John Mason, president of Chemical Bank, organized the New York & Harlem Railroad to construct the world's first street railway. Writing of these new horse cars which ran from Fourth Avenue and Fourteenth Street to the Bowery at Prince Street, the New York *Courier & Inquirer* complained that the line "will make Harlem a suburb of New York." Since Harlem was at that time a distant village to the north, the prediction seemed to many quite farfetched. But at the launching of the street railway at the end of that year, Mayor Walter Bowne proudly announced that "this event will go down in the history of our country as the greatest achievement of man."

The notion of public transportation caught fire over the ensuing years, so that, although no further horse-car tracks were laid until the mid-1850s, 593 omnibuses served the city on 27 routes, most of them converging on Broadway. Traffic was so congested, in fact, that an 1852 survey showed that omnibuses passed the intersection of Chambers Street and Broadway at the rate of one every fifteen seconds in each direction! Crossing the street on foot had become an act of extraordinary courage and agility. But New Yorkers were even then a breed of rare fortitude—after all, fresh water had come to them only ten short years before; they were battered this way and that by warring gas companies; their streets were ripped open and turned into muddy trenches for the purpose of laying pipes and mains. And now New Yorkers could suffer the added violence of recklessly driven horse cars amid cutthroat competition. "No tracks hampered the operations of the stages, whose drivers ran over men, women and children in their haste to beat competitors to waiting passengers," wrote Robert Daley. "Burly conductors shanghaied people into coaches and forced them to pay, so that heavy profits could be shown. Drivers were picked for heft not courtesy.... Axles broke, horses shied and policemen on boxes at intersections spent more time separating slugging rival drivers than directing snarled traffic."

So when the Michigan railroad man Hugh B. Willson tried to gain a charter in 1864 to build a subway modeled after London's one-year-old steam-operated underground, the public was ready. Unfortunately, the New York State Legislature was not. It did not help that the New York *Herald* described the plight of public transportation as "a perfect Bedlam on wheels," whose crowded passengers hung from straps "like smoked hams in a corner grocery. ... The foul, close, heated air is poisonous. A healthy person cannot ride a dozen blocks without a headache." The following year the Legislature relented and did pass a subways bill, but this time Governor Reuben E. Fenton took it upon himself to veto the suggestion of tunneling underneath Manhattan. "I cannot consent ... to such use of these grounds without feeling I had violated the trust reposed in me by the people," he said, and so the matter was dropped for the moment, while the "trusting" people were randomly killed above the ground for another two years.

Then, in 1867, a State Senate Committee on Rapid Transit decided that underground railways were the only quick solution to the city's need for "safe, rapid and cheap transportation of persons and property," and proposed construction of two lines—one on the East Side and one on the West Side. The committee also supported a proposal for an experimental elevated cable railroad on Greenwich Street. With a speed of ten miles per hour, this line opened on July 3, 1868. By 1871 it extended to Ninth Avenue and Thirtieth Street, and a steam locomotive had replaced the earlier cable propulsion system which had been driven by stationary steam engines.

Suddenly, one February morning in 1870, New York-

ers read a most startling headline in the *Herald:* "A FASH-
IONABLE RECEPTION HELD IN THE BOWELS OF THE EARTH!"
it screamed almost hysterically. New York had a subway—
312 feet of it! Under Broadway! One block between
Murray and Warren streets!

There, deep in the earth, the tracks inside a single
tunnel, nine feet in diameter, carried a small twenty-two-
seat "richly upholstered" car propelled by a large blowing
machine called the Roots Patent Force Blast Blower, at
a top speed of ten miles per hour. This fan, which the
workmen had nicknamed Western Tornado, was operated
by a stationary steam engine which drew air in through
a valve and with a forceful blast drove the single subway
car to the other end of the line. When the car reached
the far terminus at Murray Street, it tripped a wire that
ran along the tunnel and rang a bell at the Warren Street
end. There, an engineer reversed the blower, and the
train was sucked back to its starting point "like soda
through a straw."

The 120-foot waiting room at one end of the tunnel
was lavishly appointed with paintings and frescoes, a
grand piano, a fountain, and even a goldfish tank. It was,
said the *Sun,* "a large and elegantly furnished apartment,
cheerful and attractive throughout," lighted by zircon
lamps. And it was all a total surprise!

The idea of a pneumatic subway had been born some
years earlier when the visionary young inventor and pub-
lisher, Alfred Ely Beach, co-publisher of the New York
Sun and *Scientific American,* came upon the idea of the
pneumatic tube as a carrier system for packages and other
mail. This had proved so successful that he sought to
adapt the design to passenger vehicles. He unveiled the
prototype of his design at the 1867 American Institute
Fair at the Fourteenth Street Armory. To the cheers and
applause of his spectators, the barely forty-year-old Alfred
Ely Beach demonstrated how his ten-seat passenger car

could be blown through a tube which stretched from the Fourteenth Street to the Fifteenth Street exits—all through the action of a huge fan which either blew the car or, reversed, sucked it back. The daily crowds and their enthusiasm were such that Beach was convinced his invention would meet with overwhelming official approval.

Before he could create a tunnel under Broadway, however, he had to perfect a means of tunnel drilling. "The result was a hydraulic shield which could tunnel seventeen inches with each press into the earth wall," as Stan Fischler reports in his book, *Uptown, Downtown.* "Workers remained inside the shield, bricking the tunnel with comparative security from cave-in. Beach's earth-gouger was flexible enough to move left or right, up or down. . . ." But if Beach's hydraulic shield bore was capable of tunneling deep through Manhattan's soil, it was unable to deal with the mountains of political obstacles that Beach encountered, beginning in 1868.

In the intervening years, quite another problem had arisen to test the mettle of New Yorkers. A former saddler and bookkeeper, William Marcy Tweed, had risen through the ranks of a volunteer fire company until he became its officer, and was eventually elected alderman in 1851. As a member of an aldermanic group popularly nicknamed the Forty Thieves, Tweed had attained a level of graft before he was thirty that made honest work quite unnecessary for him. By 1855, preferring municipal to state politics, he was well on the road toward establishing what was for many years afterward known as the Tweed Ring. Through tolls and taxes levied on all who did business in New York City, through the Ring's insistence that all bills rendered against the city be fraudulently increased by fifty or even eighty-five percent to provide ample kickbacks for the Ring's members, Tweed was, by 1870, not only the dominant figure within the Tammany Hall

Democratic machine—the boss of all bosses—but also a millionaire. No single business in New York City escaped the clammy tentacles of the corrupt Ring.

Knowing that he needed a franchise to construct and operate his subway, and that Tweed would blackmail every penny from him, Beach decided he would simply not make his plans public until they were a *fait accompli*. And so, he launched his work in secret, in the dark of night. He rented the basement of Devlin's Clothing Store at Murray Street and Broadway and began work on his tunnel. With his twenty-one-year-old son Fred as work-gang foreman, Beach watched the solid wall of earth and stone become first a cavern and then a tunnel. From over-head, the clip-clop of horses' hooves echoed through the stillness of every night, as workmen below loaded the dirt they had dug into large bags and carried them above ground for furtive removal in carts with muffled wheels. The workers were constantly afraid that the tunnel would collapse on them, and claustrophobia drove many away altogether. But still, work progressed, with Beach always there to advise, to supervise, to work feverishly toward completion of his dream. He had set February 27, 1870, as the date for the opening and had already sunk a fortune of his own money into the project. He estimated expenses would reach some $350,000, of which a considerable por-tion was to be spent on furbishing the lavish underground waiting room. The digging and brick reinforcement con-tinued for fifty-eight nights, and when the tunnel was finished according to Beach's plans, work began on the waiting room, while Beach himself prepared the car which was to fit snugly into the nine-foot cylindrical tube.

And then at last came the day Beach had waited for. The pneumatic subway would surely become such a popular success, a source of such awe, inspiration, and enthusiasm that not even Boss Tweed himself would dare oppose it.

There was no doubt that Beach had accurately predicted the reactions of the public and the press. Not
surprisingly, *Scientific American* jubilantly hailed the
subway's practicality: "This means the end of street dust
of which uptown residents get not only their fill, but
more than their fill, so that it runs over and collects on
their hair, their beards, their eyebrows and floats in their
dress like a vapor on a frosty morning. Such discomforts
will never be found in the tunnel!" Beach, a small, bird-
like man, proudly led groups of dignitaries through every
inch of his tunnel. He was already thinking in terms of the
future, of expansion to Central Park, a distance of five
miles. He talked of such a subway being able to carry
as many as twenty thousand people a day at a speed of
up to one mile per minute! With such a heady prospect,
he had little time left to worry about Mr. Tweed.

But Mr. Tweed worried a good deal about Mr. Beach.
His minions had kept him completely informed of the
inventor's every move, his every word. And so, with
political power and the city's purse on his side, Tweed
merely waited, like a great hooded cobra, for his prey to
cross his path. Beach, in his naïveté, had thought that the
needs of the public would come foremost at such a time.
What he did not consider was that Tweed would hardly
forgo the handsome profits he was making annually from
the "tributes" paid him by the streetcar and omnibus
companies in favor of a subway whose secret construction
had made a fool of him. Beach, though he did not realize
it yet, was finished.

When the Beach Transit Bill backed by overwhelming public support came before the Legislature in January
1871, Tweed made his move. Both the Senate and Assembly cast a landslide vote in favor of the Beach bill. But
they also passed the Tweed-backed Viaduct Plan, a design
that called for a series of elevated railway lines to run the
length of Manhattan mounted on forty-foot stone arches

—at a cost of $80 million, as compared with $5 million for Beach's subway! Only one of the transit bills could be approved. The final decision was up to Governor John T. Hoffman. It was now that Tweed played his trump card. Governor Hoffman owed his high position in state government largely to Tweed. The decision was a foregone conclusion.

However, even in defeat, Beach refused to give up. Again and again, he sought to gain official approval. To no avail. In the meantime, Thomas Nast, a political cartoonist, had taken it upon himself to expose the Tweed Ring's corruption by mercilessly ridiculing Tweed in *Harper's Weekly*. Shortly afterward, *The New York Times* began a similar campaign of its own. It was not long before a groundswell of public anger and resentment surged through the city, and Tweed was indicted at the end of 1871. Hoffman was voted out of office and replaced by Governor John A. Dix. And then, just when Dix endorsed Beach's subway plan, engineers began to argue that the hydraulic shield would be ineffectual in tunneling through rock. As public enthusiasm and curiosity dwindled, Beach eventually resolved to close his subway and continue his struggle by switching to the more generally accepted "cut-and-cover" tunnel construction technique: a large trench dug from the surface, with the railroad built at its base. But he had lost favor among the city's capitalists in the meantime, and could not raise the necessary funds. In 1873, Governor Dix withdrew the charter for Beach's pneumatic subway.

And so, New York's first subway was walled off and forgotten for forty years, until it was discovered by chance in February 1912, when a subway construction crew working on the Brooklyn Rapid Transit (later BMT-Broadway Subway) dug through Beach's tunnel wall. And there, to their utter amazement, they stumbled upon the splendor of the inventor's salon-waiting room, its

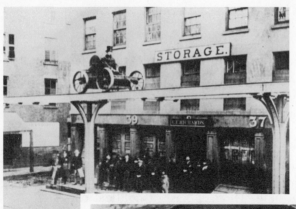

Above left: One solution to New York's desperate need for "safe, rapid, and cheap transportation" seemed to be Charles T. Harvey's experimental cable-operated El on Greenwich Street in 1867. *New York City Transit Authority*

Above right: In 1870 Alfred Ely Beach surprised the population with his secretly built subway under Broadway, between Warren and Murray streets. Abandoned soon afterward, it was accidentally rediscovered during construction of the BMT line in 1912. *Museum of the City of New York*

opulence undiminished except for some rotted wooden fixtures. Beach's small railroad car was still on its tracks. Today, a plaque on a wall of the lower level of the BMT City Hall station, which incorporates a part of the pneumatic tube, commemorates the man who began it all— Alfred Ely Beach.

In the years between 1872 and 1904, a forest of columns and girders stretched north, carrying elevated railroads—Els—along Second, Third, Sixth, and Ninth avenues. And with them came the steam locomotives which belched their thick, acrid smoke over the city, creating slums wherever they went, the soot mixing with street dust and covering buildings inside and out with a permanent film of grimy dirt. Only Fifth Avenue was protected from this modern horror when the Fifth Avenue Transportation Company, Ltd., incorporated in 1885, restricted traffic on the avenue to omnibus lines. Then in May 1886, the city's rapid transit was extended across the Harlem River when the El lines of Second and Third avenues connected Manhattan with "suburban Bronx."

By 1889 things had become so desperate that Mayor Hugh J. Grant appointed a five-member Board of Rapid Transit Commissioners to design rapid transit routes for the city—above or below the ground. More than a decade passed, however, before the question of an underground railway was resolved. Although the board decided on an underground road, it failed to receive satisfactory bids. Absolutely nothing was done until the State Legislature was forced to abolish the board in 1894. In the meantime, the many El lines streaking through Manhattan were merged by the Manhattan Railway Company under the leadership of financiers Jay Gould and Russell Sage, while the people of New York continued to cough and sputter through their daily lives, finding what comfort they could in their electrically lighted homes, and bathing in fresh

Croton water (which was by then threatening to run scarce).

It was that same year, 1894, that the subway issue was put before the voters. Since private capital had proved unwilling or unable to finance the construction of New York City's underground railroads, the voters overwhelmingly approved the Rapid Transit Act. This meant that the city would pay private contractors to build the subways, and then lease the facilities to private companies for their operations and maintenance. Nevertheless, five more years passed before the first contract for the city's first subway was awarded to John B. McDonald. A year later, on March 24, 1900, work was officially begun. To provide McDonald with additional financial backing, financier August Belmont organized the Rapid Transit Subway Construction Company, in exchange for seventy-five percent of McDonald's interest in the contract. And in 1902 the Interborough Rapid Transit Company (IRT) was incorporated by McDonald, Belmont, and Cornelius Vanderbilt (the "Commodore" 's grandson), among others, to operate the subway which was to run between City Hall and 145th Street.

Immediately, the financially overextended Manhattan Railway Company recognized the trend of the future and offered to merge with the IRT. As a "persuasive" tactic and to counteract its financially weak position, the Manhattan threatened to obtain a franchise to build a competitive subway, and to give its passengers free transfers to the company's surface lines. Reluctantly, the IRT consented to the "shotgun wedding"—a 999-year lease, backdated to November 1, 1875.

The general plan called for a tunnel to run northward from City Hall as far as Grand Central Station, then west along Forty-second Street (now the Times Square–Grand Central shuttle) as far as Times Square, and then north under Broadway to Bailey Avenue in the Bronx—a total of thirteen and a half miles, a little more than half a mile of this to be across a viaduct over Manhattanville. Because it was much easier, faster, and cheaper, it was decided to use primarily the cut-and-cover method of tunneling. Steel girders were then emplaced to reinforce the walls and to form the subway roof. The roof was ultimately covered with several feet of fill and topped with paving.

To the tune of pick and shovel, hundreds of sandhogs dug their way north, their work constantly frustrated by the ever-varying topography of the island. In the lower sections of Manhattan they were forced to shore up the sides almost as quickly as they dug them to prevent the wet sand and soil from seeping into the trench, while hard rock formations lurked directly beneath the streets above Twenty-seventh Street. The workers had to divert or dig around and beside a jumbled network of steam pipelines, gas and water mains, sewers, electrical conduits, and pneumatic tubes; skirt and shore the underpinnings of the Els; and take care not to be roasted by electrical cables, scalded by steam, or blown into the air by exploding gas. It was an obstacle course of fiendish proportions for engineers and workmen alike. Truckloads of earth and rock were piled alongside the trench and later dumped as landfill along Manhattan's shores. Wooden planks here and there formed rickety bridges. In other places, where there were no overpasses, the excavation formed a chasm separating one side of a street from the other, exposing a rough and dangerous bridgework of pipes and mains. Shopkeepers were enraged, as their businesses declined. Some offered special sales to stimulate trade. Others were forced to close altogether. To them, the construction method of the tunnel was more cut than cover. Eventually, heavy planks were thrown over the gaping wound through Manhattan, and even trolley tracks were laid across, so that life could go on more or less normally. Sometimes, for instance near Canal Street at what had once been Collect Pond, the subway tunnel dipped below the tidewater level. Every twelve and a half hours, water had to be pumped from the trench until its walls could be buttressed with heavy timbers, after which the subway was waterproofed with a concrete sheath. In other sections the subway was blasted out of rock and lined with concrete. Working eight-hour shifts, work gangs dynamited the rock in the early morning hours, after which the day gangs brought the rubble to the surface in mule-driven cars.

For two years sandhogs (mostly immigrant Italians) and engineers avoided what they feared most—an underground explosion. Even though there were gas main leaks, time and again they managed to avoid having their picks strike a spark which would ignite the gas. For two years, workmen, city officials, residents, and shopkeepers alike prayed that another day would come and go without a blast ripping through the air. And for two years, the threat remained constant, although perhaps the fear of it subsided with passing time.

When it did finally happen, it was not from the hazards of the work itself but through incredible carelessness and stupidity. On January 27, 1902, powderman Moses Epps lighted a candle a few feet away from 548 pounds of dynamite in the IRT storage shed above the subway tunnel at Forty-first Street and Park Avenue. It was a cold day, and he wanted to warm his hands. His paper-wrapped lunch lay beside him on the floor. After some minutes, Epps walked out of the shed to get some air. The candle fell to the floor and fed eagerly on his lunch wrapper. When Epps turned and saw what was happening, he grabbed a nearby bucket of water and threw it on the flames. It was not enough. He ran to refill his bucket. Halfway, he spun around to make sure there was time. But the flames were already licking at the dynamite. Dropping his bucket, Epps fled from the shanty, screaming at passersby to run for their lives. A moment later the entire midtown area of the city seemed to explode. Walls caved, plaster crumbled, glass splintered and crashed. Unsuspecting residents and pedestrians were hurled through the air and crushed by debris. Five people were killed, more than 180 injured, although Epps himself suffered only minor bruises. The IRT tunnel was virtually undamaged. Repairs took a week.

Mayor Seth Low immediately appointed a Municipal Explosives Commission to establish stricter regulations for the storage and use of high explosives within the city limits. For more than a year, work progressed without further mishap, except for a rock slide deep under Park Avenue between Thirty-seventh and Thirty-eighth streets which, although it seriously damaged the construction, took no lives. Then, in October 1903, workmen were tunneling through the deepest part of the subway road, sixty feet below the ground, at 145th Street and St. Nicholas Avenue. They faced solid rock, at the end of a tunnel fifty feet wide and fifteen feet high. The Italian work crew had already drilled the holes into the rock face, readying it for demolition. Under the direction of foreman Timothy Sullivan, they inserted the sticks of dynamite into the holes. Then Sullivan cleared the tunnel, ordered the detonation set, and waited. A few moments later, he heard the deep rumblings below ground, the distant rolling thunder he had heard countless times before—the sound of exploding dynamite. And so he ordered his men, all thirty of them, back into the tunnel, himself in the lead. A moment later there were three sharp blasts, some remaining dynamite exploding. The rock heaved and swelled. The ground rose from beneath the men. Choking their screams of terror, the tunnel roof came down on Sullivan and nine of his workers. Some men were trapped under boulders weighing as much as two

Immigrant labor to drill and blast the underlying rock was cheap and plentiful. With unsophisticated equipment, workers forged the paths that have remained testament to their skill and daring. *Museum of the City of New York*

tons. "Three men hung head downward while rescuers attacked with drills the rock which crushed the lower part of their bodies," wrote Robert Daley. "A fourth man was caught by the leg. At last a doctor amputated the leg." The man died en route to the hospital. It took days to identify the eleven dead and countless injured. Complicating the process was the fact that the Italians were recent immigrants, known only by numbers.

The remaining months of construction passed uneventfully. At last, after ten thousand men had excavated more than 3.5 million cubic yards of earth and rock over a period of four years, New York's first regular subway was ready to roll. "Twenty-five minutes to Harlem" had become a popular slogan, and the dream had finally become a reality.

"Subway Day," as the New York *Journal* called the inaugural event set for October 27, 1904, proved to be a cool, brisk autumn day. The newspaper's headlines proclaimed: "Enormous Crowds Gather to See the Opening Ceremonies—Mayor to Start First Train at 2 o'clock—Only Invited Guests Carried until 7 P.M., When Public May Buy Its Way In—Every Employee at His Post Awaiting the Signal to Begin—Great Salute Promised for First Train." Elsewhere the paper reported that "while completing the electric arrangements for the public opening of the subway today ... two electricians were badly burned and shocked near the City Hall underground station. ..."

Hours before the first train was to roll, crowds were gathering to cheer it on its journey. Church bells rang, and foghorns echoed across the harbor. Flags and colorful pennants and bunting danced in the wind. New Yorkers prepared for a celebration such as the city had not witnessed since The Great Water Celebration of 1842. There were speeches by dignitaries and officials and a benediction delivered by Archbishop Farley. Mayor George B. McClellan himself closed the ceremonies with a simple statement: "Now I, as mayor, in the name of the people, declare the subway open." To the roar and thunder of the public's cheers, he took the controls of the eight-car IRT train which was jammed with invited guests. Before him through the darkness to the north and west ran 9.1 miles of electrified tracks, from City Hall to Grand Central, west across Forty-second Street to Times Square, and from there north under Broadway to 145th Street.

The first run did not quite live up to the slogan—it took twenty-six minutes instead of twenty-five. But that was close, and nobody quibbled. Until that evening, thousands of invited guests traveled free to 145th Street and back to City Hall, while police at both ends of the line were forced to use their nightsticks to keep the press of large crowds from pushing on the train. The first full day of the IRT's public operation was October 28, and the fare was five cents per ride.

In January 1904, Mayor McClellan (seated first row, right, beside Alexander E. Orr, president of the Rapid Transit Commission) and other dignitaries set out from City Hall station for an inspection tour of the first completed portion of the IRT. *Museum of the City of New York*

Almost as though it were foretelling the future, one newspaper headline of October 29 reported, "Rush Hour Blockade Jams Subway; Other Delays Day and Evening, 350,000 Passengers; 17-Minute Delays." By the end of 1904 the daily average of New York's subway passengers was 300,000, with the Brooklyn Bridge stop being the busiest station of all.

In the meantime, work progressed on the first underwater link between Brooklyn and Manhattan. From the moment rail traffic across the Brooklyn Bridge, completed in 1883, had made the two boroughs accessible to each other, Brooklyn had begun to experience growth at an unprecedented rate. The planned IRT extension to Brooklyn's Borough Hall was to be a major step in the city's expansion. Driving the tunneling shield under the East River between the Battery and Joralemon Street, some thirty feet beneath the riverbed, workmen were rapidly approaching the midriver point in 1905 when a most astonishing accident took place. Working inside the safety of the shield chamber—a large-diameter pipelike device which was driven through soft earth or mud by jacks or compressed air (and fitted over the completed tunnel in the rear much like a thimble over the finger)—the sandhogs suddenly heard a great hiss. But they had been carefully drilled and instantly knew what to do. They grabbed the sandbags always on hand for such an emergency and began to plug the blowout in the roof which was rapidly sucking the air out of the chamber with a deafening scream. Dick Creedon was one of the men who grabbed a bag, but when he started to throw it into the breach, he was sucked up with it. With incredible speed, he was yanked up through the riverbed and then through the river itself. The sandbag was torn from his hands somewhere along this fantastic journey, and he soon found himself swimming unharmed on the water's surface. Before long, a boat picked him up.

Eleven years later, in 1916, during the tunnel construction between Manhattan's Whitehall and Brooklyn's Montague Street on the IRT's sister line, the Brooklyn Rapid Transit Company (BRT)—it became the Brooklyn Manhattan Transit Corporation (BMT) in 1923—a sudden leak again sucked the compressed air from the tube. Again there was a screaming whistle followed by a great rush of air. Before they could reach for their sandbags, three men were sucked through the hole at the top of the tube. One of the men, Marshall Mabey, was lucky. It is said by those who saw it happen that Mabey shot through the surface of the water like a cannonball held on top of a forty-foot geyser—and lived. The others were dead. One had drowned, the other had struck his head on something in the riverbed.

Great though the achievement of New York's intricate and massive subway system is, it took a heavy toll in human lives during construction. Four workers were suffocated in 1906 when a blast set off by a fire caused a cave-in. In 1913 eleven men were buried by a hundred tons of sandstone, following a cave-in at Lexington Avenue near Fifty-sixth Street.

Disaster struck again on September 22, 1915. A crowded trolley was headed north along Seventh Avenue, approaching Twenty-third Street, traveling on tracks laid over the planks covering the north heading of the new Seventh Avenue subway excavation. Heavy timbers supported the tracks and planks. Suddenly, there was a blast deep below, just south of Twenty-fifth Street. Ever so slowly, the planks and tracks lifted into the air. And then the street began to disappear, sinking into a yawning hole, crushing and dislodging the timbers below, the trolley still approaching. Five workmen at the bottom of the exposed tunnel looked up, dazed and blinded by the sudden daylight. They had mere seconds to watch death come rushing upon them. Still on its rails, the wooden trolley

The scene after an underground blast lifted support beams and tracks into the air on Seventh Avenue, between Twenty-third and Twenty-fifth streets. Five workmen below lost their lives as an oncoming trolley fell into the exposed tunnel, killing twenty of its passengers and injuring dozens of others. *Museum of the City of New York*

lunged into the depth of the tunnel, jumped its tracks, and landed on its side with a hideous crunch. A twenty-four-inch gas main lay broken and exposed, sending its gas fumes into the air. A moment later, screams rose to the street. Those of the trolley's passengers who were able to move tried to escape. Rescuers—police, firemen, amateurs—appeared from all sides, flung heavy ropes from the street, and slid into the cavity, working feverishly to raise the injured. Amid the terror of an explosion from the escaping gas fumes, hundreds of curious onlookers nevertheless rushed to the scene to gape. When it was over, twenty people were found dead, dozens injured.

Three days later it happened again. A fault in the underground rock wall north of Thirty-eighth Street brought on a sudden landslide. In moments, seventy-five feet of Broadway began to collapse—just as another loaded trolley was approaching. Motorman Malachi Murphy and his passengers were inches away from disaster. Already the trolley was beginning to slide. Instinctively, Murphy acted with almost superhuman strength. His every muscle tensed, his knuckles turning white, he threw his gears into reverse, willing the trolley to obey his body. For endless seconds it teetered on the edge of the descent. And then, at last, the wheels gripped. Sweat running over his face, Murphy backed his car from the chasm. For his presence of mind in the face of almost certain death, Murphy was later handsomely rewarded by the trolley company.

Although the IRT had by now been running daily without incident for a decade, New Yorkers were beginning to realize there was a heavy price to pay for their subways. But even though public faith was severely shaken by these repeated disasters under the streets, by the loss of lives and property, the subway lines grew steadily. As the years passed they extended deep into the Bronx and fanned across the East River into Brooklyn and Queens, through tunnels and over bridges. Even before their tentacles had stretched to the far and uninhabited reaches of the borough, speculators and contractors were busy selling large tracts of Brooklyn swampland and cow pastures to the public. With each new wave of immigrants, the different nationalities settled into pockets of the growing city which they made their own. Even today, whole sections of New York retain their ethnic flavor, where a short bus or subway ride leads to a variety of communities in which English is seldom spoken.

An important consideration of the early subways was

the design and function of the stations. Although nobody dreamed of duplicating Alfred Ely Beach's sumptuous waiting room, considerable thought was given to the stations. Particularly attractive and ornate were the early, semi-Oriental kiosks. The old IRT City Hall station, which has been closed since 1945, sported vaulted ceilings inlaid with colored tiles and glass. Mosaics formed the focal points of many early subway stations. Several of them still exist today.

The Seventh Avenue IRT's South Ferry loop (turnaround) station is identified by a bas-relief of a Hudson River sloop, a seventy-foot boat with a large mainsail, a small jib, and, sometimes, a topsail. Until the 1850s such craft made regular runs to and from New York's markets and towns upriver. Whitehall Street station is decorated with a mosaic featuring Peter Stuyvesant's Great House, built in 1658. When the English Governor General Thomas Dongan later derisively called it White Hall because of its whitewashed walls, the name caught on (the house itself was destroyed by fire in 1715). The IRT Fulton Street station depicts Robert Fulton's 150-foot steamship *Clermont,* perpetuating the myth that Fulton invented the steamboat. A $350 prize was awarded to a Frenchman named Joseph Mangin and a Scot named John McComb, Jr., for their design of a new City Hall. The building was officially opened in 1812, and it is this design which graces the BMT's City Hall station. There is a depiction of a beaver at Astor Place and Eighth Street, because, as every New Yorker knows, John Jacob Astor was known not only as the Landlord of New York, but also as the Beaver King of the World.

The Christopher Street station was decorated with a mosaic of the city's penitentiary which was located there before the prison was moved to the town of Sing Sing along the Hudson (whereupon that town promptly changed its name to Ossining). The front view of a

"balloon-stack" locomotive with its "cow catcher" has decorated Grand Central station since 1918 when the Lexington Avenue IRT opened, completing the H design of the
line through Manhattan. "The World's Eighth Wonder"
when it was opened in 1883, the Brooklyn Bridge is featured in a bas-relief at the Chambers Street station. Christopher Columbus, who discovered neither the Orient for
which he was looking nor New York for which he was
not, is commemorated at Columbus Circle by the charm-
ing bas-relief of his caravel, the *Santa Maria*. The IRT
station of Borough Hall is decorated with a representation
of what was once Brooklyn's City Hall. Then in 1898,
when Brooklyn joined Manhattan and the other boroughs
to become Greater New York, the structure became known
as Borough Hall.

Many of the early mosaics have been covered by new
facings in the trend to modernize the stations. Others are
hidden from view in disused stations. The remaining designs are quaint reminders of a bygone age, relics of a
time when New York was truly a melting pot, home for
millions from across the globe to whom English was an
alien tongue.

Most of the IRT and BMT lines which exist today
were established in the span of about twenty years. Extensions were added as the population swelled in the outlying boroughs. Only Staten Island remained immune to
the advancing tunnel bore (although in the 1920s an abor-
tive effort was made to link Brooklyn with Staten Island),
with the result that it has retained its rural aspects.

One of the earliest lines to serve the city was the
Hudson & Manhattan Railroad Company, also known as
the H & M tunnels or Hudson Tubes. Begun in 1874, it
was the first tunnel link—actually two tunnels—between
New Jersey and New York, each tunnel consisting of two
tubes crossing under the Hudson River. Beset by accidents,
legal suits, and financial troubles, the H & M's progress

The Fourteenth Street subway construction in July 1921—a cast-iron ring section of the north tube. *Museum of the City of New York*

was painfully slow. Again and again work was suspended, then begun once more, while the embryonic line fought off contentions that it would compete with existing ferry lines across the Hudson. Its reputation was not enhanced by a blowout under the river which took twenty lives in 1879.

It was an ambitious young lawyer, William G. McAdoo (later United States Secretary of the Treasury), who undertook to complete the line by electrifying it, thereby resolving the serious ferry congestion across the Hudson River. Under his leadership, starting in 1902, the H & M began to make dramatic headway. According to Anthony Fitzherbert, "the tunnel was built by pushing a shield through the silt at the bottom of the river. As the mechanical shield was pushed through the mud, every thirty inches the door was opened and the displaced mud placed into the chamber, where it was shoveled into small cars which hauled it to the surface." Huge hydraulic jacks rammed the shield through the mud and silt at the rate of seventy-five feet a day. It was, in fact, "the first time in history that a tunnel was bored without laborers having to excavate and remove the displaced earth. All the work was done under an air pressure of thirty-eight pounds per square inch." The terminals were to be located at Hoboken in New Jersey and at Thirty-third Street in Manhattan, with extensions along Manhattan's West Side and stations at Ninth, Fourteenth, Nineteenth, Twenty-third, Twenty-eighth, and Thirty-third streets, all served by the two northern Tubes.

Engineers ran into difficulties, however, when they encountered a reef on the Manhattan side of the river. So they devised a plan whereby they would dump clay on the reef from barges, allowing the reef to be dynamited without danger of a tunnel blowout. The blasted rock was then removed through the doors of the shield's bulkhead. One man, however, did lose his life during one of several blowouts when, sucked through the hole, he was weighted down by the clay above him. Several months before the IRT was opened for regular service in Manhattan, the first of the two H & M tubes was "holed through" on March 11, 1904. (Its parallel mate was holed through on September 24, 1905.) Accompanied by a group of invited guests, McAdoo walked from New Jersey to Manhattan via the Tube, through the doors of the two shields where they met at the center, deep under the Hudson River.

The Hudson Tubes were ready for regular service on February 25, 1908. The darkened train stood in the darkened Ninth Street station with its cargo of dignitaries. Then, at 3:30 P.M., a telegraph operator sent a signal to

President Theodore Roosevelt, who was waiting at his desk in the White House. A few moments later the president pushed a button which turned on the electric power. Instantly, the train and station were flooded with light to the cheers of four hundred guests. A few moments later the train picked up speed deep under the Hudson. As it approached the halfway boundary line between the two states, it slowed to a halt amid a circle of red, white, and blue lights in the Tube, to allow New York Governor Charles Evans Hughes and New Jersey Governor Franklin Fort to shake hands. At Hoboken, twenty thousand cheering and whistling spectators crowded into the square outside the terminal, accompanied by the sound of church bells and foghorns from the harbor. That night fireworks lit the sky, while thousands waited to enter the station. Within twenty-four hours, fifty thousand people had ridden the eight-car train, and by morning the ferries stood forlorn and empty, as commuters crowded to avail themselves of the eight-minute ride to Ninth Street.

That day's *New York Times* hailed the event as "one of the greatest engineering feats ever accomplished, greater perhaps than the Panama Canal will be when opened, considering the obstacles which had to be overcome." Little more than a year later, in 1909, the downtown or southern Tubes were opened, providing the important link between the Erie Terminal in New Jersey and the Pennsylvania Railroad's Exchange Place Terminal on Cortlandt Street.

It was not until 1932 that a completely new subway line, the Independent City-owned Rapid Transit Railroad (IND), the Eighth Avenue line, made its appearance. Serving the West Side of Manhattan and later the Bronx, Brooklyn, and Queens, it became the only line under city management (until the city acquired the BMT and IRT in 1940).

Then in 1940, Manhattan's last completed major trunk

line, the IND's Sixth Avenue line, was ready for service. It is a line which perhaps more than any other is truly "woven" into the fabric of subterranean New York, and it represents an engineering feat of rare proportions. Begun in March 1936, as the Depression was nearing its end, the last subway road, like the others before it, was faced with several formidable obstacles. First came the need to relocate the vast tangle of utility lines, conduits, cables, and mains which would be displaced by the subway. Because of the already overcrowded conditions on existing subways, it was imperative that the Sixth Avenue elevated line be kept in operation throughout construction of the subway below. Therefore, each of the 670 columns supporting the El had to be supported from the sides while the subway trench was dug. The weight of each column was then transferred to temporary concrete-and-steel piers sunk into the pit. As the structure of the subway moved slowly along the avenue, the weight of the columns was transferred to the roof of the tunnel. All this work was achieved while the Els continued their scheduled runs, carrying thousands of New Yorkers to their destinations. Then, just when all the underpinnings were completed and the painstaking and costly task of keeping the El running had been accomplished without mishap, the city, in its imponderable wisdom and timing, bought the El and demolished it!

A profile of the Sixth Avenue IND line from West Fourth Street to Fiftieth Street is much like a roller coaster. The West Fourth Street station is quite possibly the world's largest, with its two levels, each a four-track station with both express and local trains—the Eighth Avenue line above, the Sixth Avenue line below—separated by an intermediate mezzanine. A system of complex track "flexing" permits trains from the lower Sixth Avenue line to be switched to the upper Eighth Avenue route south of West Fourth Street, and vice versa. What few people realize is that this design was necessary because the H & M enters Sixth Avenue from Christopher Street at the mezzanine level of the station.

Between Ninth and Thirteenth streets, the two local tracks were tunneled through soft clay and sand by the shield method under compressed air. From Thirteenth to Twenty-sixth streets, the tunnels, constructed in separate cut-and-cover trenches, flanked the H & M. Above Twenty-sixth Street, the deep rock tunnels dipped to sixty-seven feet below street level. As the Sixth Avenue line passed over the Pennsylvania Railroad and Long Island Rail Road between Thirty-second and Thirty-third streets, their respective roofs had first to be removed, then replaced with shallower roofs which, in turn, served as the floor of the new subway. At the same time, the original H & M Thirty-third Street terminal had to be completely demolished and rebuilt at a higher elevation to allow the Sixth Avenue line to squeeze between it and the two railroads. Since the BMT also crossed here, its floor had to be rebuilt to allow the Sixth Avenue subway to tunnel under it. Monumental as this task was, the entire job was done without interruption of service on any of the affected lines. Small wonder that the two-and-a-quarter-mile Sixth Avenue subway cost $60 million—even at Depression prices!

It took four years to complete this work, and when Mayor Fiorello LaGuardia took the controls of the first Sixth Avenue train on December 15, 1940, he opened service on what was then expected to be the last major trunk line in Manhattan. In 1968, however, the Board of Estimate approved the construction of twelve new subway routes as well as additions to existing lines, at a total projected cost of $1.3 billion. The Second Avenue subway, a major trunk line with connecting service to Brooklyn and Queens, was begun in 1972. The route was designed to stretch from the southern tip of Manhattan into the

Bronx, where it would feed into three branch lines. It would relieve overcrowding on the Lexington Avenue IRT and provide additional service between the city's financial and civic districts and upper Manhattan's office and residential areas. Another major route is the Sixty-third Street crosstown line under Central Park, providing connections to existing subways at Fifty-seventh Street and Sixth and Seventh avenues in Manhattan and Sunnyside in Queens through a 3,140-foot East River tunnel. Construction began on the underwater tunnel in 1969. For this, four 1,100-ton, 375-foot tubes sealed at both ends by temporary steel bulkheads were towed from Maryland to Virginia. There, concrete was poured between the hollow double skin to form a three-foot-thick steel-concrete-steel tunnel wall. The tubes were then towed to New York. Work was started on the subway connections under Central Park in 1971. But as the city entered a period of serious financial troubles, progress on these lines became increasingly stop-and-start, and completion dates have been pushed further and further into the 1980s.

The total construction and equipment cost of New York's operating subway systems—the largest in the world —was $2.5 billion. Replacement today would add up to well over ten times that amount. It is a system whose tracks, laid end to end, would 'reach Detroit. In all, it covers 230 route miles, or 710 track miles. (A line extending 10 miles consists of 10 *route* miles; the same with four tracks consists of 40 *track* miles.) In Manhattan alone, there are 66.99 underground route miles, while Brooklyn is next with 43.11. Queens has 15.17 and the Bronx 11.78. (The remainder of the trackage is at ground level or elevated.) It is possible to travel more than 32 miles for one fare and without a change of trains—from Washington Heights in the Bronx, through Manhattan and Brooklyn, to Far Rockaway in Queens. Two of the city's underwater subway tunnels span more than a mile, and all of them are made of cast iron or steel sheathed in concrete, or of concrete alone.

Some 6,300 trains operate daily throughout the entire system, and they stop at 265 underground and 158 elevated stations. The busiest of these by far is the double-level West Fourth Street station with an average of seventy-seven trains per hour during the daily morning and evening rush, followed closely by Brooklyn's single-level, six-track DeKalb Avenue station with rush hour traffic of seventy-five trains. The system's newest 1,909 stainless-steel cars represent the world's largest such fleet, with an average weight of some 77,500 pounds per car. The newer R-44s and R-46s are capable of a speed of eighty-three miles an hour—a speed which they will never be allowed or required to attain in the city's subway system, though it is nice to know they can.

New York's daily 3.5 million subway riders drop their tokens into more than 3,000 turnstiles and change their money at 777 change booths. More than 81,000 passengers daily travel the five subway lines to and from Grand Central Station. Eight lines carrying more than 64,000 passengers and nine lines carrying more than 61,000 passengers each converge daily at Thirty-fourth Street and Sixth Avenue and at Times Square, respectively.

Travelers can read their morning or evening papers as they dip as much as 180 feet below the surface at St. Nicholas Avenue in Manhattan. Others can pause in their reading for a moment at Brooklyn's Smith and Ninth streets, 87½ feet above street level, to catch a glimpse of one of the most spectacular panoramic views, particularly at sunset, of lower Manhattan, the Statue of Liberty, and the harbor. On clear days they can also see the New Jersey shore, the arch of Bayonne Bridge on the shore of Staten Island, or the majestic span of the Verrazano-Narrows Bridge.

To electrify the subway system, the New York City

Transit Authority (TA) purchases approximately ten percent of all the power produced by Con Edison. Although alternating current is used for all the system's signals, station and tunnel lighting, ventilation, and some line equipment, the remainder is converted to direct current. DC is used for the operation of all trains, which draw about six hundred volts from the contact, or third, rail.

New Yorkers frequently complain about the dirty subways and stations, but they rarely give thought either to how this dirt is created, or what happens to it. A staff of more than five thousand men collects *thirty-two tons per day* of gum wrappers, beer and soda cans and bottles, cigarette packs, and sundry trash, as well as two thousand tons of newspapers yearly! In addition, these work crews are charged with cleaning, sweeping, and washing station platforms. Another five thousand men clean, inspect, repair, and service the rolling stock in thirteen shops spread over four boroughs. Still other men clean and scrape the tracks, removing the steel dust created by the friction of the wheels and the tracks, and other debris—up to 1,000–1,500 fifty-pound bags per night—all of which can cause track fires and shorted electrical circuits.

The TA, which was placed under the management of the Metropolitan Transportation Authority in 1968, numbers some twenty-six thousand employees in its rapid transit system, of whom more than three thousand are motormen and nearly an equal number are conductors. When a motorman turns the master-controller in his cab to the "power" position, a signal is sent to each car's motor-control unit to feed electric power to the traction motors, and the train moves. When the motorman turns off the master-controller, braking occurs in two stages: first, the motors act as generators to produce deceleration; then, when the train has been slowed to about ten miles an hour, the air-brake shoes press against the wheels, and the train is brought to a full stop. Traction is provided by four 100-horsepower motors under each car (115 h.p. for the R-44s and R-46s), one for each axle, or two for each four-wheel truck. Contact shoes projecting from the wheel trucks draw six-hundred-volt direct current from the trackside third rails. The automatic couplers that hold the cars together also link air hoses for the braking system and electric lines, so that acceleration, or deceleration and braking, take place simultaneously on all cars of a train.

When Transit Police began protecting the public in 1935, they did so just on the IND line, the only city-owned underground road at the time. The Transit Police grew into a full-fledged department, entirely independent of the New York City Police Department, when the city took over the remaining subway lines. Today it forms a body of more than 3,000 men—the eighth largest police force in the nation—who regularly "ride shotgun" to ensure passenger safety. More than 6,500 maintenance-of-way employees are constantly alert to trouble on the lines themselves. They clean, inspect, repair, and service tracks, signals, and structures. The Training Center in the Fourteenth Street/Eighth Avenue station teaches the intricacies of power equipment and switches, as well as such skills as construction carpentry.

There are fifty-nine console radio dispatchers working eight-hour "tricks," or shifts, around the clock, manning the command center's fifteen radio console desks at the NYCTA headquarters at Jay Street, Brooklyn. Each dispatcher covers a section of the system, and each base section consists of several segments. With the touch of a button, the dispatcher can locate and talk by two-way radio or telephone to every train proceeding through a given base section. Every train moving throughout the system can be traced visually by indicator lights on the schematic track layout on the giant command-center board. The dispatcher keeps the trains running safely and as near as possible to schedule. When a train is stalled with a shoe-beam short circuit, for instance, or there is a sick passenger, the motorman immediately notifies the dispatcher. The latter at once locates all following trains and arranges for reroutes and service adjustments. An important aspect of his job is the coordination of his planning and actions with radio dispatchers in other sections whose service will be affected. When the trouble is corrected, he must notify all concerned and reestablish normal service. "It isn't the kind of job you can pick up out of a book," says Hank Herte, who has been on the Flushing line for ten years. "You have to know the location of the switches, emergency stairs, pumps, and ventilating fans. You have to know the men on the line and who you can count on."

Let a train stall or develop mechanical trouble, and the RCI, or road car inspector, the TA's doctor-on-call, rushes to the scene—on foot, catching a passing train, hailing a cab. The trouble can be anything from flat wheels or locked brakes to a lack of motor power. During nonrush hours, he takes his post on a station platform and observes passing trains for defects, repairs these when possible, or notes them for prompt correction in the yard or shop. He files meticulous reports into a computer in order to provide a complete profile of each car's history, its defects, repairs, and replacements.

There are about a hundred specialists in the Materials Inspection Division (MID) who spend their working lives testing, analyzing, dissecting, squeezing, poking, crushing, grinding, breaking, and burning an array of thousands of products so varied that a listing would resemble a Sears, Roebuck catalog. They monitor the manufacture of Transit Authority purchases in some 450 plants in 250 cities, 27 states, and 3 different countries. They buy between seven and ten thousand railroad wheels per year, in plants as far away as Japan.

The Power Department's Cable Section maintains a

2,000-mile network of power lines that snakes under the city's streets and sidewalks and also on overhead structures. This is equal to nearly 9 miles of power cable for each of the 230 miles of track. Often, the cause of cable failure is moisture which has corroded the insulation of copper conduits carrying as much as twelve thousand volts. However, the greatest single cause of power failure is heat. Cables burn out with heavy usage and the added power demands made by air-conditioned cars.

Among the TA's rolling stock are such service cars as flat or gondola cars to transport materiel, pump cars used in times of subway floods, hopper cars which deposit ballast (rocks) along the tracks and rail ties, tower cars which repair and replace overhead lights, garbage cars and tank cars, rail testers, rail grinders, and weed sprayers. There are dump cars, vacuum cars which remove the dust and grime from tunnel walls, a steam car which cleans the tunnels and stations, crane cars which pick up rails and machinery, and signal supply cars.

When the weather forecast predicts temperatures below freezing, winds gusting to thirty miles an hour, freezing rain or snow, the TA's operations and maintenance crews know the time has come to roll out the Snowfighters. These diesel-powered, triple-action snowplow-snow-blower/alcohol-spray/third-rail-deicer machines serve as the system's armored patrols in the winter battle to keep the subways running on time. "We must make our moves before the storm hits," says former maintenance-of-way chief John J. Quinn. "Hourly weather reports keep us on top of the situation, and at the first storm warning, we alert our storm control center and get the show on the road." A crew of nine, including two motormen certified to operate diesel locomotives, mans the Snowfighters. An AC generator driven by a propane engine powers the air-blowers which blast snow from the right-of-way, while jet sprays apply an antifreeze mixture of alcohol and diesel fuel oil from 270-gallon tanks to prevent the third rail from icing up. When conditions require use of the snow-plow or blowers, which are mounted on a rebuilt subway car, the unit operates in reverse, with the locomotive pushing the Snowfighter. A motorman in the head cab directs the diesel operator in the rear by telephone headset. When the snow is too much even for the Snowfighters, a small army of sturdy trackmen takes over with yellow shovels made of plastic to prevent the kind of warm greeting the third rail would extend.

But the rarest car of all, the "phantom" train, is the one which flies through the darkness of the system, never on the same schedule twice, slipping into and out of stations with hardly a stop, protected by a small army of invisible guards. It is the money train, the train which safely carries the system's subway token revenues to a hidden terminus.

One of the most exacting and unusual TA jobs is held by Henry Ruschmeyer, who drives a signal car. In fact, he has driven it since 1944, when he took over from his predecessor who had held the job since 1926. It requires special skills to travel the dark tunnels alone, staying out of the way of scheduled trains, switching to another line with sufficient speed and control to be able to "coast" without power during the crossover, since the third rail breaks at switches. He must do his work of checking and repairing line signals with the precision of a scientist, knowing every inch of the subway map. And Henry Ruschmeyer does. He and his signal car scoot alone through the darkness—they keep the rolling stock rolling safely.

Perhaps the most colorful character ever employed by the Transit Authority was "Smelly" Kelly. Irish-born James Patrick Kelly's job for more than thirty years, until the late 1950s, was to patrol the IND subway tracks sniffing for gas and water leaks. The TA had such faith in

Kelly that if his nose told him there was gas, the power would be immediately shut off.

Kelly's nose and know-how were uncannily accurate. So was his knowledge of what lay above the surface. He gave particular attention to areas under service stations, chemical works, and storage areas for manufactured gas. "You check areas known to form pockets of sewer gas, and areas beneath new construction jobs where a steam shovel might scrape gas mains," he once commented. In as unlikely a place as the New York subway, he found a thirty-inch eel, a ten-inch trout, and dozens of killifish during his career. Not to mention rats.

Once in his career he was faced with a mystery even he was hard-pressed to solve. People were complaining that there was a distinct odor of elephants in the IND's Forty-second Street/Sixth Avenue station! With a good deal of skepticism, Kelly proceeded to check out that unlikely rumor. To his amazement, he found there was indeed a smell of elephants. But how could this be, he wondered. Elephants in the subway? And so he went on a careful inspection tour of the streets above, studying the buildings, trying to fathom the cause. It was then, thanks to his interest in the city's history, that Kelly remembered that the New York Hippodrome had once been situated at the corner of Sixth Avenue and Forty-third Street. Many circuses had performed there—and so had elephants! Their dung had been buried in the Hippodrome's basement, and there it had rested without troubling a soul—until a water main burst. The water had seeped through the dung, releasing its fumes into the station below.

Before he retired, Kelly trained sixty sniffers to take over his work. Old Smelly Kelly was quite a legend in his time.

The New York City subway system is three-quarters of a century old. Since its inception, it has carried hundreds of thousands, eventually millions, of people in swift safety every day. On the single busiest day in its history, December 23, 1946, the system established an all-time record. In that twenty-four-hour period, 8,872,244 people rode the city's rapid transit.

This remarkable statistic would be impossible without the "tripper," a sturdy metal arm which lies docilely alongside the tracks, at least one in every station. It is a part of one of the world's most extensive rapid-transit signal systems. Intrinsic to the signal system is its capability of allowing trains to follow each other safely at close distances; to permit trains to move safely through junctions and crossings (interlockings); and, in the event of an emergency, a breakdown of equipment, or any other interruption of service, to permit trains to be quickly rerouted around the obstruction. Since modern ten-car trains are capable of nearly double the acceleration rates of the older six- to eight-car trains, the introduction of the automatic block signal system provides a greatly improved minimum zone of protection behind each train, so that the following train will have sufficient braking distance in which to stop.

In automatic block signaling, the track is electrically divided into sections, or blocks, whose average length is some six hundred feet, although the length of a signal block varies, depending on whether the track is level, curved, or on an upgrade or downgrade. Longer blocks are used on level tracks than on curves, grades, or station approaches. The entrance of a train into a block is governed by a signal with three lights—red, yellow, and green—mounted on the wall on the right side of the tracks. Should a motorman ignore a red stop signal, for instance, the automatic tripper will rise to an upright position and instantly release the train's emergency air brakes, bringing the train to a halt. On the other hand, the introduction of the yellow light signal permits the motorman to maintain scheduled speed when trains are close together, as they are during rush hours, yet keep the trains sufficiently spaced to prevent a rear-end collision. After a train has passed through the block, the wayside signal turns red, and the tripper arm rises automatically to its upright position above the top of the rail to prevent a following train from passing the signal. The tripper remains in that position until the preceding train is safely beyond the next *two* signals.

In addition, the New York City Transit Authority's safety system also includes interlocking signals which govern routes at junctions and track crossings. These signals are mechanically and electrically interlocked, requiring manipulation in a predetermined order. They work in conjunction with so-called home and approach signals, all of which are interconnected and centrally controlled to permit trains to pass safely through interlocking territory, over switches, and from one route to another. Although signal modernization has reduced headway from three minutes to ninety seconds, train service is, in fact, scheduled at a two-minute headway to allow for delays in the loading and unloading of passengers at stations. Should there be a signal interruption at any time, the automatic fail-safe nature of the signal system will instantly stop all train movements on that particular line until the cause of interruption is removed.

Complain about the subways, but bless those dirty little trippers. There are thirteen thousand of them lurking beneath the city, and they have made New York's rapid transit safer than any other form of transportation. The electropneumatic interlocking signal system was called a "marvel of the times." That was in 1904, when only the IRT ventured to use it. It has been modified and modernized over the years and copied by every railroad in the world, but its most important element is still the tripper.

Despite all mechanical safeguards, however, it was

perhaps inevitable that there would be some accidents on the city's subways. The first of these happened on November 1, 1918. SCORES KILLED OR MAIMED IN BRIGHTON TUNNEL WRECK, reported *The New York Times*. "First Car Crashes Into Tunnel Pier and Other Cars Grind it to Splinters.... Dispatcher, as Strike Motorman, Sends Crowded Train to Doom at 70 Miles an Hour.... Rescue Hindered by Jam of Debris in Narrow Tunnel—Hardly a Soul Escapes from First Car."

The motormen of the Brooklyn Rapid Transit Company (forerunner of the BMT) had gone on a wildcat strike. And so the inexperienced twenty-three-year-old Edward Luciano (identified in early dispatches as Anthony or Ed Lewis), a dispatcher for the BRT, was pressed into service. With two days' training behind him, he took the controls of the five-car wooden train. A sign in the approach to a sharp curve before the tunnel at Malbone Street in Brooklyn clearly warned motormen not to exceed six miles an hour. Luciano later admitted to taking the curve at thirty miles an hour, although a surviving passenger, a naval officer, testified it was closer to seventy miles an hour. Speeding into the curve, the train rammed into a concrete partition between the north- and southbound tracks. Within seconds, "almost every man, woman and child in the first car was killed, and most of those in the second were killed or badly injured ... the counting of the dead proceeded slowly." And Edward Luciano had disappeared. Nearly twenty minutes passed before word of the nature and location of the accident reached the surface. Scores of doctors and nurses, firemen and police rushed to the scene, but forty-five minutes went by before organized rescue attempts could get underway, and then they were hampered by crowds on the street. Brooklyn residents thronged to discover the fate of husbands, fathers, sons, and daughters traveling home in the evening rush hour. Others streamed to the scene as onlookers. Police from six precincts were needed to contain the screaming, surging mass. Blood was everywhere.

"Firemen who took part in the rescue work said the second and third cars had fallen over so that one side formed the floor, and the passengers were heaped upon one another, some dead, some dying, some slightly injured and some unhurt, but all so tightly gripped in the wreckage and so menaced by steel and wooden splinters, that movement was impossible," reported the *Times*. The rest of the train, still traveling at high speed after its impact with the first car, had crashed into a series of pillars supporting the tunnel roof, and the pillars had gouged deeply into the cars. People were flung on the tracks and killed instantly under the wheels, or impaled on the jagged metal of broken seats and rails. The third rail was ripped up and short-circuited.

A warrant was issued for the arrest of the motorman. All BRT officials even remotely responsible were arrested for criminal negligence in hiring the inexperienced man to run a train. At two o'clock on the morning of November 2, as a result of the wreck and just seven hours after it occurred, the motormen called off their strike pending an adjustment of their grievances by the Public Service Commission. One hour earlier, Edward Luciano had been arrested at his home. He could not remember how he had extricated himself from the wreck or how he got home. When detectives found him, he was "pale as death . . . on the verge of collapse."

Luciano was tried for manslaughter, as were the BRT officials held responsible for ordering a "green" recruit to run the fatal train. In the end, after six months of trial and legal maneuvers, all the accused were acquitted. But the accident spurred heated demands for increasing the BRT's safety measures. It was then that the line installed the tripper, long used by the IRT, to prevent any train from ever again running through a red signal above a prescribed speed. However, it did not help the 102 who had died. Today, Malbone Street no longer exists. The name itself struck such terror in the hearts of New Yorkers that it was changed to Empire Boulevard.

Nearly five years went by without further incident. Then on June 25, 1923, a two-car BRT train fell "like a plane" from the Fifth Avenue elevated railway tracks in Brooklyn. As it entered the curve toward the intersection of Atlantic and Flatbush avenues, the train derailed, sending the cars over the top and into the street thirty-five feet below. One of the observers in the street said later that "the forward car left the rails, and after bumping along the ties for fifty feet hung for a moment on the edge of the structure and then toppled over, pulling the second car after it." Miraculously, only six persons were killed, although countless others were injured.

Yet another five years passed before catastrophe struck once more. This time it was the IRT. A train had just left the Forty-second Street station. It was about three blocks south of Times Square when a boom reverberated through the tunnel. The platform and tunnel went dark. Nothing could be seen of the wreck, and yet "women called wildly and men cried hysterically and cursed." When the lights came on again, they revealed a tangled mess of twisted steel, cars smashed and ripped like crumpled paper. A switch just outside the station had malfunctioned. Motorman William McCormick had pulled his nine-car train cautiously out of the station, anxiously listening for the sound of the two wheel trucks which supported each of the nine cars as they cleared the switch. He heard the first truck of the ninth car clear the switch's straightaway position. Then there was a sudden dreadful hissing sound—the switch was moving from straightaway to curve as the rear truck of the ninth car approached it. The rest was inevitable. Half of the ninth car was pulled south, the other half yanked into the curve. Car 9 was ripped apart. That Friday, August 27, 1928, sixteen people were killed and more than a hundred injured in the city's second-worst subway disaster.

Forty-two years went by without further mishap. Then on May 20, 1970, as *The New York Times* reported, two people "were killed and at least 71 were injured when an empty IND subway train smashed into a crowded rush-hour train" at Jackson Heights, Queens. And on October 25, 1973, a crowded IRT express train smashed into the rear of the train ahead of it, which had been stalled by a fire. This time, straphangers were fortunate. None of them were killed, although more than 150 suffered from severe smoke inhalation. A rush-hour derailment of the sixth car of an eight-car BMT train on April 12, 1977, caused only minor injuries. There have been a few other minor mishaps since then.

Fewer than a dozen accidents in all. Most of them could have been averted. The 126 lives lost cannot be replaced. But in the words of one transit official, "The safest railroad in the world is one on which trains do not run." Even so, billions upon billions of people have traveled the New York City subways safely since 1904.

six

FROM THE HARLEM CORNERS TO CASSATT'S PALACE

———————⚓———————

Few things produced as much derisive laughter throughout New York in 1869 as Cornelius Van Derbilt's conceit to build what he tenaciously referred to as a Grand Central Depot at Forty-second Street. The site was so obviously "the end of the world" that hardly any of the public doubted that the "Commodore" was in his dotage. He was seventy-five at the time, large, cantankerous, and self-willed, a hardheaded, outspoken businessman whose word was his honor, a man whose courage and vision were tinged with a ruthless determination.

Van Derbilt's ancestor, Jan Aertsen van der Bilt, had emigrated from the town of Bilt in Holland in the seventeenth century to become one of the early Dutch patroons who settled on Staten Island. By the time Cornelius, one of many children, was born in 1794, his family had not only become poor but had also changed the spelling of its name to vander Bilt. Cornelius attended school until he was eleven, and then began to work on his father's farm. But he had dreams of a more adventurous future. At the age of sixteen, he borrowed $100 from his father and bought himself a piragua, a small two-masted sailing vessel with which he planned to ply the waters between Staten Island and New York, carrying passengers and freight. This venture proved so successful that, within a few short years, he expanded his business to Long Island Sound and the length of the Hudson River to Albany, and engaged in active trading. He also changed the spelling of his name again, this time to Van Derbilt. In the meantime, he had built two schooners and become captain of the larger one.

It was in the early 1830s that he met his nemesis, Daniel Drew, a competitor in the Hudson steamboat trade and the man who would spend the remaining years of his life trying to bring about Van Derbilt's downfall. Trade was rich along the Hudson, and competition between the two as well as among their many rivals was fierce. The result was a rate war that finally depressed the rate between New York and Albany to twelve cents per fare! It had clearly become not only an intolerable situation, but also one which was likely to ruin all competitors. At last, in 1834, Drew was forced to sell out to Van Derbilt. It was a defeat Drew never forgave. However, being a shrewd speculator and capitalist, a manipulator of stock, he next turned his attention to Wall Street and the Erie Railroad.

Van Derbilt, in the meantime, expanded his steamboat business in size as well as scope and was responsible for many design innovations. He had long become known as Commodore, had amassed a great fortune and considerable stature. But the one thing for which he thirsted more than all else—acceptance by New York society—

continued to elude him. Even when he built an elegant townhouse on New York's fashionable Washington Place in 1846, he failed to dent the barriers between him and the city's scions.

Van Derbilt was nearly seventy when he divested himself of his steamship holdings at the beginning of the Civil War. He sold his entire line to the government for $3 million. The following year, in 1862, he decided to carve out an entirely new career for himself in railroads. With an energy and drive seldom rivaled, and with alarming ignorance of the field he had chosen to enter, he threw himself and his fortune into the new venture. He wanted to own a railroad.

It is an affirmation of his brilliance that in a span of less than fourteen years he built an empire that put to rest for all time any doubts about his visionary genius.

As early as the 1830s, New York City, still firmly rooted below Fourteenth Street, had been linked with the mainland by the New York & Harlem Railroad and the New York and New Haven Railroad. Their locomotives chugged down the center of Manhattan Island, along Fourth Avenue, belching soot and cinders as far as the railroad buildings at Forty-second Street. From there, the passenger cars were individually pulled by horses to the city's Madison Square terminal at Twenty-sixth Street. Madison Square itself was on the outskirts of town. Then, in the 1850s, another railroad began to serve New Yorkers. The Hudson-River Rail-Road was the best-built and best-equipped railroad in the country at the time, with tracks along the Hudson River from Albany to its terminal at Tenth Avenue and Thirtieth Street. Yet even though New York had long since grown into a prosperous city, all three railroads were in poor financial health.

Van Derbilt wanted the New York & Harlem Railroad. For a long time, Harlem stock had held at a fairly steady low of $9 per share. But in the fall of 1862, financial observers began to notice that Harlem was very quietly, very steadily climbing—to $10, to $12, to $15. Since there had been some talk of extending the line along Broadway to the Battery, experts felt these rumors might have spurred renewed interest in the stock, although they knew that the Harlem lacked the necessary financial backing for the extension ever to come about. So when the Harlem reached $18, they rushed to sell and turn a handsome profit.

To their utter amazement, however, the wave of selling which should have plummeted the Harlem stock back to $8 or $9 had virtually no effect on it. Instead, it was over $20 within a week.

Wall Streeters blinked, and conducted some fleet research. They discovered none other than old man Van Derbilt behind the scenes. By the time Harlem reached $40, Wall Street was seized by a fit of glee. Clearly, both the stock and the old Commodore were headed for a delicious crash.

Undeterred by all the laughter, Van Derbilt went on buying all the shares he could find. He even used them as collateral for loans to buy still more shares. Wall Street watched with bated breath, waiting to pounce and profit. And still the stock rose. The old man was obviously senile, hell-bent on losing all his steamboat millions. Wall Street loved it.

Harlem climbed to $50.

By April 1863, Van Derbilt owned more than 55,000 of the 110,000 shares outstanding, and the New York & Harlem Railroad was his. And so, in his customary forthright manner, he applied for a franchise from the Common Council to extend the tracks to the Battery. The franchise was granted. Harlem shares shot to $75. And then it happened.

Under the careful tutelage of Daniel Drew, Van Derbilt's former steamship rival, the city's aldermen began to sell. Harlem's $75 had already begun to waver when Van Derbilt heard what was going on. Instantly he knew what the aldermen had known from the start—that the franchise they had granted him was illegal. He also knew that if Harlem dropped too precipitously, the value of his collateral at the banks would be impaired and he could lose his fortune. But the old man still had a major trump. That trump was his broker, the brilliant young Leonard Jerome (the grandfather of Sir Winston Churchill). Jerome advised Van Derbilt to buy.

As quickly as the aldermen sold, the Commodore bought. In fact, the aldermen were selling shares they did not even have, "selling short." They did so on Drew's advice, in order to buy back cheaply once the Harlem had crashed and before delivery fell due. It was to be Drew's revenge.

But the crash did not come. Harlem dropped only three points—and held.

And then came the day for delivery of all the shares the aldermen had sold short, all the shares which Van Derbilt had, in turn, bought, all the shares which they had to deliver to him at $75. But the impact of their sudden rush to buy sent the value of the shares skyrocketing to $179 per share! What had such a short time before been an irresistibly sweet proposition, a foolproof get-rich-quick scheme, was now the overnight ruination of every single alderman. Van Derbilt was the undisputed master of the railroad, although he did lose the franchise for the extension which, in the meantime, had been granted legally to another company by the State Legislature.

A year later Van Derbilt set his heart on acquiring the Hudson-River Rail-Road. He planned to combine it with his own line as the New York, Harlem & Hudson-River Rail-Road. Openly, he applied and paid for a consolidation franchise from the State Legislature. Harlem shares rose sharply. It seemed a perfect time for another raid. Under the direction of an unrepentant Daniel Drew, the legislators swarmed into Wall Street on a mad selling spree, again selling short as the city aldermen had done a year before. This time, Harlem dropped to $90. And because it fell, the Legislature voted down the consolidation bill! Drew assured his greedy clients that long before their notes were due, Harlem shares would be down to $8 or $9. The scheme could not fail. And so, the legislators sold thousands upon thousands of Harlem shares.

Van Derbilt once again was forced to buy, buy, buy, straining even *his* resources to stay afloat in this sea of avarice. Bankruptcy became a distinct possibility for him. Then one day, he added up all his shares. They numbered 137,000—27,000 more than existed! It was time for the legislators to make delivery. That is when they discovered to their horror that there was only one man in town from whom shares could be bought—that "senile" steamboat captain who knew nothing about railroads.

Van Derbilt set the price at $1,000 per share. The legislators and all Wall Street gasped. It would be their collective ruin. Leonard Jerome acted as mediator and urged Van Derbilt to show mercy, if for no other reason than to keep Wall Street itself alive. At last, the Commodore compromised at $285 per share. Even so, several legislators were bankrupted. The Commodore's astuteness was never again questioned, and these two battles went down in Wall Street history as the Great Harlem Corners.

Van Derbilt needed one more railroad to complete what by now even skeptics could see would inevitably become a profitable network, something no other railroad in the country could boast as yet. That railroad was the New-York Central, which ran between the prosperous Hudson River port of Albany and the Great Lakes port of Buffalo, carrying a lucrative trade which was transferred at Albany to and from the Hudson River's steamboat services. If Van Derbilt could link up with the New-York Central, his railroads would gain undisputed supremacy all the way to Canada, and profit from New York State's vast trade.

But his nemesis lurked once again in the wings. Although the Central made a deal with the Commodore to accept Buffalo-to-New York freight and passengers "all the way by rail" and to engage in an active interchange between the respective lines, the Central also formed the People's Steamboat Line with Daniel Drew. Through this agreement, freight would be accepted at Buffalo to go "all the way by rail," but would in fact be transferred at Albany and carried downriver to New York. There was little that Van Derbilt could do. Central shares were not to be obtained on Wall Street and, although he fulfilled his part of the bargain, feeding business to New-York Central, the Central failed to reciprocate.

Fate played into the Commodore's hands, however, with the sudden death of the railroad's president and, soon afterward, with the onset of winter. As the Hudson began to freeze, freight which had been accepted by Central at Buffalo to go "all the way by rail" began to stack up at Albany. Now that the river traffic was halted by ice, Van Derbilt simply abrogated his agreement with Central, refusing to accept any of its freight. New-York Central's managers panicked, knowing they could not hope for legal support, and also knowing they would shortly be ruined by liability suits for undelivered freight. On Wall Street, Central stock began a nosedive.

And then, miraculously, after an interruption of only twenty-four hours and the exchange of a fortune in cash, the traffic agreement was in effect once again, New-York Central's future was assured—and so was that of its new owner.

In 1869, only seven years after he had launched his railroad career, the seventy-five-year-old Cornelius Van

Derbilt consolidated his three railroads by forming the New-York Central & Hudson-River Rail-Road, an enterprise worth well over $20 million. Renamed the New York Central Railroad in 1914, it was to become the most extensive, most efficient, and most profitable railroad in the world.

During this time, Van Derbilt had also bought up twenty-three acres of land between Madison and Lexington avenues, from Forty-second to Forty-eighth streets, in readiness for his Grand Central Depot. The whole idea of calling it *central* anything was so absurd that newspapers jeeringly called it End-of-the-World Station. There was little in the surrounding area besides a few houses, an occasional country estate, some outlying farms, and, of course, the fashionable promenade around the Croton Reservoir. A whole new generation would grow up before the city sprawl engulfed Forty-second Street. Undaunted by the jeering, however, the old man knew that one day there would be no question about the centrality of his depot. The first foundation stone was laid on September 1, 1869. That same year, he commissioned a huge bronze statue of himself, standing tall and erect, which dominated the roof of the Madison Square terminal for sixty years. Called "a biography in bronze" when it first appeared, it was moved in 1929 to its present site, in the middle of Grand Central's main facade, gazing over the viaduct across Forty-second Street down the length of Park Avenue.

By October 1871 the station was completed, ready to handle its daily average of 164 long-distance and commuter trains. Architecturally indifferent, the depot's most startling aspect was the huge train shed at its northern end. A cylindrical vault 530 feet long and 100 feet high at the crown, and lighted by three enormous glazed monitors, it was supported and framed by thirty arched wrought-iron trusses. Entering Manhattan from the north, the coal-powered puffer-bellies ran over a raised viaduct as far south as Ninety-sixth Street. From there, where the terrain rises sharply, the tracks ran through an open rock cut as far as Sixty-eighth Street, below which they traveled on the surface to Forty-second Street. It was this last stretch which was soon condemned as "a great blunder." William J. Wilgus, who thirty years later redesigned the track system as it is today, wrote that "the yard tracks on the surface acted as a veritable 'Chinese wall' to separate the city into two parts for fourteen blocks—nearly three-quarters of a mile—between 42nd Street and 56th Street, and forced the discontinuance of a leading north and south thoroughfare, then known as Fourth Avenue, between 42nd and 49th Streets." Here, in addition to the train tracks, were the railway yards with their engine houses and machine shops, and countless tracks spread between Lexington and Madison avenues.

No sooner was the depot completed, however, than it became evident that traffic would soon exceed its present capacity. So between 1872 and 1874, construction was undertaken on "four-tracking" the depot's approaches as far as the Harlem River. Although the tracks south of Fifty-sixth Street were dropped to below grade, they were not low enough to allow street-level bridges across the tracks, and eight elevated footbridges had to be built across the yards, two of them capable of carrying vehicular traffic.

Designs were also drawn up for improving Fourth Avenue between Fifty-sixth and Ninety-sixth streets by creating a landscaped park strip along the center. These planted garden plots served not only as a lid to the open cut tunnel but also to frame the large smoke vents in their center. This design provided a perfect opportunity to change what had become a grimy shantytown stretch into the fashionable Park Avenue it became at the turn of the century. But while efficiency was no doubt increased, the added smoke in what was now a two-mile, four-tracked open cut tunnel became the nearest thing to a modern death ride. As Wilgus recorded it, "The products of locomotive combustion in the two single-track side tunnels were imperfectly discharged by natural ventilation into the double-track center tunnel, from whence smoke, gas, and cinders from all three tunnels were shot upward through longitudinal openings between the streets into the faces of passers-by and the occupants of the abutting property."

Throughout the few years that were left to him, the old Commodore remained actively involved with railroads. He was not to live to see the day when his arch-rival, Daniel Drew, died in poverty, having speculated, manipulated, and finagled once too often. The Commodore himself died on the afternoon of January 4, 1877, as a fine snow began to fall. Just sixty-seven years after he had borrowed $100 from his father, he was worth $100 *million*.

By the late 1880s seven new tracks were added to Grand Central's yards, making a total of eighteen. In 1898 the depot itself was enlarged. A massive reorganization of the station's space was undertaken to provide a central concourse which would help keep the daily masses flowing and eliminate the various points of congestion. A special waiting room for immigrants was built in the station's basement to relieve "the main waiting room and rotunda of this class of passenger entirely," as one contemporary phrased it, and the depot was even given a new name—Grand Central *Station*. Still it was not enough.

As the century neared its end, the city experienced a surge of growth such as it had never known before. New York's population was expanding at the rate of more than thirty thousand people per year. Railroad traffic was at a constant peak of nearly five hundred trains daily. Day and night the acrid black smoke of the locomotives hung in the air over the city, endangering the health of the populace. Burning cinders and sparks threatened life and property along the right-of-way. In the two-mile Park Avenue tunnel, smoke was so thick that visibility was often reduced to near zero. It was dense smoke that obscured a red signal in January 1902. The result was an accident that took the lives of seventeen people.

Public pressure began to build against this smoke-breathing monster, the locomotive, which spewed its blanket of soot over the northern reaches of the island. New Yorkers were also demanding the restoration of cross streets below Fifty-sixth Street. The time had come to banish the locomotive from the city. To do so, there appeared to be only one answer—to drop all tracks deep underground and to electrify all trains. This now became a plan to which William J. Wilgus, vice-president and chief engineer of the New York Central Railroad, was to devote many years.

Adding to the New York Central's pressures was the announcement by its chief rival for traffic to Chicago, the Pennsylvania Railroad, that it planned to enter Manhattan through a tunnel across the Hudson River and construct a through station on Manhattan's West Side. Equally pressing was the construction that had already begun on the city's first subway and which might well course under the station and thereby forever rob Grand Central of a chance to sink its own tracks.

Although electrification of Grand Central had been under consideration as early as 1899, such a project posed major, seemingly insurmountable difficulties from the standpoint of logistics. Electric traction itself was a field still in its infancy. Barely a decade had passed since its pioneer, Frank Sprague, had unveiled the first electric street railway system in Richmond, Virginia. Nevertheless, it was recognized from the start that electrification would permit engineers to eliminate the Park Avenue smoke vents necessary for coal-powered locomotives. It would also let them increase track space by installing a two-tiered system, thus avoiding the prohibitive expense of acquiring additional real estate. Since Grand Central was to become a *terminal* station, its design must include a turn-around loop for each of the two decks. It was Wilgus's plan, therefore, to push the smoke-belching locomotive beyond the city's outskirts so "that the outward limits of the electric zone for both express and suburban service should be established at Croton-on-Hudson and North White Plains."

Born in Buffalo, New York, Wilgus was a self-made engineer whose education ended with a correspondence course in drafting at the age of twenty. Having worked his way up from surveying and drafting positions in the Midwest, he joined the New York Central as assistant engineer in 1893. Six years later he was named chief engineer, and in 1903, at the age of thirty-seven, he became one of the railroad's vice-presidents.

On March 19 of that year Wilgus revealed a detailed scheme which he had drawn up—a scheme unique in railroad history. As he explained it:

> the objects were the erection of a suitable fifty-seven-track, all-electric, double-level terminal with a suburban loop, and a future rapid-transit connection should one be found to be desirable; the utilization of air rights producing income sufficient to pay interest on the cost of the terminal, the depression of the yard with street crossings restored from 45th Street to 55th Street, inclusive, and the attendant electrification . . . the erection of a hotel and other means of attracting travel and revenue; the creation of a new north and south elevated city artery circumscribing the station

building, extending over 42nd Street on the south . . . and ramps connecting car-floor-level train platforms with the concourses.

His estimated costs were $43,460,000 (almost $30 million below its actual final cost).

So impressed was the city's Board of Estimate that its chief engineer, Nelson P. Lewis, remarked that the plans provided "perhaps the finest railway terminal station in the world." Wilgus planned for express trains to approach the terminal on an upper tier which, twenty feet under the city's streets, would gently fan out into thirty-one tracks, beginning at Fifty-seventh Street. Inbound trains would then discharge their passengers in the Arrivals Building under what is today's Biltmore Hotel (Forty-fourth Street and Madison Avenue), permitting the easy flow of people without conflict between departures and arrivals. Also at Fifty-seventh Street, a gradually sloping ramp would carry suburban trains to a lower deck, forty feet under the street, which would fan out into seventeen tracks. Loops on both levels at the southernmost end of the terminal would then allow the inbound trains to turn around, ready for outbound service, without impeding either inbound or outbound service.

Deep below both track levels, Wilgus planned the construction of a luggage tunnel which would allow loading and unloading of luggage without encumbering passenger traffic. His plans also included heating plants, electric power facilities, steam, water, sewage, and electric mains. Rights had to be secured from the city to build a sewer six feet in diameter below the lower level, more than eighty feet under Forty-fifth Street. In all, twenty-five miles of pipes and sewers had to be replaced or relocated. For a distance of only 2,049 *feet* from Forty-second to Fifieth street, Wilgus's plans called for 27 *miles* of tracks. By double-decking all tracks, Wilgus gained 66½ acres for the new terminal, or almost three times the space of the original depot and yards. Altogether there were to be 81 tracks—passenger, storage, and other miscellaneous tracks—on the two levels, providing accommodation for 1,071 cars.

The key to the real brilliance of Wilgus's plan, beyond the ingenuity of its arrangement of tracks, lay in its concept of creating revenue-producing "air rights" space. A grid of rectangular open spaces left between the restored avenues and streets, which themselves were to form the "lid" over the railroad's operations below ground, would become made-to-order building sites. Tall buildings, straddling the steel-work roofs over the railroad tracks, could occupy these spaces. Instead of basements, these buildings would have a railroad in their cellar. For the ground on which the buildings stood and for the air rights above, the New York Central would realize huge rentals—enough revenue to offset the entire construction cost!

The work was to take a long ten years, beginning in 1903 and ending in 1913. This pace could not be accelerated since uninterrupted service had to be maintained throughout, at a daily volume which had reached more than six hundred trains by 1906. Actual construction began with track changes on July 18, 1903. On August 17, the demolition of buildings on Park and Lexington avenues between Forty-fifth and Fiftieth streets was begun. The yard excavation was planned to "be made in three successive 'bites,' each to be completed before another was undertaken, working westward from Lexington Avenue," so that railroad traffic could continue unimpeded. Seventeen additional acres along the eastern line had to be acquired and added to the original twenty-three-acre site. Some two hundred buildings had to be demolished, "a veritable slum clearance" that included smoke-stained churches, hospitals, and stores. Proceeding east to west, a pit forty feet deep was excavated from Forty-second to

Forty-fifth streets, from Lexington almost to Madison Avenue. Between Forty-fifth and Fiftieth streets, the excavation narrowed to the full width of what is today Park Avenue.

Wilgus wrote that by 1907

> the major portion of "Bite No. 1" on the easterly side of the terminal area along Lexington Avenue from 50th Street to 43rd Street had been completed with its yard, substation, heating plant, express facilities, street viaducts, drainage sewer to the East River, and a temporary passenger station—all in actual use by the New York Central's electrified suburban service. . . . The terminal building was nearly completed on Lexington Avenue between Forty-fourth and Forty-fifth streets. The entire yard, old and new, had been electrified.

In all, three million cubic yards of rock and earth were excavated and carted off for landfill along the island's shores and elsewhere. Some one hundred thousand tons of steel were used to build the two-tiered structures and substructures.

Deciding whether to use direct or alternating electric current to power the third-rail conductors was a major problem. George Westinghouse favored alternating current "supplied to overhead working conductors instead of direct current fed to a third rail." The discussion was to blossom into a cause célèbre and was still not resolved by the 108th meeting on October 5, 1906, when the initial electric zone was already completed and ready for the running of the first electric train.

The footbridges across the old terminal yards had to be kept open throughout construction. At Forty-fifth Street, where the excavation dropped to a seventy-foot pit (for the baggage tunnel), this required considerable ingenuity. And so the engineers devised a plan in which not only the footbridge but a gas main they had found under it were suspended from a wooden truss mounted on wheels. As the excavation proceeded, the truss was rolled from east to west. Engineers gave particular care to the underpinnings of buildings along Park Avenue by installing a system of "needle beams." By converting the Grand Central Palace on the corner of Lexington Avenue and Forty-third Street into a temporary terminal, work could begin at last on the demolition of the Commodore's lofty train shed and depot. That was in 1910.

It was a job that required a daring plan, as well as iron nerves for workmen and the daily thousands of passengers alike. To remove the 1,700 tons of wrought- and cast-iron trusses, beams, and supports, the 150,000 square feet of roofing and glass, the thousands upon thousands of bricks, without one slip, without one moment's danger to the passengers swarming in and out of the station every day, was an enormously challenging task. A huge traveler was constructed to conform to the curve of the train shed, a hundred feet high at its apex. Beginning at the northern end of the shed and slowly working their way back toward Forty-second Street, the day crews carefully demolished the structure, placing the materials on the platforms of the traveler. During the night, other crews lowered the debris into freight cars for removal.

Once the train shed was eliminated, work could begin on the terminal building as we know it today. Minnesota architects Charles Reed and Allen Stem submitted the winning design for the new terminal. It was they who came up with the concept of ramps for the station's interior and for the elevated roadway that runs like a ribbon around the circumference of the terminal, connected by a ramp with Park Avenue both at Fortieth and Forty-sixth streets.

Although Reed and Stem had won the design competition, they were soon urged to share the project with Warren and Wetmore—a move which filled neither Reed nor Stem with enthusiasm. Charles D. Wetmore, a lawyer, was not likely to be a threat to their design, but they could readily foresee problems with the flamboyant, artistically brilliant Whitney Warren. He was not only a cousin but also the best friend of William K. Vanderbilt (as the name finally came to be spelled), chairman of the New York Central and son of the old Commodore. Reed and Stem's original design was soon scrapped in favor of Warren's idea of creating a "monumental" terminal. Warren had pursued his architectural education mostly in Paris and had taken the Beaux Arts school of design to his bosom. Now he wanted to introduce it to New York. Although his revised design failed to gain approval, and new plans drawn up in 1909 reverted in large part to the competition-winning original, Warren was determined to gain complete control over the project. This became a reality when Reed died in 1911. When the building was completed two years later, Whitney Warren was generally hailed as its architect. Although there is no doubt that it was Warren who was responsible for the terminal's artistic refinements and Beaux Arts splendor, it was unquestionably Charles Reed who conceived its fluid, functional innovations.

Stem took the matter before the courts, and the judgment that was eventually handed down in 1922 required Warren to make a settlement of almost $400,000.

Today, coursing forty feet below the street are the tracks of the suburban line, with the express tracks twenty feet above them. From Grand Central as far as Fifty-seventh Street, Park Avenue, itself a skin of steel and asphalt no more than eighteen inches thick, forms the roof of the express line. Together these lines carry 140,000 people per day.

Even though the loop tracks on the terminal's two tiers were not completed until 1927, the newest and grandest terminal of them all, Grand Central Terminal, was opened to the public on February 2, 1913, exactly as planned, ten years after the start of construction. By the end of that day, more than 150,000 people had wandered through its vastness, following the ramps through the huge waiting room, past ticket windows, down the natural flow to the Concourse, that magnificent vaulted structure with its painted cerulean blue firmament in which all the constellations except Orion are painted in reverse and in which the sun would rise in the west and set in the east. (It is based on a design by the French artist Paul Helleu and, although dozens of conjectures have been offered over the years, the most likely explanation for the reversed constellations is that Helleu was inspired by an illuminated manuscript from medieval times, when it was common to depict the heavens as though viewed from outside the celestial sphere.)

The particular beauty of Grand Central's Concourse is the access it provides not only to all trains and to the Arrivals Building but also to the surrounding streets. The grand staircase at its western end and all the ramps produce a natural delivery "chute" to departing trains, as well as to transverse foot traffic. Directly below the main Concourse lies the suburban Concourse, an entirely independent and separate station. The Arrivals Building exits take yet another path, through which passengers can easily reach the street surface or enter directly into the Biltmore Hotel.

But for anyone who wants to spend a little more time in the terminal, just one level below the street is a network of shops and amusements, a variety of banking, betting, and eating places. Most famous among the latter is the Oyster Bar & Restaurant which, as the name sug-

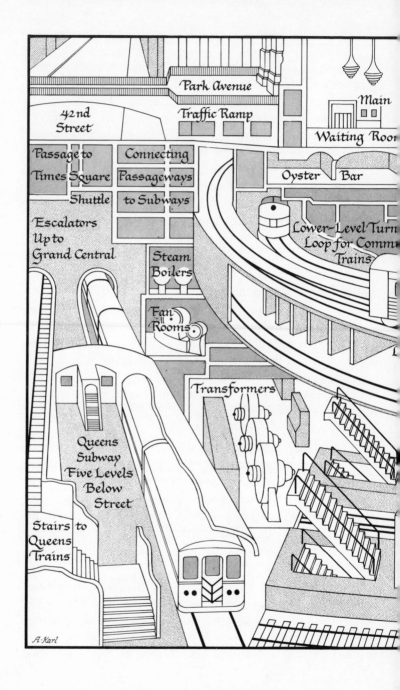

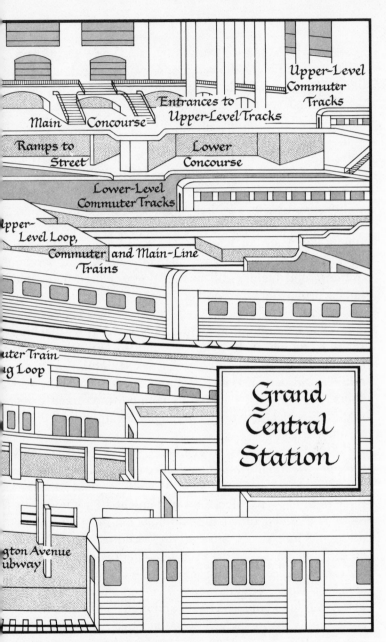

The genius of William J. Wilgus's 1903 plan for Grand Central Terminal was its use of vertical space within a forty-acre area.

gests, is most noted for its oysters—nine varieties of them. An average of eight thousand oysters is served here every single day, or nearly three million per year.

In their rush through the terminal's concourses, few of the estimated 250,000 people who daily use Grand Central have time to wonder how it all works. Below the suburban level, three and four stories under the surface and stretching from Forty-third to Forty-ninth street, lies a vast network of pipes and mains, electric and telephone utilities, and steam and hot-water conduits which service the station as well as many of the buildings between Lexington and Madison avenues. The power for all these services is generated in a vast, distinctly Rube Goldbergian underground facility still farther down, where giant machines drone and whirr and chug with pent-up energy day and night.

Another underground tunnel is lined with machine shops in which all the work is done to keep the power flowing. Here, in the dim glow of naked lightbulbs, is another world, a world of dark green doors, gray walls and floors. Men transport materials in huge motorized carts, materials which arrive via enormous elevators deep under the city streets.

Still farther down, *seven* levels below the streets, is the electrical substation which contains the ultimate power that makes Grand Central work, a giant chamber the length of a city block and perhaps half its width. The room is so deep down that its only air must be forced through funnels, down from the terminal's roof, while other funnels take up the used air. There is no heating in winter, no air-conditioning to cool the summer heat. The men who work here know that when summer comes they will spend long hours each day and night bathed in sweat. Here they spend every working moment listening to the constant thunder of towering ten-foot-diameter circular rotary converters which convert the alternating current

Ten-foot rotary converters (right side of photo) thunder day and night converting AC into DC to feed the third rail and signal systems. A signal control board and electrical switches (left side) constantly monitor Grand Central Terminal's railroad conditions. *Pamela Jones*

supplied by Con Edison into the direct current which is then fed into the terminal's third-rail and signal system. Opposite the converters is a signal control board, a wall banked with a long row of electrical switches whose flashing lights alert the engineers to all railroad conditions within the terminal. A row of meters allows them to keep constant watch over the system's amperage, alerting them to the need to adjust or regulate.

It is possible to walk from Lexington Avenue nearly to Madison, from Forty-third to Forty-ninth street *underground*, along dark, hot tunnels packed with mains from floor to ceiling. Some of these tunnels also provide a dark, dirty, rat-infested refuge for a number of homeless hoboes.

In the years since 1913 a long line of buildings has grown along what has become that elegant and fashionable thoroughfare called Park Avenue. Their elevators begin on the second floor, and elevator housings are on the main floor, since the buildings lack basements. Real estate values have soared from about $3 million per block in 1913 to more than $20 million today. Perhaps the most famous building along the street is the Waldorf-Astoria, a hotel which had lived at two previous addresses. It was erected on the east side of Park Avenue between Forty-ninth and Fiftieth streets in the 1920s. What distinguishes the Waldorf from all other hotels in the city is its very own railroad spur, Track 61 in Grand Central's storage yards, which it has used on occasion for the delivery and departure of distinguished guests. Probably the most notable among these was President Franklin D. Roosevelt, who arrived via this route when he visited the Waldorf to deliver a speech on foreign policy during his 1944 presidential campaign.

As early as 1929 it was thought that the New York Central Building which straddles the terminal's ramps at Forty-sixth Street occupied the last of Wilgus's air-rights space. But then, in the 1960s, the fifty-nine-story Pan Am Building rose sharply into the sky just north of the main Concourse. Its bleak modernity shattered the elegance and aristocracy which had allowed the terminal to be both grand and central to the eye traveling the island's natural upward grade north along Park Avenue. As if this insult were not enough, a campaign has been launched to obliterate the last vestige of air and sunlight by erecting a tower over the final air-rights space left—over the Concourse itself.

Fifty million commuters stream annually through the terminal, a number far beyond any William J. Wilgus could have anticipated at the turn of the century. Yet even then his plans included a direct link between Grand Central's tracks and what was to become the Lexington Avenue subway and the Forty-second Street crosstown shuttle. There was only one provision which Wilgus did not include in his plans. For decades, trains have discharged their passengers in the terminal. Those seated in the last car of the trains walk the long distance to the front, and up to the street. Many of these passengers must then retrace their steps above the ground to reach their offices. To alleviate the inconvenience this poses, as well as the rush-hour congestion within the terminal, the Metropolitan Transportation Authority, which now controls all city transit, has undertaken plans to provide a series of exits as far uptown as Forty-ninth Street. As commuter traffic has increased, the suggestion has evolved to create a combined concourse and shopping mall from the terminal to Forty-ninth Street, with connections to adjacent buildings. They are plans which, in a sense, drive Grand Central, that End-of-the-World Station, still deeper into the outlying "wilderness," an idea which would surely amuse that old steamboat captain, Commodore Cornelius Van Derbilt.

As the crow flies, Hoboken, New Jersey, is about a mile from Manhattan. It was in Hoboken that the idea of trains of cars pulled by mechanical power was born in 1812. Having become interested in John Fitch's steamboat designs as early as 1788, John Stevens, a former colonel in the Continental Army during the Revolutionary War, devoted most of his life to the development of mechanical transportation on water and land. An experimental steam locomotive he built and ran on a circular track on his Hoboken estate in 1825 was, in essence, the progenitor of what would soon become a major industry in the nation— the railroad. Because of this early trial and a charter he had been granted some years before by the Pennsylvania State Legislature to build a railway, Stevens can be considered the father of what came to be known as the Pennsylvania Railroad. Although a number of lines, the Pennsylvania among the largest, crisscrossed various parts of the country as the nineteenth century advanced, it was nearly a hundred years, in 1910, before Stevens's brainchild linked the short distance across the Hudson between New Jersey and New York City.

By the late 1870s Van Derbilt had already extended his railroad empire beyond the initial three for which he had fought so bitterly. In the end, he had also wrested the important Erie Railroad from Daniel Drew, even though Drew had enlisted the help of such financial giants as Jay Gould and James Fisk. And so the way to Chicago was now open. It was here that William K. Vanderbilt, the Commodore's grandson, met the Pennsylvania Railroad. It was rivalry at first sight, "a clash of great enterprises, and of the hopes and expectations of men. It was on both sides the usual sordid fight for riches; but on both sides, too, it was also a struggle to create and build what men had set their hearts upon. Therefore it was a passionate struggle." What it actually became was a mad race for supremacy which involved cutting travel time, cutting fares, cutting freight rates. By 1883 the two railroads were invading each other's territories. "Striking at the heart of the Central-Hudson's monopoly of the Hudson and Mohawk valleys, the Pennsylvania was furiously building a new line to Albany and Buffalo," while Vanderbilt was hacking out a new trunk line from New York to Pittsburgh. In 1887, Congress established the Interstate Commerce Commission which was at long last to govern fixed fares and freight rates as well as general railroad business practices. It was a move that took the passion out of the competition and marked the end of unrestrained warfare among railroad giants.

The two lines locked horns once more when the Pennsylvania decided to enter Manhattan and establish a terminus at the same time Grand Central Terminal was under construction. To add momentum and gain public support for its plan for a New York City through station, the Pennsylvania acquired the Long Island Rail Road in 1900.

During the two hundred years of the city's existence, a certain insular pride and snobbery had developed in the minds of New Yorkers whose magnificent harbor, capable of handling half the country's foreign shipping, placed them at the center of the nation's commerce. The congested traffic on all the surrounding waters was testament to that. Grand Central Terminal served to reinforce that view. All the roads at the turn of the century did lead to the Rome of the New World, New York, the center of commerce and finance and newness. Its efficient railroads had made New York the greatest terminal passenger and freight traffic center in the country. In manufacturing variety New York ranked first among American cities. It was hardly surprising, therefore, that some citizens viewed the Pennsylvania's proposed incursion from the mainland with a certain anguish and resentment, perhaps best expressed by a New York *Herald* man who cried out, "They're reducing New York to a two-minute stop on the line from Long Island City to Rahway, New Jersey."

For years, passengers and freight carried by the Pennsylvania had been forced to reach the island's west shore across the Hudson by car-floats and ferryboats. River traffic had become not only dangerous but obstructive, occupying space along the waterfront which could be more profitably occupied by long-distance ship commerce. Bridges across the East River had relieved much of the congestion in that waterway, but the much wider Hudson, the more important river of the two with its heavy traffic of oceangoing vessels, made the construction of

bridges impractical. Underwater tunnels for the diversion
of passenger and freight traffic were, therefore, the only
means of relief. Already, the Hudson & Manhattan line,
opened in 1908, was demonstrating the practicality of such
a solution. The Pennsylvania alone was daily ferrying some
ninety thousand people across the Hudson. Thousands
more poured into the city from Long Island. Tunnels
under both rivers would eliminate virtually all these
water transportation problems. Even so, until other tunnels could be built across the Hudson to carry the sizable
vehicular traffic, large numbers of ferries would still continue plying their trade across this waterway. (Under the
Hudson, the Holland Tunnel, named for its chief engineer
Clifford Holland, was not opened until 1927, and the
Lincoln Tunnel's three tubes opened successively in 1937,
1945, and 1960; the Queens-Midtown Tunnel and the
Brooklyn-Battery Tunnel were ready for service under the
East River in 1940 and 1950, respectively.)

In 1907 it was estimated that the population density
per acre in the five boroughs was as follows: Manhattan,
157; Brooklyn, 29; Bronx, 14; Queens, 3; Richmond
(Staten Island), 2. A connecting line through Manhattan
between Long Island and the mainland would thus considerably increase the population in all boroughs, and increase accessibility to outlying parts. Already the great
commercial houses, banks, brokerages, and retail and
manufacturing plants in Manhattan were moving above
Twenty-third Street, a movement largely stimulated by
the development of the telephone and the advent of the
city's first subway. A major railroad station at Seventh
Avenue and Thirty-third Street would, therefore, deliver
passenger traffic into the heart of the city, its commercial,
shopping, and hotel center. Newark, the Pennsylvania's
nearest terminal to the city, would be only seventeen
minutes away, and passengers would enjoy the added con-

venience of not having to change their mode of transportation.

At an estimated cost of $150 million for building the necessary extensions, improvements, and electrification, the Pennsylvania's directors expected the line to be in full operation by 1910. The Manhattan station itself was to occupy two city blocks between Seventh and Ninth avenues, an area of approximately eight acres. Below the streets were to be eleven passenger platforms and the entire station and yard area containing some sixteen miles of track within a twenty-eight-acre site. Unlike Grand Central, the power service plant for lighting, heating, and ventilation of the station was to be located in a separate building to the south, with electrical energy for the third-rail conductors supplied by a power house in Queens.

The moving force behind the concept, design, and execution of this project was the railroad's president, Alexander Johnston Cassatt. An engineer with the Pennsylvania Railroad since 1861, he was a man with uncommon knowledge of every aspect of railroad construction, operation, and management, a man respected by railroad men throughout the country. When Cassatt appointed a Board of Engineers in 1902, he instructed them that "in view of the magnitude and great cost of the proposed construction, and of the novel engineering questions involved, your studies should be thorough and exhaustive, and should be based upon absolute knowledge of the conditions."

To build the connecting links across the East and Hudson rivers, Cassatt and his engineers planned two pairs of cast-iron, single-track tunnels twenty-three feet in outside diameter which, once they reached Manhattan from the east and west, would merge into one pair of two-track tunnels in their approaches to the station. In their early designs, the engineers considered constructing "floating plants" (tunnels) through the water, but they soon decided that this method would serve only to obstruct the free flow of river traffic. They therefore recommended that the shield method be used to drive the tunnels below the bottom of both rivers. This presented several problems when work got underway, particularly in the East River, where the underwater conditions varied widely from seamed and fissured rock—covered by boulders, gravel, and sand often ten feet thick—to thick clay. The tunneling under the Hudson River was frequently interrupted by blowouts in the shield chamber when fissures in the riverbed ruptured during the work. To check the escape of air from the chamber, the river bottom which lay above the tunnel had to be continually blanketed with clay. When it became apparent that these difficulties would continue over the full distance, the engineers in charge tried to make tunneling less dangerous by freezing the ground around the shield to facilitate its advance. By driving a seven-and-a-half-foot-diameter pilot tunnel in front of the shield, they proposed to freeze the ground to a distance of over eleven feet around it by circulating very low temperature brine through a system of pipes within the pilot tunnel. However, they soon realized that, promising though this method was, it required far too much time and would thus be far too uneconomical.

Soon another concern arose. Because the tunnels would be lighter than the materials they displaced, even with the added weight of a live load, it was feared that the actions of actual traffic as well as the tide might displace them. The type of underwater materials found in the East River indicated that this would not be a serious problem there, but the Hudson was another story. The tunnels progressed the full width of the river through an envelope of soft silt, and so the engineers thought at first it might be necessary to provide a system of supports to insure against tunnel displacement. To meet this contingency, they proposed to sink cast-iron screw piles through the bottom of each tunnel, through the underlying silt, and into the bedrock below. The tunnels would thus form an underwater "bridge" supported by a network of girders across the bottom of the river. But a close and careful examination of the H & M tunnels to the south convinced the engineers that such a measure was not called for after all.

For added safety to passengers and employees in case of an accident, as well as for the convenience of inspection, it was at first deemed advisable to build underwater cross-passages between the tunnels. This was done at regular intervals in the land sections. Although one cross-passage does exist under the East River, the engineers later concluded that such passages underwater would, if anything, increase instead of decrease danger.

Once the East River tunnels were brought on shore in Manhattan, they encountered what has long been acknowledged by New York's contractors as an age-old problem. In order to reach the Seventh Avenue station, the tunnels had to be dug across the right-of-way of an ancient buried U-shaped stream which dips to its southernmost point between Thirty-first and Thirty-second streets on Park Avenue, where it widens, like a pendant on a chain, into Sunfish Pond. Compared with the diversion of this stream, the remainder of the crosstown cut was relatively smooth work.

In the meantime, in readiness for the vast station and its approaches and railway yards, a large number of private homes and apartment houses and several church properties had to be acquired and demolished.

And now, at last, the house-wrecking could begin in earnest. Since materials from the buildings being demolished became the property of the contractors, it was a sufficiently profitable business for them to pay the railroad company for the privilege of doing the work. Most of the demolition was completed between April and August of 1906. Bricks were cleaned and sold at the site and so were most of the building fixtures. The laths and other small timber were sold or given away for firewood. In order to remove the rubble and excavation materials, a deep cut was dug between Ninth and Tenth avenues and a trestle constructed to the disposal pier at the foot of West Thirty-second Street.

The excavation for the station and its approaches was begun on May 11, 1906. Work was done in ten-hour shifts, day and night, six days a week, for almost three years. The pay for laborers was $1.75 per shift, or $10.50 per week. Foremen were paid as much as $3.50 per shift. Fifty scows were used to remove thousands of tons of rock and earth from the site. Huge derricks mounted on piers were used to load these sturdy craft which then chugged off on their three-and-a-half-day round-trip journey across the harbor to dump the debris in Greenville, New Jersey.

The rock which the work crews encountered varied from granite to mica schist, with isolated seams of pyrites, hornblende, tourmaline, and serpentine. They also found veins of quartz and even some glacial markings. Where the rock broke sharply along the lines of stratification, work progressed without much fear of a mishap. It was only where the ground was soft that the danger of land-slides existed and it became that much more difficult to reach a firm base before retaining walls could be built. The worst slide occurred on July 3, 1909. Great care had been taken during the blasting, as it was evident from the beginning that the rock was unstable. Nevertheless, the engineers felt sure it would hold. Instead, a sudden rumble shattered the stillness of that night as hundreds of tons of earth and rock crashed down into the pit. Fortunately, no one was killed.

Under Ninth Avenue the excavation plummeted to a depth of fifty-eight feet. Here it was necessary to construct an all-steel viaduct twenty-four feet below the surface for the eventual support of the avenue's structures. At the same time, the overhead three-track elevated railway structure, the Ninth Avenue El, had to be continuously braced and supported while work went on beneath it. A variety of pipes, mains, and conduits had to be temporarily broken until they could be relaid elsewhere. Although this section of the avenue was closed to all vehicular traffic, a trestle footbridge for the city's pedestrians was built across it.

To fracture the rock, "spring holes" twenty feet deep were drilled, with two or three sticks of dynamite exploded at the bottom. Once the downward cavity grew, it became possible to drill and break up chunks of rock fifteen feet thick. The average rate of progress was some thirty feet per shift. Nearly all the earth excavations were done with steam shovels. Loaded on side-dump cars and taken to the disposal pier, the earth was dumped through chutes to the decks of the scows and used for "padding" under the rocky debris.

Where workmen encountered quicksand, excavation was not only impossible but also threatened to undermine adjoining buildings. In such areas a wooden cylinder was sunk through the sand by excavating the material inside it. The cylinder was weighted with pig iron, and men gradually worked it down to reach gravel below the quicksand. Water was then pumped from the base, and the excavation work could continue. In one instance, however, sand bubbled up from under the cylinder at such an alarming rate that the front walls of several adjoining houses were severely cracked and had to be taken down and rebuilt.

As soon as the excavation was completed, a concrete retaining wall, two feet thick, was constructed against the surface of the rock. In order to prevent an accumulation of water (and consequent pressure) against the back of the wall, box drains fitted with pipes which led through the base of the wall were placed between the retaining wall and the rock face. The major considerations throughout this phase were to construct a wall capable of withstanding whatever stresses could be reasonably expected in the future and which would least interfere with or undermine abutting properties during construction. Built in fifty-foot sections, each of the wall's monoliths was tongued-and-grooved. Near adjoining buildings and for softer ground materials, three-inch-thick steel sheeting was used to create the wall.

A total of twenty-eight acres was readied within the approach and station areas, with tracks at least forty feet below the street surface. Gas, water, and sewer mains had to be relocated. Service mains no longer in use were removed. Room had to be left between the subsurface structures and the streets to permit new and future mains to be laid.

To provide drainage for the tunnels, an underground sump with a pump chamber above it was constructed for each pair of tunnels at regular intervals. Forty-four feet long and with a ten-foot outside diameter, these short tunnels were placed underneath the main tunnels. The pump chamber directly above the sump and between the tunnels pumped out the water that dripped from the rail tunnels into the sump. A cross-passage was built above the pump chamber, between the walls of each pair of tunnels, with access not only to the railroad tunnels but also to the pump chamber and sump. The walls of each sump and pump chamber formed what is essentially a waterproofed concrete-iron-concrete sandwich.

Heroic as was all the work done during these years, most of it has never been seen by the outside world. Those sections which were bared to the daily commerce of the city during construction were regarded more as a nuisance than as a tribute to man's ingenuity.

At last, in 1910, the "Pennsy" was ready to serve its far-flung communities with direct and uninterrupted service between Long Island, the New England states, and the entire Pennsylvania Railroad system. For the following half-century, New Yorkers descended the sweeping breadth of stairs which led from the street down into the lofty and austerely classic beauty of the station's concourse. For the first time in their history, they began to feel the impact of their city's oneness with the nation. Comparable in size with the nave of St. Peter's in Rome (and, in fact, designed on the lines of the Caracalla Baths), the Pennsylvania's concourse was 340 feet long

When the "Pennsy" began service to and from Manhattan in 1910, no other public building in the city could equal the classic grandeur of the Pennsylvania Station concourse, seen here in part with the westbound track level. *Museum of the City of New York*

and 210 feet wide, with a crown 153 feet high. Its exterior grandeur provided small indication of the majestic steel-columned domes and arches inside, which were covered with acres of sun-filtering glass. Its very size muffled the sound of the thousands of travelers who daily entered and left the station, a sound which, filled with a distant echo, seemed to promise the wonders to be found across the great nation. Open stairs with polished brass railings led down to the tracks that opened the way to the far reaches of the Western world.

Cassatt did not live to see the completion of his grandiose plan, nor could he have suspected that, little more than fifty years after his engineers had placed their architecturally grandiloquent station in the heart of New York City, it would fall victim to progress.

In 1963 the wreckers came. A concrete slab was lowered to within eighteen feet of the concourse floor. Above the former station rose a complex of buildings indifferent to and yet dependent upon the 650 trains which daily deposit 200,000 commuters from as far away as Philadelphia, Washington, D.C., and Boston, as well as the suburbs of New Jersey and Long Island. At the center of the huge complex, and towering fifty-seven stories above is One Penn Plaza, a streamlined business community. On its perimeter are Madison Square Garden, the smaller Felt Forum, and the Exposition Rotunda Cinema. Just below ground is a shopping arcade directly accessible from the Penn-Central and Long Island Rail Road stations, with connecting underground corridors leading to the BMT, Sixth, Seventh, and Eighth Avenue subways, and the PATH (the former H & M) system. This sprawling transportation network receives and disperses a daily swell of half a million people.

Beneath all these structures, under the concrete slab which became its roof, the old Penn Station was transformed into a busy underground thoroughfare, a space-age piazza surrounded by a city in microcosm. Long gone is the old elegance and grandeur of 1910. Their place has been taken by a fast-moving, streamlined city beneath the city that caters to a population of transients. In this city which never sees the light of day, trains come and go every minute of every day, destinations flashing like stars on a huge computer board. On their way to Long Beach, Long Island, or Long Beach, California, thousands of people rush or wander, far removed from the crush and noise of the city above them, down escalators which glide silently on rubber soles to the tracks below. But here and there, a few staircases remain with their polished brass rails.

seven

WHAT COMES IN...MUST GO OUT

Sewage is a subject few people like to discuss. Even the city department responsible for it is called the Department of Water Resources, a part of the Environmental Protection Administration. Nevertheless, whatever the euphemism, sewage is a very real part of our daily lives.

Every day 1½ *billion* gallons of fresh and wholesome water enter New York City—and virtually all of it goes down the drain. Whenever we shower, bathe, flush the toilet, wash dishes, clothes, or the car; whenever we hose the garden, douse a fire, turn on a fire hydrant, wash down the street; whenever we run water for any reason; whenever it rains—the water instantly becomes waste. And it all flows into the city's 6,500-mile sewer system. Sewer pipes and mains discharge on a three-degree downward grade into large individual pipes called interceptor sewers.

A number of interceptors may join to form a trunk line which then discharges sewage into the pollution-control or treatment plants. But where does it go from there?

The answer was a long time in coming. One of the reasons for this delay is that New York enjoys what was for too long considered an ideal situation—countless rivers and waterways, a vast harbor, and, beyond this, the sea. Eventually, however, even New York's waters became deficient in oxygen. The result was pollution.

Almost since the beginning, pollution had been a concern of the city fathers, even though the word itself did not gain coinage until the twentieth century. Barely forty years after Manhattan Island was first settled, the English found it necessary to cover the Dutch canals which had already become open sewers. First among these was Heere Gracht, under Broad Street, once a beautiful tree-lined Dutch residential area. It was the English who also built the town's first sewer in 1696. Even so, pigs and goats continued to roam freely through the unpaved streets, feeding on the offal and refuse which the inhabitants tossed in front of their houses.

It was not until 1744 that hatters and starch-makers were forbidden to pour their dyes into the gutters. In 1789 the Common Council passed an ordinance requiring householders to have the dirt from their yards and cellars and from the street in front of their homes collected near the gutter on alternate Fridays (in poor sections, once a month). This proved to be a somewhat less than successful sewage system. The city's wealthy residents devised their own solution. Long lines of black slaves could be seen late at night, wending their way to the river banks with tubs of refuse and "nastiness" upon their heads. While this may have eased the civic conscience of the rich, it did nothing to alleviate the sanitary problems of the large majority.

By 1789, when New York's population stood at about

sixty thousand, the streets and canals had become such breeding grounds for every kind of disease that visitors to the city were often forced to hold their noses against the evil stench or lavish heavy perfumes on themselves. The streets were a network of open sewers, awash with putrefying debris of every description. The ruts down their unpaved center carried the city's filth downhill to the nearest waterway or allowed it to seep into the ground, headed toward surrounding springs, pumps, and wells, where it was often drawn up again for fresh water.

Ten years later, in 1799, the Common Council, with its long-established penchant for appointing committees, was finally moved to more radical action when it decided that New York needed a system for collecting and selling "Street Dirt and Manure."

Provision was made for the hiring of two men to be supplied with carts equipped with bells, whose daily task it was to go through the streets "collecting the Garbage and Offals from Yards and Kitchens for which purpose they shall Ring the Bell at suitable Distances to Notify the Inhabitants to bring out the same and put it in the Carts." This may have been in part the result of a committee investigation into the causes of yellow fever— judged to be "Deep Damp Cellars and Filthy Sunken Yards," "Burial Grounds," and "Sailors Boarding Houses and Tipling Houses." The first of these is self-evident. The second contention is based on the fact that, where water was drawn from the vicinity of a burial ground, as was true in at least one instance, the water, though clear, "was overcharged with phosphate of lime and an extremely fetid animal matter," which was hardly surprising. The third supports the view of a Dr. Samuel L. Mitchell that "the long use of strong malt liquors, Wines and distilled Spirits" had lowered the imbibers' resistance to disease.

One suggestion put forward for the removal of filth

in the streets was that intersecting streets might "easily be overflowed, by making a small temporary Dam of old blankets, &c. below the part to be washed." Three years later, in 1802, the city's street commissioner, Joseph Brown, offered yet another proposal. Why not dig a canal from north of the Fresh Water Pond (which it was no longer) to the North River (the Hudson, so called because it formed the northern border of William Penn's territory of which the Delaware River was the southern border), with an intersection at Leonard and Chapple streets and sluices along the way which would allow fresh water (as Brown persisted in calling it) from the Collect to clean out the ditch. Brown advised, however, against making the canal wide enough for shipping because of "the distructive [*sic*] influence of the Sun on the putrefying mass contained in it." As an afterthought, he also recommended extending the canal, in the form of an open circular brick tunnel six feet in diameter, as far as the East River, through Roosevelt Street. He feared that without such an extension heavy rains could cause massive overflows.

In due course a committee voted in favor of such an open canal, to pass through a street a hundred feet wide. That was in 1805, and today's busy Canal Street is still much wider than its neighbors—although, mercifully, the sewer was enclosed long ago.

In an 1825 Report of the Street Committee made to the Common Council, the committee stated that it had given the subject of removing

> Filth and Dirt from the streets in this city . . . that attention which it so much merits, as connected with the health and convenience of the citizens as well as others who visit us on business or otherwise. . . . Heretofore, the Street Manure has been a subject of revenue; and in order to obtain the largest sum, con-

tracts have been made with *one* (seldom more than *two*) persons for the whole city. Those few having the monopoly, and paying a large sum for the privilege . . . the filth and dirt [was] removed, only when [their] interest was best subserved, notwithstanding the citizens duly and faithfully swept and heaped the manure as by law they were directed.

The committee, therefore, recommended that the city be divided into nine separate districts for the purpose of sanitation.

Even so, conditions continued to deteriorate. An official report presented by the Lyceum of Natural History in 1831 described them with the following matter-of-factness:

> Into the sand bank, underlying the city, are daily deposited . . . about 100 tons of excrement every 24 hours. In these deposites [*sic*] we may find all the ingredients . . . which destroy the purity of our waters. But in this estimate we do not include an equal amount of urine, for the following reason: This liquid, when *stale* or *putrid*, has the remarkable property of . . . [making] hard waters soft. Although the fastidious may revolt from the use of water thus sweetened to our palate, it is perhaps fortunate that this mixture is daily taking place, for otherwise the water of this city would become, in a much shorter space of time than it actually does, utterly unfit for domestic purposes.

The report went on to remark that the public had become so inured to the foul taste of the city's water that, of truly fresh spring water, it was commonly said with bitter humor, "This water is like wind—there is nothing substantial in it; nothing to bite upon." By this time, the city's population was 202,500.

Sewer systems have been used since ancient Greek and Babylonian times, although no effort was made to introduce them to modern cities until the mid-nineteenth century. New York's earliest application of sewer engineering occurred in Brooklyn in 1857. Before the Greater New York Charter uniting all five boroughs went into effect in 1898, each township had its own local government, and each community had its own method of sewage disposal. Most of it was simply funneled through sewer pipes into the nearest river or harbor.

In its June 1873, issue, *Scientific American* observed:

> The death rate from zymotic [infectious or contagious] diseases alone averages 9,000 a year within the corporate limits of New York City. . . . Old marshes that, in the overwhelming desire to raise grades and make streets, were filled up with sand and stone, have asserted their existence and converted the land into a sponge, absorbing the filth which flows from the faulty sewers. Burying a nuisance is not abating it. It is an urgent necessity to thoroughly overhaul and, if need be, entirely alter our sewerage.

It was only after the 1898 Charter established Greater New York that a unified and collective effort could be made to deal with the city's waste. But even then waste disposal was not thought to be much of a problem. It was commonly accepted that sewage flowing into the nearest body of water would become harmless through dilution. Although Manhattan was densely populated, large parts of the other boroughs were still farmland and open spaces.

There was still plenty of good fishing in the rivers and harbor, and fine beaches abounded. New Yorkers worried little about polluted waters. But as the population expanded and the waste effluent from industries increased, people began to realize that before many more years passed, the city's drinking water would be contaminated, beaches would be condemnable, and fish and waterfowl lost forever. The grandeur of New York's harbor, its rivers and shorelines, would be little more than a memory; they would become unsightly, festering blots on the landscape.

On any hot summer day, a million people crushed together on a one-mile stretch of beach at Brooklyn's Coney Island, a five-cent subway ride from the city's congested centers. For most people, Coney Island was the only recreation they could afford. Yet, jammed together along a shoreline which was itself contaminated, they were exposed to enormous health hazards. From all around, raw sewage flowed freely into rivers and waterways, along the shores and into the ocean. Water-pollution control became essential.

In 1909, as the population swelled to unprecedented numbers, farsighted biologists and engineers recognized the potential hazards to the city's waterways and its inhabitants. Through surveys they undertook in the harbor, they could clearly see that the dissolved oxygen content of the water was falling rapidly. Following World War I, more industries sprang up along the waterfronts, adding still greater pollution. The oxygen level began to plummet. The situation became urgent. A population that had been over three million in 1900 had doubled by 1930.

In the intervening years, a master plan for the containment of New York City's water pollution was developed. By the mid-1920s the city with singular foresight had acquired a series of waterfront sites for the eventual development of sewage treatment plants. In spite of the Depression and a lack of municipal funds for major public-works programs, sewage treatment received top priority. There was virtually no oxygen left in the waters of the Harlem River. The flow in the East River which is, in fact, not a river at all, but a tidal strait, was so minimal that raw sewage merely sat there, contaminating not only the water but the air itself.

The first of the city's thirteen sewage treatment centers, the Coney Island plant, was opened in 1935. Others have followed on the city's perimeter in the decades since. While there are many systems of sewage treatment, including septic tanks, trickling filters, sand filter beds, or plain sedimentation, to name a few, New York's circumstances required a special approach, since the type of sewage treatment used had to be determined on the basis of volume, the kind of surrounding waters for effluent discharge, and the available land. With only limited space in New York's congested urban center, treatment plants often had to be located close to residential sections of the city. Under these circumstances, and considering the volume of sewage that had to be processed, the so-called activated sludge process seemed the most efficient treatment.

Water pollutants fall roughly into three categories: oxygen consuming, synthetic organic chemicals, and sediments. In order to decompose, organic wastes use up oxygen in any body of water. The degree of pollution can be measured, therefore, by the amount of oxygen the pollutants use—that is, their biochemical oxygen demand or BOD. Thus, the primary function of any sewage treatment is to reduce the BOD to an absolute minimum. Synthetic organic chemicals are far more difficult to deal with. Although New York City's treatment plants employ primary and secondary treatments, they cannot rid the water of detergents, pesticides, or industrial chemicals. Despite regulations which limit the amount of toxic waste which industries are permitted to

Top: Aerial view of one of New York City's thirteen sewage treatment plants. *Pamela Jones*

Center: In the aeration tanks, impurities are converted into particles that will quickly settle. *Pamela Jones*

Bottom: At left, diffusers pump compressed air into the aeration tanks. The additional oxygen accelerates flocculation. On the opposite side of the tank, fine sprays reduce detergent billows. *Pamela Jones*

discharge into the sewer system, a certain percentage of synthetic organic chemicals flows into the waterways even after treatment. The new law passed in 1971 requiring reduction or elimination of phosphates has markedly lowered this harmful outflow. Sediments—soils, sands, grit, and minerals—are the least harmful but most expensive pollutants to process.

New York's sewage treatment process is divided into three separate stages—preliminary, primary, and secondary. When raw sewage is delivered to the treatment plant through the network of interceptor sewers or trunk lines, it first passes through bar screens. A series of upright metal bars spaced one and three inches apart separates large objects such as sticks, logs, cans, and rags, which arrive with the influent. These are automatically removed by raking devices, while the sewage flows on into the preliminary settling tank. Older plants contain grit chambers, designed to slow the sewage flow to about one foot per second to prevent damage to the plants' machinery and to allow heavier particles—sand, grit, soils—to settle, while lighter impurities remain suspended in the sewage flow. The grit is then scraped from the bottom of the grit chamber and removed for landfill. In newer plants, however, the grit chamber is no longer used. Instead, grit and sewage flow together through a preliminary settling tank. While the heavier grit instantly settles here, the remaining sewage flows into a primary settling tank. After about an hour, one-third of the suspended organic impurities settles at the bottom and forms a sludge which is then removed by pumps. A rotating mechanism skims the surface for the small amount of scum and grease which rises to the top.

The sewage is now ready for its secondary treatment. It is introduced into an aeration tank, where it remains for about three hours. During this time, diffusers near the base of the tank pump compressed air into the tank. The impurities which remain after primary sedimentation are thereby freely suspended or dissolved, as the aeration tank converts them into particles which will settle quickly. Because of the additional oxygen supplied by the compressed air, aerobic (oxygen-dependent) bacteria are able to consume the organic waste at an accelerated rate. In fact, they thrive on it. They gather around the particles of organic matter which they consume, causing it to accumulate into clusters called floc. Once flocculation has taken place, the sewage is directed into the final settling tank. Here, within two or three hours, the suspended solids, or floc, settle to form a sludge, which is then removed by pumps. The clarified liquid at the top becomes the final effluent which is discharged into the waters of the harbor.

The settled solids next undergo the activated sludge process. Although the conversion of suspended solids into sludge is achieved very efficiently by aerobic bacteria, these bacteria are constantly being washed away with the clarified liquid. Therefore, some of the sludge in the final settling tank has to be returned to the aeration tank for more concentrated bacterial activity.

As soon as this phase is completed, the sludge bulk must be reduced. This is achieved by placing the sludge in a special settling tank called a thickener, where it is held for periods of twelve to twenty-four hours. During this time, a considerable amount of water separates from the sludge. While this water is returned to the sewage flow at the beginning of the plant to go through the whole process again, the thickened sludge remaining at the bottom of the thickener is pumped into a digester. Because it consists of raw putrescible solids, the sludge cannot be used for landfill, nor is it ready to be dumped at sea.

The digester is a large, enclosed, circular tank in which the sludge is detained for several weeks at a temperature of about ninety-five degrees. Under these conditions and in the absence of oxygen, vast numbers of *an*aerobic bacteria begin to proliferate. By feeding on the organic compounds of the sludge, these bacteria break them down and convert about fifty percent of the organic compounds into various gases and water. The gases produced by this digestion process are essentially methane and carbon dioxide, which in turn are used to generate all or most of the power for some of the treatment plants.

Then and only then, the remaining digested sludge, a dark, relatively inert liquid containing some three to four percent solids, is pumped into sludge storage tanks where it awaits shipment out to sea. It is then carried by one of the city's four sludge vessels to a fourteen-square-mile federally approved area about twelve miles out to sea, east of Sandy Hook, New Jersey. This sludge dumping site has been used for more than forty years, but studies have been made recently to see if ocean disposal can be eliminated altogether. One recommended alternative is the thermal destruction of sludge in an oxygen-deficient atmosphere (pyrolysis) combined with accelerated composting.

Thorough as New York City's water-pollution controls are, even the most efficient treatment will not remove certain pathogenic bacteria from the sewage discharged into the waters around the city. In order to protect local beaches from possible contamination, New York's treatment plants subject all effluents to one final process during the summer months. Although chlorine is by far the most efficient and economical disinfectant available for sewage treatment, it is also extremely dangerous in its liquid and gaseous states. Therefore, the city's plants house special tanks containing sodium hypochlorite, in which form chlorination of all effluents can take place during a thirty-minute detention period. As frequent samplings have demonstrated, nearly one hundred percent of the bacteria are destroyed in the process.

With the rapid disappearance of available landfill sites for New York's waste, studies are underway to determine how as much as twenty percent of the waste could be used as fossil fuel to generate electricity. Because New Yorkers produce, in addition to sewage waste, an average of *thirty thousand tons* of garbage *per day* —more than any other city in the world, and more than London and Tokyo combined—this is a very serious consideration for the future. It is estimated that 1,000 tons of garbage power could equal 1,400 barrels of oil. As world oil resources are increasingly depleted, so New York's garbage power may provide an alternative.

For many years the city's treatment plants contended with the voluminous billows of white fluffy detergents that floated atop the dozens of connecting tanks and screening devices through which New York's waste was largely freed of odor and dangerous bacteria before it entered the harbor. The detergents had to be diluted and reduced to liquid waste by hundreds of fine-spray jets, filtered down from one tank to the next below it. Thanks to the law prohibiting the use of phosphates, much of this dangerous nuisance has been removed.

A major consideration for the city, however, has always been the control of industrial waste. Since industry forms a vital mainstay of the urban structure, it was necessary to establish guidelines that were firm but not so restrictive as to force industry out of New York. Through a surcharge on sewer rates for above-normal waste flowing into the sewers, the city was able to process the added volume without requiring industries to undertake individual pretreatment. At the same time, the city prohibited the discharge of inflammable, explosive, obstructive, or toxic wastes. It also regulated the amount of metals, oil, and grease to be discharged, subject to change, as new knowledge became available. Should any industry regularly ignore these guidelines, the city reserves the right to shut off not only the offender's water supply but also his access to the sewer system. It is in this manner that the city is able to honor its responsibility to the public to keep New York's waters clean—as clean as possible.

Lest it be thought that the horrors of plague and contamination are a thing of the past, on Long Island, where some townships still depend on wells for their fresh-water supplies, an outbreak of several cases of cholera was recorded as recently as 1971—when untreated sewage found its way to the water table. The communities involved were promptly forbidden to draw water from their wells, and the town councils moved with remarkable swiftness to construct a comprehensive sewage treatment facility.

Even though New York has the heaviest population concentration in the entire United States, promised federal funds in support of sewage treatment plant construction and improvements under the Clean Water Restoration Act of 1966 have been all too frequently unavailable. The result has been long delays in the completion of work. In a suit brought by the city against the federal government, the Supreme Court ruled in favor of New York, but the delays cost the city dearly in advancing its program of building separate sanitary and storm sewers in addition to special storm water treatment plants.

In the last century, so-called combined sewers to carry both sanitary waste and storm water proved extremely economical and efficient. But with today's concentrated population, even a moderate rainfall raises the volume carried by those combined sewers from five to fifteen times the normal amount—a volume with which treatment plants are unable to cope. Consequently, the system was equipped with regulating devices that allow such storm waters mixed with sewage to flow directly into the waterways without treatment during heavy rains.

It has, therefore, been long recognized as imperative that new facilities must be built to separate the two types of waste. But as the city's economic health has suffered dramatic setbacks, so have its public-works programs been slowed to a snail's pace. Furthermore, although a sewer's average life span is about a hundred years, funds are regularly diverted from new projects to make necessary replacements and repairs.

Coupled with the continual lack of funds is public fear and ignorance of the effects of a sewage treatment plant upon the community. This has been most dramatically illustrated on Manhattan's West Side. Since the city was first settled, through the more than three hundred years of its history, all the sewage from Bank Street to Spuyten Duyvil and as far east as Fifth Avenue has been discharged directly into the Hudson River. Fortunately, that river is blessed with a strong tidal current. To cope with the enormous volume of waste from approximately one million people, the city set plans in motion to construct the North River plant between 137th and 145th streets. They were greeted with public uproar. Community opposition and demonstrations, even the threat of riots, not only caused a series of dangerous delays but also forced the city to present entirely new plans for construction.

As a result, what will distinguish this plant from all others is the fact that it will be wholly out of sight, its roof especially reinforced to support a newly created park occupying thirty acres partly alongside and partly in the Hudson—at more than triple the original cost! While such a revision is without doubt more pleasing to the community eye, the net result poses potential problems which far outweigh aesthetics. In most cases, New

York's open-air sewage treatment plants abut residential areas. Yet, because of the sprawl of the settling and aeration tanks out in the open air, there is no buildup of noxious fumes or gases. In fact, what mild odors do exist around a working plant more resemble the smell of musky earth in the country than sewage. Since the plants always face the nearest waterway, it is virtually impossible to detect their purpose from an inland viewpoint.

By being forced underground with vastly reduced ventilation, the North River plant will inevitably generate and contain far more noxious gases, create both undesirable and uncomfortable working conditions, and accelerate the corrosion of equipment. Finally, just at a time when the world is becoming aware of an increased shortage of energy and the need to conserve, the out-of-sight North River plant will be forced to expend considerably more than normal electric power for added ventilation and equipment maintenance. But unless a largely uninformed general public can come to understand the step-by-step workings of sewage treatment, it will continue to sacrifice its long-term best interests to the more immediate expedient of aesthetics.

The North River plant itself will provide primary and secondary treatment to 220 million gallons of sewage daily. Its six digesters and four aeration tanks will be capable of removing ninety percent of BOD and suspended solids from the sewage, in accordance with the city's overall program to give secondary treatment to all sewage generated within New York.

Perhaps because they are not usually a topic of everyday conversation, sewers have been occasionally featured in some interesting myths. One fanciful story which has circulated around New York for many years is that the city's sewers are literally infested with alligators up to five feet in length.

Families visit Florida, so the story begins. Their children fall in love with a darling baby alligator and bring it back to New York. But the baby alligator keeps growing until one fine day it grows so large that it has to live in the family bathtub. Finally, after a good deal of discussion and deliberation, father one dark moonless night takes the alligator under his arm and stealthily tiptoes to the nearest street corner, where he throws the beast into the local sewer. Or . . . anticipating that the baby alligator will grow up to live in the family bathtub, father waits until the children are asleep one night and then flushes the alligator down the toilet. Both versions of the story end the same way: New York's sewers become the breeding ground for a thriving population of alligators. Poppycock and balderdash. There are some excellent reasons why alligator survival in the sewers is highly *unlikely*. The sewer pipes range from twelve to fifty-four inches in diameter. All are usually three-quarters full, and all have a three-degree downward grade, since sewage is discharged under the force of gravity. This produces a rate of flow so intense that, by the time it reaches the interceptor sewers, it is comparable with Niagara Falls. Although interceptor sewers are larger (as are storm sewers—one in Queens, for example, can comfortably accommodate two Mack trucks side by side), an alligator could never reach them alive. Even if it could avoid being wedged in a twelve-inch pipe, it would drown, since alligators are air-breathing creatures. Furthermore, even if the heat in July and August does seem to belie it, New York simply is not a semitropical climate, nor do the sewers much resemble the Everglades. And even if some West Side alligator were miraculously to survive the harrowing trip to the Hudson, it would soon die in the river's cold waters. Of the four or five alligators ever reported found in Manhattan—all of them near death—only two were in sewers, and they were tiny, pitiful two- to three-inch specimens. Finally, no alligator, dead or alive, could ever escape the city's pollution control plants, although none has ever tried. In all the years they have been in operation, no screening mechanism has ever caught an alligator, although tragically, aborted fetuses or full-term babies are occasionally washed into the treatment plants. But there *are* waterbugs in the sewers—millions of them.

There is also a less well-known corollary to the alligator story: that Public Works inspectors armed with .22-caliber rifles regularly used to go on alligator hunts. Apart from the obvious dangers of firing a rifle inside a pipe or main, the flow velocity in pipes which are three-quarters full makes it neither possible nor desirable for a man to stand still long enough to take aim—in spaces that are not exactly brilliantly lighted or of sufficient girth. The most fanciful stories of all, however, revolve around Teddy May, the longtime and legendary sewer "king." Teddy May was real enough—a short, feisty, colorful fellow, who took great pride in "his" sewers. But that he used to swim or take leisurely Sunday afternoon strolls in them allows for only one conclusion: Teddy May was either a terribly small man or a terribly large legend.

On the other hand, the wildlife specimens that *do* travel through the city's sewers inspire no legends. They are a society of outcasts, members of a large and mostly unseen population numbering in the millions, shunned, hated, and feared by almost every citizen. They are the Norway rats, genus *Rattus norvegicus*, which have lived and bred under New York probably as long as human settlers have done so above ground. Why they are called Norway rats is not entirely clear, since they are of a variety believed to have migrated west from Asia during the early eighteenth century—cold-weather rats as opposed to the so-called Mediterranean, or warm-weather, rats found in the southern states.

New York's very own rarely exceed sixteen to eighteen inches in length, tail included. Their average weight is one pound. It is, of course, impossible to take an absolutely accurate census of the city's rat population, since they are not only rather skittish beasts, but far more intelligent and cunning than people might think. Conservative estimates place the rat population at half a million; others say there is one rat for every human inhabitant. Surveys have indicated that there is probably a constant population of four to five million—about one rat for every two persons living in New York. (And New York has just as many mice as rats.) However, densities vary. Norway rats, for example, are particularly partial to the moist underground conditions of the Lower East Side with its high water table and channeled rock as well as the many substructures dating back to the city's earliest days. Here, the rats find countless hidden passages and "runs" in relative safety from the Bureau of Pest Control.

It is a sobering thought that one single pair of rats, if left unmolested, is capable of realizing a hundred family members within one year. Each female is capable of bearing young at the age of three months and of becoming pregnant again within forty-eight hours after giving birth. Each litter produces between seven and twelve offspring. It is not difficult to see that if left to their own devices, without interference from the city's Bureau of Pest Control, the rats in New York could very easily outnumber the human residents.

In New York—where else?—even a "super rat" was discovered some years ago. It was a kind of rat that proved immune to what is still the most deadly weapon against these rodents—namely, Warfarin. An odorless, tasteless anticoagulant, Warfarin produces internal hemorrhaging that quickly causes death. When it was discovered that the super rats (a mutant strain apparently confined to a roughly five-block area in the South Bronx) resisted Warfarin, the Bureau of Pest Control turned to zinc phosphide—a quick-acting poison with a strong garlic odor—only to find that it too had little effect on the rats, who were able to recognize its presence in the remains of their dead friends and thereafter shun all baits. The department's "chefs" then substituted Lorexa on the rat menu. This less detectable vitamin D_2 product met with great success. Heavy doses of vitamin D unaccompanied by vitamin A could be harmful even to humans, and it was precisely this recipe that became the undoing of the super rats.

Rats are unable to see very well, but they have a keen sense of smell, and their sense of touch is remarkable. Their whiskers and the hair on their bodies are their ultimate sensors. They are family-oriented beasties which move in packs and care for their young, although many of these die early. Rats seek familiar smells, are rarely seen in the open unless they are frightened or near death, and leave a trail of body grease from which they recognize their territory. They generally confine their activities within a radius of 150 feet.

Although the heaviest concentration of rats is supposed to be in the city's poor sections, rats are also found in the cellars of fashionable apartment dwellings around Central Park. On the first frosty autumn night, the rats migrate in large numbers from the pleasant wilds of Central Park to the snug warmth and comfort of these "winter resorts." Returning to the familiar runs along underground pipes, through crevices in the walls, going from building to building, the rats seek out their favorite haunts.

In the spring, these "jet-setting" rats, like the wealthy inhabitants living above them, begin to flock to their summer retreats. Back in the park they scuttle about their business, burrowing trails and nests as far as eighteen inches under the surface, always with sufficient foresight to provide several escape routes. (In some sections, they are capable of burrowing to a depth of ten feet!)

And so, New York's Norway rats add constantly to the maze of natural and man-made underground passages within the city. Wherever they go in their furtive life, be it cellar, subway, or sewer, theirs is a life no human seeks to share—yet another compelling reason why even Teddy May, the brash sewer king, would have hesitated to swim or stroll among them.

Sewers even assumed a certain fleeting glamour in the 1950s. One of the hit tunes of that great musical comedy *Guys and Dolls* celebrated the privacy and shelter they offered for "the oldest, established, permanent, floating crap game in New York." Sewer humor was also provided by the long-running television series "The Honeymooners." Art Carney in his role as "sewer snipe" Ed Norton spent long, happy, off-camera hours in New York's sewers, indulging in such lunch-break diversions as "wet cards wild" poker games.

Generally, however, sewage is serious business, a business that costs the city of New York millions of dollars every year. Since 1909, biologists and engineers have been gathering data from New York's harbor. Although far too much raw sewage is still discharged into this body of water, much of it from communities outside the city, the 1970s have brought encouraging signs that the extreme dangers of pollution may have been halted. There is a marked increase in the harbor water's dissolved oxygen content. Even the Harlem River, which was once virtually devoid of oxygen, is showing signs of improvement, as is the East River. As treatment plants gain in greater efficiency, as construction of new plants nears completion, so the residents of New York can perhaps again eventually look forward to seeing the variety of fish that the Indians enjoyed three centuries ago.

eight
ROCKBOTTOM

———◆———

Before a contractor digs a hole anywhere in Manhattan, it behooves him to consult what most engineering and building experts consider a one-page "bible"—the Viele-MacCoun map. The reason is water. Quite a lot of it. Three hundred years' worth of construction has steadily pushed most of it deeper and deeper underground, often hiding it forever from view. Except during excavations.

Brigadier General Egbert Ludovicus Viele was a man of many talents and accomplishments. Descended from one of the earliest Dutch settlers in Nieuw Amsterdam, he studied law, graduated from West Point, participated in the capture of Norfolk, Virginia, during the Civil War, and became its military governor for a time. Viele was also a civil engineer and, as chief engineer of New York City's Central Park, was placed in charge of the park's development until his design was superseded by that of Frederick Law Olmsted and Calvert Vaux. In 1856 he began to study the original topography of Manhattan. He recognized even then that it would be important to plan all future streets and sewage systems in accordance with the island's natural drainage. His *Topographical Atlas of the City of New York,* showing the original water courses as well as early landfill areas, was published in 1874. His map showed the ponds and streams and marshes as the earliest inhabitants had known them. Then in 1909 a land surveyor named Townsend MacCoun came along and improved upon this map by superimposing Manhattan's street plan and adding the latest man-made land areas along the shoreline.

Few city engineers or contractors can afford to ignore the Viele-MacCoun map, and few of them do. Many, in fact, have copies of it hanging on their office walls, mounted and framed. Even if they do not all agree that the water they encounter under the ground stems from original springs or streams—there is even a tiny controversy over whether to call them "streams" or "ground water"—none disputes that there is water. Borings and careful tests of subsurface conditions, together with coordination with the utility companies and city agencies, help determine their findings.

Test borings, however, do not always tell the whole truth, as was discovered during the excavation for Public School 174 at Columbus Avenue between Eighty-third and Eighty-fourth streets. While the Viele-MacCoun map quite unmistakably indicated the presence of a stream, the borings came up with little more than rock. "So we assumed that the old stream was now nothing more than a little flow of water in a seam of that rock," recalled Eugene E. Hult, the Board of Education's Superintendent of Design, Construction, and Physical Plant at the time. Instead, as the excavation progressed, workers discovered

a pond barely fifteen feet under the surface which, together with several other "little" problems, necessitated
a complete revision of the designs at a cost of $100,000.
Another school under construction between Seventh and
Eighth avenues, 120th and 121st streets, was found to be
sitting in the middle of a swamp, quite a sizable one in
fact, near the source of what had once been one of Manhattan's mightier streams. Navigable half a mile inland,
and called Monteneys Creek, alias Harlem Mill Pond,
alias Harlem Creek, it was no less than twenty feet deep
and a hundred feet wide in parts.

And then there was the contractor preparing to build
the Criminal Courts Building at Foley Square. He went
bankrupt at the turn of the century because of the un-
foreseen quantities of water that flooded the site—he was
digging at the northeast end of none other than Collect
Pond. Uptown, near the end of the nineteenth century,
another contractor suffered a similar fate. The boating
lake in Central Park, although man-made, lies in the
watershed of several streams which unite at Fifth Avenue
near Seventy-fourth Street, becoming the Saw Kill Stream.
But the contractor chose to ignore the stream's natural
drainage to the East River and erected his houses directly
in its path. Trapped by walls of concrete, the Saw Kill
Stream welled up to the surface and flooded the buildings, until it found an alternate route to its destination.
As one contractor observed recently, "You have to work
with nature. If there's water, give it somewhere else it
can go, and in return it won't interfere with your work."
Unfortunately, that turn-of-the-century builder learned
his lesson too late.

On the following pages, the "bible" that contractors and engineers
rarely ignore—the Viele-MacCoun map—clearly shows the hidden
waterways that continue to flow under the city.

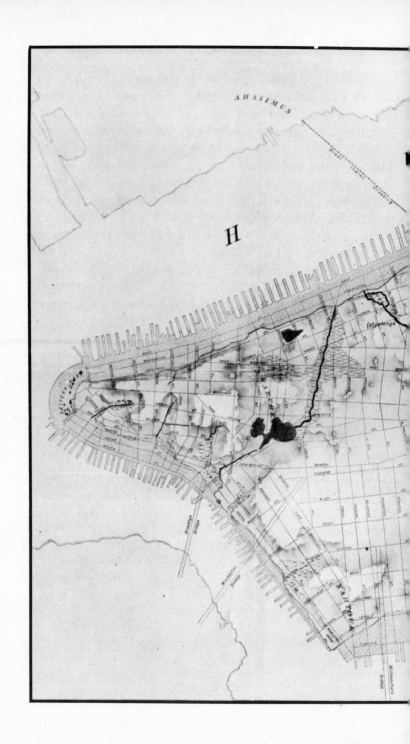

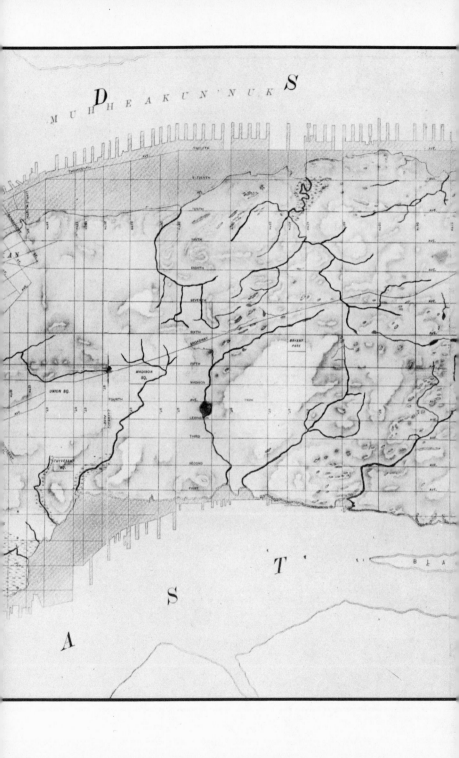

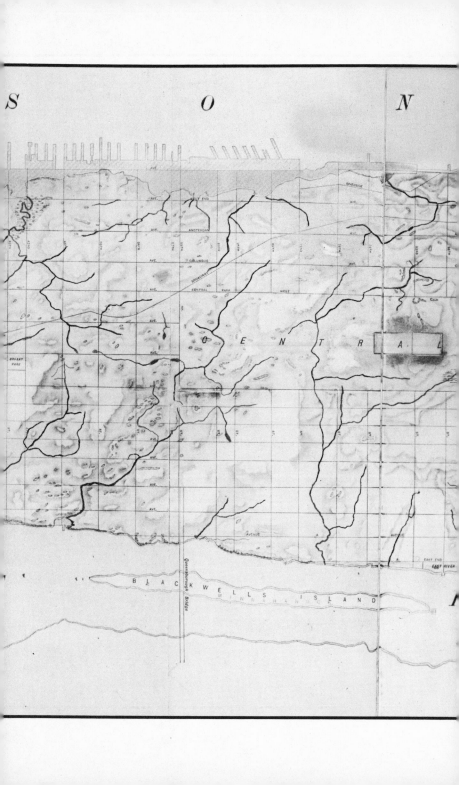

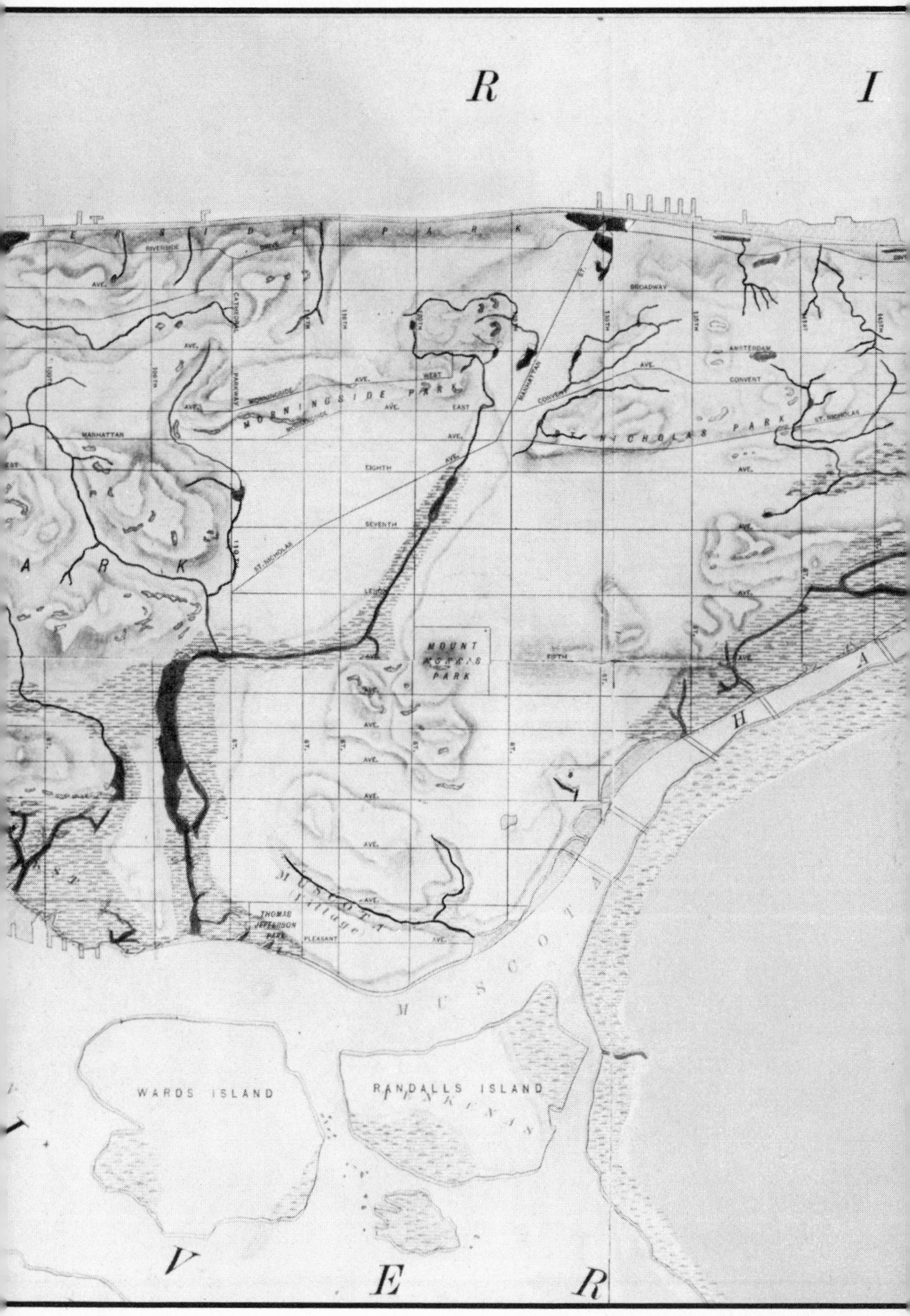
R
I
RIVERSIDE
DRIVE
BROADWAY
CATHEDRAL PARKWAY
MORNINGSIDE PARK
AMSTERDAM
CONVENT
ST. NICHOLAS PARK
MANHATTAN
EIGHTH
SEVENTH
ST. NICHOLAS
MOUNT MORRIS PARK
FIFTH
THOMAS JEFFERSON PARK
PLEASANT
WARDS ISLAND
RANDALLS ISLAND
V
E
R

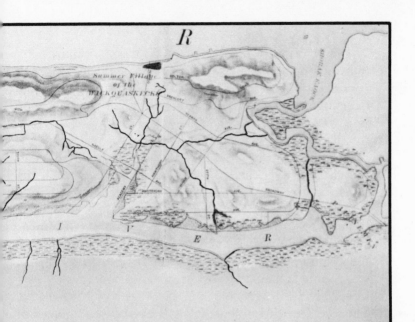

1609

THE ISLAND OF MANHATTAN

(MANNAHTIN)

AT THE TIME OF ITS DISCOVERY

SHOWING ITS ELEVATIONS, WATER-COURSES, MARSHES, AND SHORE LINE

BY

TOWNSEND MacCOUN

This map is based upon the early colonial surveys of Ratzer, Montresor, Knypthausen, Bradford, Dayekinek, etc. and the Survey of 1867 by Genl. E. L. Viele

On the other hand, Horace C. Grant, Empire City Subway Company's former chief engineer, did try such cooperation some years ago when working near Harlem Creek and still nearly found himself with a brownstone in his excavation. The company was digging a manhole for the New York Telephone Company when the workmen suddenly discovered that, for every shovelful of sand they heaved over their shoulders, two slid back from the sides. Realizing that before long this would undermine a nearby building, they braced the excavation with interlocked steel sheeting. Even so, they could not dig as deeply as they had planned since the sand at the base of the cylinder began to "boil"—that is, the steel cylinder was no longer equal to the pressure of sand and water outside it, and the sand began to bubble from the bottom. The site? Once again those friendly neighborhood marshes surrounding Monteneys Creek.

Excavations for the Chase Manhattan Plaza in New York's financial district in 1957 revealed "no more than the usual ground water," according to the project manager at the time, although eventually it was found to be a good deal more than "usual." The building site was, in fact, on the western edge of what used to be Smit's Vly, just south of the little stream along Maiden Lane where Dutch women used to launder their linens. But thanks to an innovative development in the chemical industry, work on the foundations could quickly resume. Solutions totaling one hundred tons of calcium chloride and fifty thousand gallons of sodium silicate were injected into some two hundred two-inch-diameter pipes which were bored between twenty and forty feet deep. The chemicals solidified the troublesome quicksand, forming a sandstone "wall" some five feet thick, within which the contractors were able to excavate the necessary ninety feet down into bedrock. (Although this may be the first time sodium silicate was used in the building industry,

In this aerial view of lower Manhattan, the solid white line indicates the island's original shoreline. Everything outside that line is filled land. *The Port Authority of New York and New Jersey*

farm women long before had stored their eggs in solutions of it called waterglass, to keep them fresh during winter.)

Perhaps the most amazing excavation story in New York concerns the World Trade Center, which was opened in December 1970. For a brief time, until the Chicago Sears building topped them, the Twin Towers, 110 stories (1,350 feet) high, were the tallest buildings in the world, a center for more than six hundred world trade organizations, a kind of supermarket for import and export businesses.

Long before it could even be dreamed of, in the days of the early Dutch settlers, much of the site on which the WTC rises today was in the Hudson River. *In* it. As the city matured, so landfill was added to its shores. Greenwich Street, for example, which had run along the river's edge in 1783, is now two blocks (seven hundred feet) inland. As wharves and piers fell into disuse, they were filled over. The island swelled, the Hudson shrank.

In the early 1960s, the Port Authority of New York and New Jersey acquired a thirteen-block area of century-old, largely run-down buildings. As these were demolished, engineers set to work, trying to solve the problem of how to dig through the reclaimed land area, through the riverbed below, into solid rock seventy feet under the surface. Because of the nearness of the Hudson and the sponginess of the fill, they knew that the river's water would seep into the excavation as fast as it could be dug. No amount of pumping could keep pace with the flow of water. It was therefore necessary to lower the ground water level to the same depth as the proposed seventy-foot excavation, so that construction could take place on dry land. Under normal conditions, a series of deep wells would provide the necessary drainage, though unfortunately this would simultaneously lower the ground water level in adjacent areas. Formerly submerged soils would dry and settle and thus affect the stability all around the site not only of buildings but of streets and those underlying utilities not directly supported by bedrock. Also, because the WTC's lowest basement would be deep below the ground water level, it would be subject to constant upward pressure from the water below. One possible method of overcoming such buoyancy was to construct a heavy concrete pressure mat at the base of the excavation. But apart from the fact that the permanence of this solution was questionable, it was also very expensive.

As in the case of the Con Edison high-voltage cable insulation, the Italians came to the rescue once again. The "slurry-trench" method they had developed was already widely used in Europe and Canada as well as in San Francisco and Boston. It required that a trench be dug around the periphery of the building site before excavation was begun. The trench was then filled in sections with slurry—a soupy porridge made of clay and water which held the ground water out. As soon as a portion of the trench was filled with slurry, concrete was piped to the bottom of that section, forcing the slurry out at the top, ready to be used in the next section. At the same time, workers demolished the old buildings within the site and relocated the various utility lines traversing it. As the concrete retaining wall rose, six-inch-diameter steel tendons were regularly placed through it at a forty-five-degree angle to brace the wall from the outside. These "tie-backs" served as external anchors for the retaining wall which, when completed, formed what was essentially a giant concrete bathtub. Only then was the inner area ready for excavation.

In the WTC saga, one of the most delicate operations was the support of the two southern H & M railroad tunnels from New Jersey. (This nearly bankrupt system was acquired in 1962 by the Port Authority's Trans-Hudson Corporation, and renamed PATH.) Since 1909 these tunnels had carried thousands of commuters every day deep under the Hudson to the city. Now they were about to be incorporated into the WTC substructure. One of the parallel tunnels crossed the site near its northern end, the other near its southern. In order to excavate around and under these tunnels, it was necessary to suspend them without interruption of service. Caissons were constructed to support pairs of steel trusses on either side of the tubes. Saddles across each pair of trusses were then able to carry the live load of the tunnels. Without a

During construction of the World Trade Center complex, one of the most delicate operations became the support of the two parallel PATH tunnels which crossed the site near its northern and southern ends. Without interruption of service for the daily 80,000 commuters, the tunnels were suspended over the base of the World Trade Center "bathtub" site. The top photo shows the early excavation with one tube partially exposed and its support framing begun; the bottom photo shows both tubes suspended and construction proceeding between them. *The Port Authority of New York and New Jersey*

minute's interruption or danger, 80,000 daily commuters pressed into the trains inside these tunnels which, exposed to the elements for the first time ever, continued their scheduled runs throughout the years of construction. Today more than 140,000 commuters ride the PATH trains under the WTC every day.

It was only after the Tubes were secured that the huge job of emptying the bathtub could begin in earnest. More than a million cubic yards of debris had to be removed. To avoid the great expense of hauling it far distances, it was decided to extend the shoreline still farther into the Hudson. To do this, a large rectangular cofferdam enclosure was constructed in the river, and the excavated materials dumped in it to create twenty-three acres of new land, now known as Battery Park City.

Today WTC is served not only by PATH but by the city's IRT and IND subway system. The enormous expanse of space under the ground, six finished levels in all, contains storage areas for WTC tenants, delivery docks for the hundreds of trucks which enter every day from a separate spur off Barclay Street, and parking facilities for two thousand cars.

Although the mighty Hudson has had to make its way to sea along an ever-narrowing path during the last three centuries, other, much smaller ancient waterways have doggedly refused to be obliterated. For example, the Great Kill. In its heydey, it was a rich source of brook trout, pickerel, and perch. Men would angle along the shores of the wily stream or hunt deer in the woods all around and take home a feast. Today the Great Kill continues its gurgle, with a little less sparkle perhaps—as it gets a free ride in the westbound interceptor sewer under Forty-second Street, which is exactly where it was going anyway. There is also Turtle Creek, or DeVoor's or Duffore's Mill Stream, a waterway which, like most others, goes by several aliases. In its meandering toward the

East River, it makes a generous contribution to the pond inside Central Park just north of the Plaza Hotel, then dips under the ground again, flows deep under the Delmonico Hotel at Fifty-ninth Street, and continues under the Park Avenue railway lines in its travels to the East River at Turtle Bay, "where it is common," wrote the Reverend Andrew Burnaby in 1760, "to have turtle feasts: these happen once or twice in a week." On several occasions in the past, the stream has also caused some floods in the basements of fashionable East Side buildings.

Cedar Creek is no mean stream either. It watered the park at Madison Square and, later, the graveyard there, on its way to the East River at present-day Stuyvesant Town. Minetta Stream or Creek, which gave its name to the street in Greenwich Village, a "turbulent brook" also called Devil's Water, rose at Seventeenth Street and Sixth Avenue and at Fifth Avenue and Twentieth Street. Once full of the finest trout on the island, it wriggled its way through such diverse landmarks as Union and Washington Squares, when the former was still known as The Forks and the latter was a potter's field for the poor, for victims of yellow fever, and for out-of-towners.

Nobody would suspect that Gramercy Park might be a corruption of Crommeshe, also known as Crommesie or Crummashie, sometimes attributed to the Indians, in which case the meaning has become lost to history, or to the Germans as being somewhat loosely translated from *Krummer See* (crooked lake). However, the Germans were latecomers to Manhattan's shores, whereas the Dutch were not and, most likely, named it for what it was— *Krom Moerasje*, a crooked little swamp. Although, of course, there are those who say that when Mayor James Duane named his country estate "Grammercie Seat" (based on the French *grand merci*, later adopted by the English as "gramercy," now obsolete, but meaning "thanks" in both languages), he needed no inspiration from the silly little brook with its silly little swamp in the middle of his orchard. Although the mayor has long since passed to his reward, the brook may well be one of the reasons why the park is always such a luxuriant green.

And who would guess that a little north of Canal Street, the Bowery (that tree-lined promenade amid sprawling *bouweries,* meaning farms) was bordered by Buttermilk Pond on one side and Sweetmilk Pond on the other. Also it may be difficult to imagine today that it might be possible to cross Manhattan Island from the East River to the Hudson through a series of streams, some of which run east, others west between 156th and 166th streets. Canoes used to do just that.

Whether New York's hidden underground waters flow through narrow cracks or stand in broad marshy fields below the surface, all of them make their way through rock. And, as every schoolchild knows, all of New York City stands on rock. But just how deep or shallow that rock is can become a source of considerable dismay for any builder, especially one who does not gather meticulous geological data.

Although one tends to think of rock as being a solid, continuous mass, the geology of New York City is more accurately described as "buried channeled scabland." In fact, there are three broad rock formations throughout the city. Of these, the so-called Fordham gneiss (predominant in the Fordham Heights region of the Bronx) is generally considered the oldest formation. Another is the Inwood dolomitic marble formation located in the Inwood section at the northeastern tip of Manhattan Island. The youngest is the Manhattan formation, a mica schist which forms the bedrock of most of Manhattan Island south of 110th Street. (Ground moraine or till underlies Brooklyn and Queens.)

Scabland consists of a network of deep underground stream channels, dry waterfalls, abandoned canyons, and steep-walled midchanneled mesas—almost all the result of massive flooding by glacial waters which produced a labyrinthine pattern of deep and shallow canyons. During geological studies at the turn of the century, it was discovered, for example, that the Bronx River which flows through Inwood dolomitic marble swings suddenly east and cuts a new channel through the much harder Manhattan schist. When the Consolidated Gas Company dug its Ravenswood tunnel across the East River in 1894, engineers found that Roosevelt Island not only divided the river into two channels but that the eastern channel ran through solid rock and was shallower than the western channel which ran through soil. Then, upon examination of borings taken on the Lower East Side of Manhattan for a proposed tunnel to Brooklyn, geologists discovered that part of the city stood on a buried preglacial channel of the East River. Whereas rock in this section was not reached for about 125 feet, the depth to rock in the nearby East River was only about 75 feet. The geologists also determined that a preglacial stream had flowed from the Hudson River to the East River, along the so-called Manhattanville Fault, present-day 125th Street. (It is along this line that some seismologists predict the inevitability of a major earthquake before the year 2000.) Yet another stream flowed from the Hudson to the East River along what is today Canal Street, while the Harlem River once flowed down the Upper East Side of Manhattan as far south as 108th Street. Soundings taken near Sandy Hook revealed a canyon cutting through the Continental Shelf some one hundred miles out to sea, which suggested that this canyon had been cut by the glacial melt waters flowing through a once greatly enlarged Hudson River, although no buried Hudson River channel has ever been found.

In Jamaica, Queens, a buried valley filled with a singular gray gravel, named Jameco, was thought to indicate that a so-called Sound River flowed through Long Island Sound and that the rivers of Connecticut had once flowed west and joined the Hudson to form a powerful river.

According to engineer Louis Binder, "The glaciers moving over the New York area deposited an unstratified coarse blanket of material called a ground moraine. When the glaciers reached their lines of maximum advance they left a ridge of material they had been bulldozing in front of them. This is the terminal moraine." With rising temperatures, the glaciers melted faster than they advanced, forming lakes betweeen the ice front and these terminal moraines. Therefore, it is believed that the Hudson River was once Glacial *Lake* Hudson, and that other, smaller glacial lakes were formed in today's Long Island Sound. These lakes were fed by flow waters produced by melting ice, and it is these currents which quite possibly cut channels through the gravel in the moraine. The combined force of water currents and gravel could quite easily have cut new channels for both the Bronx and East Rivers as we know them today. Certainly, the glacial lake sequence of the subsoils under Manhattan's Lower and Upper East Side lend credibility to such a chain of events.

It is quite possible that future geologists will be momentarily startled to find a piece of England—Bristol Basin—in the middle of New York. An engraved bronze plaque along the East River tells how this came about.

When the East River Drive was being constructed during the 1930s and 1940s, it followed the contours of Manhattan's East Side on largely man-made landfill. Then, after the Japanese attack on Pearl Harbor, and entry of the United States into World War II, a steady line of troopships sailed from New York toward England. For ballast on their return journey these ships carried, according to the dedication written by Stephen Vincent

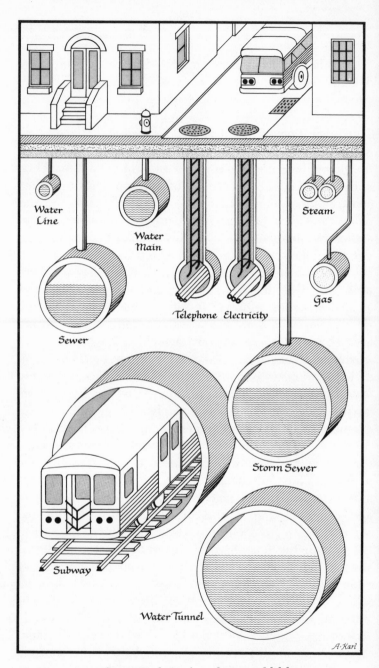

A cross-section of New York City's underground lifelines.

Benét, the "stones, bricks and rubble from the bombed city of Bristol in England . . . fragments that once were homes. . . ." It was this rubble which became landfill for the East River Drive between roughly Twenty-third and Thirty-first streets; and it was to commemorate "the resolution and fortitude of the people of Britain . . . the valor that kept them free" that this stretch of New York City is known today as Bristol Basin. For some years during construction of the Waterside apartment complex, the plaque itself disappeared from view, kept safe for its rededication in 1974 on a low wall overlooking Waterside's windy plaza, with its back to the East River.

Most of the time, historians and archaeologists must move swiftly if they wish to catch a quick glimpse into New York's past before it is built over in the city's constant upward thrust. This was most dramatically shown at the time the site of the World Trade Center was excavated. Since it is located in one of the oldest areas of the city, archaeologists and historians were on hand to salvage what they might before twentieth-century technology shattered or carted it away. Considerable excitement ran through their ranks at the discovery of such diverse historic objects as medicine bottles, shoes, silverware, chamber pots, a Portuguese fisherman's fork, and a few coins in mint condition, not to mention anchors and cannonballs. One anchor alone was no less than ten and a half feet high and six feet wide across the flukes! (It rests today, ignored and rusting, seven levels below the World Trade Center.) The finds were all quite logical. Before landfill began to extend the shoreline into the Hudson, there had been piers and wharves and wooden houses along the water's edge. As these fell into disuse, rotting and crumbling, they became a part of the manmade land.

But what the historians were really looking for were signs of the seventeenth-century Dutch ship *Tijger*, which

Already in 1917, as in this northeasterly view of the corner of Wall and William streets, Manhattan's subsurface resembled an impenetrable bowl of spaghetti. Today, more than sixty years later, engineering ingenuity must continue to find new paths for conduits to satisfy New Yorkers' ever-increasing demand for modern services. *Con Edison*

left Amsterdam in October 1613, four years after Henry Hudson's discovery of Manhattan. With Adriaen Block as its master, the vessel made its way across the Atlantic to trade for furs with the Indians. Early in 1614, the *Tijger* was accidentally burned. Exactly *where* it was burned is not known, although many historians believe it happened near what became the site of the World Trade Center. The eminent historian I. N. Phelps Stokes, however, insisted that there is no evidence to support such claims, but that there "is strong circumstantial evidence . . . that Block was in the vicinity of Albany" at the time of the disaster. It is, of course, entirely possible that the ship might have burned near Albany and been carried south by the strong currents and tides of the Hudson River.

Whatever the answer may be, it is a fact that James

A. Kelly (not to be confused with Smelly Kelly) was foreman of a construction crew digging for New York's Seventh Avenue subway at the present-day Cortlandt Street station in 1916. One day in May, his laborers' pick-axes struck solid wood instead of the accustomed soft earth. They quickly scraped and shoveled the soil from what soon emerged as the partial outline of an old ship's bow and keel. The heavy oak was badly charred. Kelly was quite baffled by the discovery and sought the advice of a number of the city's historians. Their reaction was hardly conducive to inspiring an enthusiastic archaeological search, although a few of them speculated that Kelly's crews just might have discovered the charred remains of the *Tijger*. After a futile attempt to pull the timbers free, Kelly ordered his men to cut them at the line beyond which they were buried in the tunnel wall, and he had the timbers taken to the New York Aquarium at Castle Garden. There, immersed in the seal tank, the bow and keel with its three protruding ribs became a favorite obstacle course for the animals. And there the mystery ship's timbers might have remained, except that the New York Aquarium was destined for the wreckers in 1943. Knowing that this included "his" ship's remains, Kelly managed to retrieve them from the already decaying building. Before long, they were moved to the Museum of the City of New York, where they are still displayed. In 1955 Kelly and the museum staff began to take steps which they hoped might bring about the systematic excavation of the ship's remainder. Dating of the wood and one iron bolt had established with certainty that the ship was between 320 and 360 years old. Whether or not it was the *Tijger*, there was no doubt that Kelly's timbers belonged to New York's earliest history. As such, the rest of the ship deserved to be excavated.

In the meantime, the World Trade Center was to be built. Through a combination of factors—the need of contractors to maintain construction schedules and lowest possible costs, the archaeological ignorance and indifference of those in charge, and the city's refusal as early as 1959 to underwrite the excavation—time ran out. Construction on the WTC complex began in 1966. The mystery of the *Tijger* remains—a legacy of academic and civic sloth—a piece of the city's earliest history sacrificed to the twenty-first century, to a complex of buildings whose architecture has lost all contact with humanity.

And yet it is somehow appropriate that this city, this former wilderness outpost which became the center of history's greatest human migration, should offer only such brief and tantalizing glimpses into its past. Throughout its existence, New York has been a symbol of the future, ever impressionable, a city in flux, whose history is reflected by the people it has molded.

BIBLIOGRAPHICAL NOTES

In writing this book I relied to a large extent on interviews with engineers, contractors, and archivists, as well as on some technical writings, to convey a sense of the vast scope involved in constructing the underside of New York City.

For the wealth of detail concerning the discovery, settlement, topography, and early history of the city, no work can compare with I. N. Phelps Stokes, *The Iconography of Manhattan Island, 1498–1909*, 6 vols. (New York: R. H. Dodd, 1895–1928). It is largely this work which permitted me to produce a sense of immediacy through the use of quotations from contemporary observations, newspapers, and town ordinances.

In addition, I relied heavily on community-research notes and booklets and the information provided by individual city agencies. To place New York City's growth in perspective with other historic events, I drew from general works of reference and American history.

In her otherwise not entirely flattering portrayal of New York,

Mrs. Frances Trollope's *Domestic Manners of the Americans*, edited, with an introduction, new materials, and notes by Donald Smalley (New York: Alfred A. Knopf, 1949 [paperback—New York: Vintage, 1960]), nevertheless offered some acute and lofty views derived from firsthand observation.

Chapters One and Two (Water)

Of the many works I consulted apart from I. N. Phelps Stokes (previously cited), I found the following most useful for its animated description of Manhattan Island's early waterways, as well as for the locations of the city's earliest wells: George Everett Hill, *Old Wells and Water-Courses of the Island of Manhattan*, 2 vols. (New York: G. P. Putnam's Sons, 1897). Another book dealing specifically with springs and wells, written from a more recent perspective, is James Reuel Smith, *Springs and Wells of Manhattan and the Bronx* (New York: The New-York Historical Society, 1938). The charms of a leisurely tour of the city's early streets and landmarks, many of which no longer exist, are delightfully described by Charles Hemstreet, *Nooks and Corners of Old New York* (New York: Charles Scribner's Sons, 1899).

For the great drama of immigration over the decades, I relied largely on the meticulous and stirring works of Oscar Handlin; see *The Uprooted* (New York: Grosset & Dunlap, 1951), and *The Americans* (Boston: Little, Brown, 1963). Thomas E. V. Smith, *The City of New York in the Year of Washington's Inauguration, 1789* (Riverside, Conn.: Chatham Press, 1972); William Chauncy Langdon, *Everyday Things in American Life, 1776–1876* (New York: Charles Scribner's Sons, 1941); Floyd M. Shumway, *Seaport City: New York in 1775* (New York: South Street Seaport Museum, 1975); Frank Monaghan and Marvin Lowenthal, *This Was New York: The Nation's Capital in 1789* (Garden City, N.Y.: Doubleday, Doran, Book For Libraries Press, 1943); and Robert Daley, *The World beneath the City* (Philadelphia: Lippincott, 1959), collectively present a most encompassing picture of the varied lifestyles, customs, and amusements of the city's residents during New York's history.

Though written in a somewhat quaint and amusing style, the sights and smells which early travelers to the New World encountered are best conveyed by Andrew Burnaby, *Travels through the Middle Settlements in North-America in the Years 1759 and 1760* (Ithaca, N.Y.: T. Payne, 1960); and Pehr Kalm, *The America of 1750 . . .* (New York: Wilson-Erickson, 1937).

For details concerning the Manhattan Company, I drew heavily from Nathan Schachner, *Aaron Burr* (New York: A. S. Barnes & Company, 1937); as well as *An Act of Incorporation of the Manhattan Company*, 1830, on file at the New York Public Library. The story of Gulielma Sands (see pp. 32–33) is based entirely on an account by Edward S. Gould, "The Manhattan Well Murder," *Harper's New Monthly Magazine* 44 (May 1872): 924–28.

The best accounts of various aspects of municipal water-systems construction from the beginning to present day are contained in Christopher Colles, "Outline History of New York's Water Supply," *The New-York Historical Society Quarterly* 1 (October 1917): 62–70; Charles King, *A Memoir of the Construction, Cost and Capacity of the Croton Aqueduct . . .* (New York: Charles King, 1843); John B. Jervis, *Description of the Croton Aqueduct* (New York: Slamm and Guion, 1842); Nelson Manfred Blake, *Water for the Cities: A History of the Urban Water Supply Problem in the United States* (Syracuse, N.Y.: Syracuse University Press, 1956); Alfred C. Maevis, "Municipal Construction in Early New York," *The Municipal Engineers Journal* 58 (1972): 163–66; Abraham Groopman, "New York City Water Supply Sources and the Need for Additional Sources," *The Municipal Engineers Journal* 60 (1974): 138–46; and Charles W. Weidner, *Water for a City: A History of New York City's Problem from the Beginning to the Delaware River System* (New Brunswick, N.J.: Rutgers University Press, 1974).

Most comprehensive for the Catskill and Delaware systems is Board of Water Supply, City of New York, *The Water Supply of the City of New York* (New York: Board of Water Supply, 1950). Additional materials that were most useful were *Report of the Board of Water Supply of the City of New York to the Board of Estimate on the Third City Tunnel, First Stage*, as well as *Sixty-Fifth Annual Report of the Board of Water Supply, 1970*, and *Sixty-Seventh Annual Report of the Board of Water Supply, 1972*.

An excellent and brief history of the plight and heroism of the early firemen is contained in *The Volunteer Fire Department of Old New York, 1790–1866* (Scotia, N.Y.: Americana Review, 1962).

Vivid eyewitness accounts of personal and public response to fresh water and The Great Water Celebration are provided, respectively, in the delightful and informative writings of George Templeton Strong, *Diary*, ed. Allan Nevins and Milton Halsey

Thomas (New York: Macmillan, 1952); and Philip Hone, *The Diary of Philip Hone, 1828–1851,* ed., with an introduction, by Bayard Tuckerman (New York: Dodd, Mead, 1910).

For information on Central Park's development and the work of Frederick Law Olmsted and Calvert Vaux, I consulted Elizabeth Barlow, *Frederick Law Olmsted's New York* (New York: Praeger, 1972); and Henry Hope Reed and Sophia Duckworth, *Central Park: A History and a Guide,* sec. ed., rev. (New York: Clarkson Potter, 1972).

Chapters Three and Four (Utilities)

By far the most informative books on the history of gas are Frederick L. Collins, *Consolidated Gas Company of New York: A History* (New York: Consolidated Gas Company of New York, 1934); and Louis Stotz, in collaboration with Alexander Jamison, *History of the Gas Industry* (New York: The Press of Stettiner Bros., 1938). However, I also drew considerable information on the use of gas and the biases against it from Committee on Education of Gas Company Employees, *The Story of Gas* (New York: American Gas Association, n.d.). For the more recent introduction of natural gas and its general background, I read Harold W. Springborn, *The Story of Natural Gas Energy* (Arlington, Va.: American Gas Association, 1974).

By far the most thorough work in existence on Thomas A Edison's introduction of incandescent lighting, adult life, and work is by Edison's chief engineer, Francis Jehl, *Menlo Park Reminiscences,* 3 vols. (New York: Edison Institute, 1937). And through his own observations, the inventor's wit and charm are at once evident in Thomas A. Edison, *The Diary and Sundry Observations of Thomas Alva Edison* (New York: New York Philosophical Library, 1948). Glimpses into Edison's early years are provided by Ernest Greenwood, *Edison: The Boy—The Man* (New York: National Light Association, 1929).

A most thorough history of the early history of steam is to be found in New York Steam Corporation, *Fifty Years of New York Steam Service: The Story of the Founding and Development of a Public Utility* (New York: New York Steam Corporation, 1932).

For details of everyday American life during this period of industrialization, I again referred to Langdon (previously cited).

No other book deals so lucidly with the development of the telephone as John Brooks, *Telephone: The First Hundred Years* (New York: Harper & Row, 1976). For an earlier accounting of a youthful industry, I consulted Frederick L. Rhodes, *Beginnings of Telephony* (New York: Arno Press, 1974). For the captivating description of telephony's earthly sounds, I am indebted to Herbert N. Casson, *The History of the Telephone* (Chicago: A. C. McClurg & Co., 1910).

Details of conduit construction, cable insulating techniques, and underground congestion are contained in a number of articles: "Early Cable Construction," *Bell Telephone Quarterly* 1 (April 1922): 29–32; "The Development of Cables Used in the Bell System," *Bell Telephone Quarterly* 2 (April 1923): 94–106; S. A. Haviland, "Some Unusual Conduit Tunnels," *Bell Telephone Quarterly* 11 (January 1932): 27–33; William Chauncy Langdon, "Myths of Telephone History," *Bell Telephone Quarterly* 12 (April 1933): 123–40; Frederick L. Rhodes, "How the Telephone Wires Were First Put Underground," *Bell Telephone Quarterly* 2 (October 1923): 240–54; Frederick L. Rhodes, "Outwitting the Weather," *Bell Telephone Quarterly* 6 (January 1927): 21–31; Louis P. Scaltro, "Coping with Growing Urban Underground Congestion," *Telephone Engineer and Management* 80 (1 September 1976): 104–8; and Kirkland A. Wilson, "The Telephone Problem in the World's Largest Metropolitan Area," *Bell Telephone Quarterly* 13 (October 1934): 233–66.

Chapters Five and Six (Transportation)

The statistics concerning New York City's public transportation systems from earliest times to the present are most concisely contained in *Facts and Figures 1976*, published by the New York City Transit Authority.

However, for the everyday and often harrowing impact of the various modes of transportation on the city's residents, the customs of the times, dangers, and inconveniences, I turned to the marvelous social fabric woven through the pages of David McCullough, *The Great Bridge* (New York: Simon & Schuster, 1972); and to the entertaining glimpses into early New York in Robert Daley, *The World beneath the City* (Philadelphia: Lippincott, 1959).

For the story about the ill-fated first subway of Alfred Ely Beach, I am indebted largely to Robert Daley and Stan Fischler, *Uptown, Downtown: A Trip through Time on New York's Subways* (New York: Hawthorn Books, 1976).

The background of the Tweed Ring and its activities are most informatively set forth by Alexander B. Callow, Jr., *The Tweed Ring* (New York: Oxford University Press, 1965). For an "insider's" view of Tammany Hall and its machinations, I read the delightful William L. Riordan, *Plunkitt of Tammany Hall* (New York: Alfred A. Knopf, 1948).

Amid the scant information available about the H & M Tubes, I found two articles most useful: Anthony Fitzherbert, "The Public Be Pleased: William G. McAdoo and the Hudson Tubes," *Headlights* 26 (Supplement, June 1964): 1–8; and Frank E. Johnson, "Eight Minutes to New York: The Story of the Hudson & Manhattan Tubes," in *American History Illustrated* 9 (August 1974): 12–23.

The beginnings and financing of the city's subways are best described in New York Interborough Rapid Transit Company, *The New York Subway: Its Construction and Equipment* (New York: Arno Press, 1969). And for an articulate and attractive guide to subway art, much of which no longer exists, I referred to John Tauranac, "Art and the I.R.T.: The First Subway Art," *Historic Preservation* 25 (October–December 1973): 26–31.

Additional information was provided by pertinent issues of *The New York Times*.

Although written in an often rambling style, no account of Grand Central's beginnings equals in sympathetic humor the story of the Harlem Corners by David Marshall, *Grand Central* (New York: McGraw-Hill, Whittlesey House, 1946). But the book is also a most fastidious tour through the entire history (until the end of World War II) of one of the city's greatest landmarks. For additional information I consulted William D. Middleton, "The Grandest Terminal of Them All," *Trains* 35 (May 1975): 22–33; and James Marston Fitch and Diana S. Waite, *Grand Central Terminal and Rockefeller Center: A Historic-Critical Estimate of Their Significance* (New York: New York State Parks & Recreation Division for Historic Preservation, 1974).

For an appreciation of the sheer magnitude of driving the terminal's services under the ground, nothing equals the understated, articulate, engineering precision of the work's designer, William J. Wilgus, *The Grand Central Terminal in Perspective*, Transactions of the American Society of Civil Engineers, paper no. 2119 (New York: American Society of Civil Engineers, 1940).

The construction of the Pennsylvania Railroad to and in Manhattan can be followed through a number of detailed, though somewhat dry, engineering reports, all of which appeared in *The New York Tunnel Extension of the Pennsylvania Railroad*, vol.

68 of the Transactions of the American Society of Civil Engineers series (New York: American Society of Civil Engineers, 1910). These are: James H. Brace and Francis Mason, "The East River Tunnels," paper no. 1159; James H. Brace and Francis Mason, "The Cross-Town Tunnels," paper no. 1158; George C. Clarke, "The Site of the Terminal Station," paper no. 1157; B. F. Cresson, Jr., "The Terminal Station West," paper no. 1156; and Charles W. Raymond, "The New York Tunnel Extension of the Pennsylvania Railroad," paper no. 1150.

Also helpful was Nathan Silver, *Lost New York* (New York: Schocken Books, 1971). For additional information I referred to Joseph R. Daughen and Peter Binzen, *The Wreck of the Penn Central* (New York: New American Library, 1971). For background on the city at the end of the nineteenth century, I again consulted McCullough, Stokes, and Langdon, all cited above.

Chapter Seven (Sewers)

No writings present the city's problems of pollution more comprehensively and soberly in terms of the need for fresh water sources than Charles King, *A Memoir of the Construction, Cost and Capacity of the Croton Aqueduct...* (New York: Charles King, 1843), see p. 216. That attention to this need was long overdue (see pp. 215–16), is evident from the Common Council Street Committee, *Report Concerning Removal of Filth and Dirt*, 3 January 1825.

To underscore the plight of New York's fresh water shortage (and resultant disease), I derived considerable insight from the comprehensive directness of the book by Nelson Manfred Blake, *Water for the Cities: A History of the Urban Water Supply Problem in the United States* (Syracuse, N.Y.: Syracuse University Press, 1956). Stokes contains a host of appeals by prominent physicians, notably Dr. David Hosack (developer of Elgin Botanic Garden, now the site of Rockefeller Center), to illustrate the urgency to control disease resulting from contaminated water. In addition, I referred to a variety of early reports submitted to and by New York's Board of Health.

For the construction and application of sewage treatment plants, I relied heavily on the following: Burton J. Fitzpatrick, "The Construction of a Tunnel," *The Municipal Engineers Journal* 61 (1975): 127–59; Martin Lang, Charles Samowitz, and Mohan S. Jethwani, "The Control of Water Pollution in New York City," *The Municipal Engineers Journal* 60 (1974): 115–37; Martin

Lang, Charles Samowitz, Mohan S. Jethwani, and Frederick Novotny, "Sewering the City of New York," *The Municipal Engineers Journal* 61 (1975): 39–54; and Martin Lang, "New York City's Water Pollution Control Program," *The Municipal Engineers Journal* 58 (1972): 199–205.

Also useful was Roy Mann, *Rivers in the City* (New York: Praeger, 1973).

Chapter Eight (Rockbottom)

For the variety and location of ancient waterways that can still plague modern contractors, I consulted George Everett Hill, *Old Wells and Water-Courses of the Island of Manhattan*, 2 vols. (New York: G. P. Putnam's Sons, 1897).

A clear and persuasive account of New York City's geological origins is contained in Louis Binder, "New York City a Buried Scabland Area," *The Municipal Engineers Journal* 60 (1974): 151–57.

The mystery of the *Tijger*, unresolved even by so eminent an historian as Stokes, continued into the early twentieth century when the first subways were constructed. For a thorough though somewhat emotional account of the possible sequence of events, I found most enlightening the following article: Christopher L. Hallowell, "Disappearance of the Historic Ship *Tijger*," *Natural History* 7 (August–September, 1974): 12–26. For further discoveries of historic objects, I referred to "Artifacts Are Dug Up at Trade Center Site," *The New York Times*, 10 June 1968.

Once again, it was Stokes who provided the most comprehensive details of ancient waterways long lost to sight.

INDEX